The Fresh Fruit and Vegetable Book

Produced by
Celebrity Kitchen, Inc.
In Cooperation with
United Fresh Fruit
and Vegetable Association

BARNES & NOBLE BOOKS
A Division of
Harper & Row Publishers

For information contact:

Celebrity Kitchen, Inc.
P.O. Box 98
Suffern, New York 10901

FOREWORD

Fresh fruits and vegetables are foods that are tasty, nutritious, enjoyable. They are easy to prepare and economical to serve.

The wonderful world of freshness is available the year around in today's retail produce departments. Modern homemakers can choose from a great variety of zesty fresh fruits and vegetables which today require a minimum of preparation.

Many fresh fruits are ready to eat in essentially the form they are purchased in the store. Fresh fruit for dessert is the easy, delicious, sensible way to conclude any meal. And there is no better way to start the day than with a piece of fresh fruit for breakfast. Nothing makes a better mid-day snack!

Vegetables, too, are better than ever. Today's fresh vegetables are available the year around in quantity that permits their being served as a matter of healthful habit. Often, fresh vegetables are ready to serve in their raw and natural state. It is easy to prepare them, for now homemakers realize that where cooking is indicated, it is not a long, time-consuming process.

The material in this cookbook taken from the extensive files of the United Fresh Fruit and Vegetable Association, is the accumulation of a great storehouse of information, recipes and helpful hints on how to select and use the products its members grow and distribute. The United's library was developed for use by home economists, dietitians, nutritionists, teachers, newspaper, magazine, radio and television writers and authorities. Now some of its resources are available to you for the first time through the pages of this book.

We feel that this cookbook will be as useful and exciting for you as it was enjoyable for us to assemble.

THE UNITED FRESH FRUIT AND VEGETABLE ASSOCIATION

CONTENTS

Delicious and Nutritious

MOTHER NATURE has blessed us with an astounding variety of delicious fresh fruits and vegetables. In addition to their wide range of taste appeal, fresh fruits and vegetables are a most important food source that is essential to good health. Today, nutritionists generally categorize foods essential to our health into four major categories: the Meat group, the Milk group, the Bread and Cereal group, and the Fruit and Vegetable group. Of these four basic food groups, the Fruit and Vegetable category contains by far the greatest number of varieties to choose from when you are planning well-balanced meals for your family. Truly, the "fresh" offers the homemaker the greatest selection of taste, texture, color and serving methods.

The key to good nutrition is: eating a well balanced diet of nutritious foods. This includes selecting many items from the fruit and vegetable category. To make this easier, this book is devoted to providing information concerning the selection, nutrition, and preparation of fresh fruits and vegetables.

DELICIOUS . . . . . YES!

Fresh fruits and vegetables can be served in a wide variety of ways: raw, boiled, baked, stewed, broiled, steamed, panned, and as beverages and sauces. In this book we shall discuss all of the wonderful ways of preparing and serving fresh fruits and vegetables—from A to Z! You'll discover recipes and serving ideas that will open a whole new world of taste delight for you and your family.

NUTRITIOUS . . . . DEFINITELY!

Fruits and vegetables provide almost all of the ascorbic acid (vitamin C) obtained from food—about 94%. They also provide almost half of the vitamin A; 20% of the iron; 19% of the thiamine; 17% of the niacin; 11% of the phosphorus; 9% of the riboflavin; 7% of the protein in all food consumed in a year. Interesting to note, fruits and vegetables account for less than 1% of the fat consumed in the human diet for a year. Yes, fruits and vegetables are virtually "fat-free," and they all contain a large percentage of water (80 to 95%) so consequently their caloric value is low.

Fruits and vegetables constitute a third of the weight of all foods used; however, they provide less than a tenth of the nation's calories. This applies especially to the fresh products which have no added sugar or starch.

Many fruits and vegetables contain "pectin," and it has been found that a diet rich in fruits and vegetables tends to reduce the cholesterol level of the blood serum by a small but significant amount. Nutritionists recommend a general increase in natural consumption of fruits and vegetables for many reasons, including the fact that they contribute such a large percentage of the important vitamins A and C and many minerals to the diet; including trace minerals. Fruits and vegetables are also an important source of fiber which is an aid to digestion. The versatility of fruits and vegetables allows you to add color, variety and taste to your diet while combining them with other important foods such as meats, fish and cheese.

Fruits and vegetables also contribute to dental care in two important ways: (1) by providing some essential nutrients for the teeth and gums; (2) by helping to cleanse the teeth in the case of crisp, crunchy or juicy fruits and vegetables. For example, a raw fruit for dessert will help clear away sticky foods before bacteria in the mouth can act on them to produce harmful acids.

DIETING AND FRESH FRUITS AND VEGETABLES

Anyone who has had occasion to investigate dieting knows that "fresh" fruits and vegetables play an important role in most medically approved diets. Canned fruits and vegetables usually have a much higher content of calories because of their syrup content.

In a word, weight-watchers would do well to discover the wonderful world of *fresh* fruits and vegetables. In this book under each listing alphabetically we have made note of the calorie counts of each fruit and vegetable, as well as mentioning the nutritional value of each item.

THE LOW-SODIUM DIET

Many patients in hospitals and many out-patients are put on "low-sodium" diets by their physicians. It is important to note that *many* fresh fruits and vegetables are low in sodium. Fresh fruits and vegetables therefore provide a variety of ways of adding flavor to meals without using salt! Lemons, limes, onion and garlic are great for adding flavor to other dishes as well.

THE PROPER SELECTION OF FRESH FRUITS AND VEGETABLES

Knowing how to select fresh fruits and vegetables of "good quality" is very important. This is covered specifically along with the description of each type of fruit and vegetable; however, here are some general pointers to always keep in mind.

1. CHECK FOR FRESHNESS—buy only fruits and vegetables that "look fresh" and are reasonably unblemished. Avoid produce that is wilted, wrinkled, drooping, insect-damaged or dirty.

2. NOTE THE COLOR—select items of "characteristic color." Color is often a good guide to quality. For example, the deeper the yellow, as in carrots and winter squash, or the darker the green, as in kale or spinach, the better the content of vitamin A.

3. NOTE THE SHAPE—grossly mis-shapen fruits and vegetables usually are inferior in texture and taste and have a good deal of waste. They are also more difficult to prepare.

4. NOTE THE SIZE—medium sizes are generally preferred for most purposes. Items which are extremely large or extremely small may have undesirable points. For example, very large fruits may be coarse and over-mature. Extremely small ones may be immature and will have too much waste.

5. CHECK THE DEGREE OF MATURITY—the proper maturity of a fruit or vegetable is the state at which it is judged to be right for harvesting in order to bring it to you, the consumer, in the best possible condition. Such maturity varies. All leafy vegetables must be immature. If they carry seed-bearing parts, they are too mature and will be tough. Some states have laws regulating the maturity at which harvesting is to occur.

6. NOTE RIPENESS—ripeness is different from maturity. For many products, "ripeness" is undesirable: for example, a ripe cucumber would have hard seeds, poor flavor and be inedible.

And finally, USE YOUR GOOD JUDGMENT! Ignore fancy claims (organically grown) which do not have the slightest factual support. Buy at produce departments which are well run—where you have a wide variety of selection and where you have made quality purchases of produce before.

NOTE: Fresh fruits and vegetables should be bought for use within a short time. Some fruits must be held to soften and ripen. HOWEVER, LONG STORAGE AT HOME IS NOT PRACTICAL.

ORGANIC FOODS—IS THERE REALLY A DIFFERENCE?

There has been much publicity and interest in "organically grown" fruits, vegetables and grains. Health food stores selling "organic" fresh fruits and vegetables have sprung up all over the land . . . and they often charge outrageous prices for these items!

First, let's understand what people mean when they use the term "organic." The health food advocate defines "organic" foods as those grown without the use of pesticide sprays or chemical fertilizers. However, the scientific definition of the horticulturist is as follows: "anything which grows, is 'organic.'" But, we're not really concerned about proper definitions—we want facts. Is there a nutritional difference between regular and so-called organically-grown foods? The answer is no. So-called organically grown foods are neither more healthful nor more nutritious than the usual commercially grown products.

The basic nutritive qualities of fruits and vegetables depend upon genetics—the composition of the seed, not the method of fertilization of the soil! Fertilization, however, does affect the yield of the crop. BUT, scientists DO NOT make any distinction between chemicals formulated in a factory and chemicals formulated in the body of living things (organic fertilizers). This means that there is absolutely no difference in the nutritive value of crops whether they are fertilized with organic or synthetic fertilizers.

But, what about the use of pesticides in the regular production of fresh fruits and vegetables? It is only because of the general use of pesticides that you are able to find abundant supplies of healthful, delicious fresh fruits and vegetables at your local supermarket! Farmers use pesticides with stringent care and they are carefully policed by State and Federal agencies in order to insure that no harmful amounts remain for human consumption. Although we don't subscribe to the "organic food" story we think that health food advocates are performing an important func-

11

tion, namely to promote "nutritional awareness" to the general public. Everyone can benefit from a greater knowledge about the nutritional values of foods . . . everyone should strive to maintain a well-balanced diet . . . everyone should demand and know how to select quality food products.

PREPARATION &
SERVING SUGGESTIONS
FOR
FRESH FRUIT

HOW TO COOK FRESH FRUIT

It is usually preferable to eat fresh fruits without cooking them. In cooking, fruits tend to quickly lose some of their vitamin content. However, fresh fruits can be baked, stewed, poached, broiled, sautéed, puréed or pickled.

The basic rule is: cook as quickly and gently as possible and use very little water.

As a general rule do not cook fruits in a pressure cooker. It's a good idea to poach fruits rather than to stew them. The poaching method helps to retain the shape of the fruit. Poaching: prepare the syrup first and when it is really hot, put in the fruit; cook gently. Soft fruits do not need any cooking; they just need to stand in the hot syrup as it cools. Stewing: when stewing hard fruits, put them into a pan with sugar and water and simmer gently. Stewing very delicate fruits is best with this method: place fruit into a double boiler top over hot or boiling water. Just add sugar and a little water to the fruit and cook gently.

Fruits that can be baked include: apples, bananas, oranges, peaches, pears, and rhubarb.

Fruits that can be broiled include: apricots, bananas, grapefruit, and peaches.

Check under alphabetical listings for other cooking ideas with fruits.

FRESH FRUIT SALADS

Prepare fresh ripe fruits heaped in a bowl, several wedges of a robustly flavored cheese, and sesame-topped bread with texture and flavor. From an assortment of fresh fruits you get a wide variety of vitamins and minerals. An orange, nutrition experts say, may well have as many as 250 substances when all analyses have been made. Apples have long been famous for their health-giving properties and most recently dentists have noticed that apple-eating children had fewer cavities than those who indulged in sweeter but less nourishing treats.

Fresh fruits will supply the vitamin C, the bulk and the fluids which are lacking in the high-protein cheese and high-carbohydrate bread. Where whole-milk cheese is a concentrated food and necessarily high in calories per bite, fresh, unsweetened fruits are amazingly low in calories. These foods complement each other, adding up to a beautifully balanced meal . . . certainly one which is easy to prepare.

The weight-watcher may want to eat cottage or pot cheese in place of the whole-milk cheddar or bleu cheese. And, of course, there are a number of specially baked low-calorie breads and wafers to round out the menu.

A fruit salad can combine the delicate colors and shapes of orange and apple wedges; pink-fleshed peach halves; ripely red strawberries, wearing their decorative little caps; blueberries; assorted melon balls, both cantaloupe and honeydew, or possibly watermelon; and, to top it all off, a drape of fresh table grapes, either red or white.

Serve this salad as the main event at a luncheon, accompanied by substantial ham or chicken sandwiches or grilled, just-melted cheese sandwiches. It makes a delicious dessert salad too, mixed with a cream or fruit-juice variation of mayonnaise.

Reducers will enjoy a mixed fruit salad as is, or accompanied by a serving of cottage cheese and a slice of low-calorie bread.

When produce counters are filled with summer fruits the following are particularly good combinations.

- Peach halves, sweet red cherries, sliced pineapple
- Watermelon balls, orange slices, apricot halves
- Pineapple wedges, banana slices, raspberries

Molded fresh fruit salads that can be made quickly in the cool morning hours are always a hit. Although they're delicious made with tangy lemon or lime gelatin, for a novel switch try using watermelon juice made from the puréed melon. It has a most delightful flavor and looks delicately cool. Served with peaches and cantaloupe rings (both stuffed with cottage cheese), as well as melon wedges and perhaps banana chunks and grapes, it is a cool-looking eye catcher bursting with good flavor.

Tossed or arranged fresh fruit salads are a blessing to homemakers because they need so little preparation. Just wash and cut the fruit into any one of many possible shapes. Combine with lettuce and the salad's made. However, when planning them remember that contrasts in color, flavor, texture and shape are very important for taste and eye appeal. For instance, watermelon balls and honeydew cubes are extra delicious when combined with tartly sweet blueberries and sliced peaches. A mixture of green and blue-black grapes, red watermelon balls and pineapple cubes is another excellent combination.

Choosing the right dressing is another important point. In general, fruit salads call for sweeter dressings than those used with vegetable salads. A fluffy cream and mayonnaise dressing flavored perhaps with fruit juice is always good. Or, try one seasoned with grated apple or pear over citrus and pineapple salads. Lightly sweetened French-type dressings are also delicious in tossed fruit salads.

FRESH FRUIT BEVERAGES

Fresh fruit juices are ideal beverages. Their tart-sweetness is delicious and, at the same time, fruit drinks contribute vitamins and minerals. We depend on fruits (and vegetables) for almost all of the ascorbic acid (vitamin C) obtained from food.

Fresh fruits have special nutritional importance, not only for the nutrients they contain but for what they do not contain. Almost all fruits are virtually fat-free and have high water content. Consequently, their caloric value is low.

LIME FROTH

⅔ cup fresh lime juice   ¼ cup sugar
1 cup finely crushed ice   2 unbeaten egg whites
Few drops green food coloring, optional

Place all ingredients in a shaker or 1-quart fruit jar. Shake well until ingredients are well blended and the mixture is frothy. Serve in fruit juice glasses or in tall-stemmed cocktail glasses. If desired, mix ingredients in an electric blender. Makes approximately 1 cup.

SOUTHERN FRESH FRUIT PUNCH

2 cups orange juice
1½ cups fresh lemon juice
   all the orange peels
   all the lemon peels
1½ cups sugar
2 quarts water

1 cup cold tea
1 cup diced fresh
   pineapple
Fresh mint leaves
Fresh lemon slices

Squeeze oranges and lemons, reserving the peels. Combine sugar and 1 quart of the water in a 2-quart saucepan. Mix well, bring to boiling point and boil 1 minute. Remove from heat. Add all the lemon and orange peels, cover and steep 5 minutes. Remove peels and drain to remove all the syrup that the peels have absorbed. Discard peels. Cool syrup. Add remaining 1 quart water, the orange and lemon juices, cold tea and diced pineapple. When ready to serve, place ice in a punch bowl and pour in punch. Garnish with fresh mint leaves and lemon slices.
YIELD: 3¼ quarts.

FRESH STRAWBERRY AND LIMEADE

1 cup sugar

5 cups cold water

1 cup fresh lime juice

1 cup fresh strawberry
   purée*
Fresh lime slices for
   garnish
Fresh mint for garnish

Combine sugar and 1 cup of the water. Stir to dissolve sugar. Bring to a boil and boil 5 minutes. Cool slightly. Stir in remaining 4 cups cold water, fresh lime juice and strawberry purée. Serve chilled or over ice, garnished with fresh lime slices and mint leaves. Makes 1½ quarts.

* Press 1 pint capped fresh strawberries through a fine sieve.

RHUBARB PUNCH

1 quart diced rhubarb	2 cups fresh orange juice
1 quart water	1½ teaspoons vanilla
1½ cups sugar	extract
1 cup fresh lemon juice	Orange slices
	Whole cloves

Combine rhubarb and water. Cover. Bring to boiling point and cook slowly 10 minutes. Cool and strain. Stir in sugar, lemon and orange juices and vanilla extract. Pour into a punch bowl over ice cubes. Garnish with orange slices stuck with cloves. Makes 8 to 10 servings.

FRESH ORANGE FROSTED

½ cup sugar	3½ cups fresh orange juice
2 cups water	Orange slices
½ cup fresh lemon juice	Orange sherbet
	Fresh mint

Mix sugar, 1 cup of the water and ¼ cup of the lemon juice in a saucepan. Bring to boiling point and boil 1 to 2 minutes. Remove from heat and cool. Add remaining water, lemon juice and orange juice. Place an orange slice in each glass. Fill to ⅔ full with the orangeade. Top each with a scoop of orange sherbet and a sprig of fresh mint. Makes about 12 servings.

BANANA FRUIT PUNCH

½ cup sugar
1 cup water
2 cups fine fresh pineapple
   wedges
½ cup cold water
3 medium bananas, sliced

½ cup fresh lemon juice
1 cup fresh orange juice
Grenadine for color
2 bananas for garnish
4 slices fresh oranges

Combine sugar and water in a saucepan and bring to boiling point. Set aside to cool. Put 1 cup of the pineapple and ¼ cup of the cold water at a time in an electric blender bowl. Turn on switch and blend 30 seconds. Pour pineapple juice into a large pitcher or large bowl. Repeat using the remaining pineapple and water. Put half of the bananas at a time in the blender bowl and blend 30 seconds. Repeat using remaining bananas. Add to pineapple juice along with sugar and water syrup, lemon and orange juices. Add enough grenadine to give the desired pink color. Peel the remaining bananas, cut in half lengthwise and place one-half in each tall glass used. Fill with ice cubes, over which pour punch. Float ½ of an orange slice over the top of each. Makes approximately 1½ quarts or 8 servings.

WATERMELON LEMONADE

2 cups fresh ripe
   watermelon purée*
½ cup fresh lemon juice
½ cup sugar

½ teaspoon grated lemon
   rind
2 cups water

Combine watermelon, lemon juice, sugar and lemon rind in pitcher. Stir well to dissolve sugar. Mix in water. Chill. Serve in tall glasses over ice cubes. Makes about 1 quart.

* To puree watermelon, remove rind and seeds. Press through sieve or put through food mill.

FRUIT DRINKS SERVED IN FRUIT

For parties and special occasions, be creative and serve these fresh fruit juices in nature's own punch bowls - hollowed - out watermelons, canteloupes, oranges, pineapples. This isn't at all difficult, although it does take a bit of planning and measuring.

Cut melon in half lengthwise. Cut out the pink fruit with a French melon ball cutter or ½-teaspoon measuring spoon, removing seeds as you go along. Scrape out all the pink pulp which is left in the shell and drain well. (Save pink pulp for use in punch, fruit cups, etc.) Using melon ball cutter, cut scallops in rim of the rind. Set cantaloupe and watermelon balls in scallops. Serve filled with punch or some other fruity beverage.

To make orange cups, slice off just as little of the top of the orange as will permit squeezing the juice from it. Mark rim of empty orange rind into halves, then quarters and eighths. Using these marks as guides, cut neat scallops with a sharp, pointed kitchen knife or kitchen scissors.

Hollowing out a pineapple to form a "cup" requires a good quality grapefruit knife. Slice off a small part of the top, just as little as will make it possible to remove pulp from pineapple. Run grapefruit knife all around pulp, about ¼-inch in from rind. With a sharp straight knife, cut pulp into narrow wedges—the way you would cut a pie. It's not going to be possible to dig out the pineapple into completely neat wedges, but it can be hollowed out well enough to yield attractive "sticks" for garnish or for use in salads while the bits and pieces are liquified in an electric blender and used in a pineapple or fresh fruit punch.

Keep a good supply of colorful fresh fruits in your refrigerator. Berries, peaches, plums and citrus fruits are easily turned into quickie coolers—perfect to serve as mid-morning boosters, afternoon refreshers or evening snacks.

FRESH FRUIT REFRIGERATOR
ICE CREAMS AND SAUCES

Some of the most flavorful treats of summer are found in the season's bounty of fresh fruits. Luscious peaches and plums, big red cherries, berries of all types, treasured melons and many more are arrayed in plentiful supply. Since appetites naturally yearn for something light and refreshing, one interesting idea is to turn these flavorsome fresh fruits into satiny smooth refrigerator ice creams. Surprisingly, they take very little effort to make since the freezing compartment does most of the work for you.

When making refrigerator fruit ice creams, be sure to chop or crush the fresh fruits finely before adding them to the cream mixture. Use only the highest quality fruits. See to it, too, that the freezing compartment is as cold as possible and also place the tray in the coldest part of it.

When serving, it's a good idea to let solidly frozen ice cream stand at room temperature to thaw for just a few minutes before dishing up. This allows the fruits to soften slightly and also makes for easy serving. Another trick is accomplished by pouring the cream mixture into an ice cube tray containing a divider. If the cubes are pierced with a stick when they're partially frozen and then dipped into chocolate sprinkles or shredded coconut, they're guaranteed to make an extra special hit with the pigtail crowd.

Homemade ice cream topped with a fresh fruit sauce is a double-barrelled treat. By taking advantage of the wide variety of fresh fruits available, there are unlimited sauce possibilities. Also try joining two or three fruits together for new flavor twists. For instance, sliced bananas stirred into puréed sweetened strawberries will rate raves when served with a scoop of pineapple or strawberry ice cream. A medley of fresh peaches, grapes and blueberries spiked with lemon juice is an elegant sauce for parfaits and banana splits.

22

FRESH FRUIT

JELLY-MAKING

There is no reason under the winter sun why you can't make jams and jellies during the long cold days when the out-of-doors isn't beckoning.

Oranges and other citrus fruit are in good supply at this season of the year. When other fruits are out of season, the faithful citrus fruits are readily at hand.

The citrus family is a fairly large one. There are oranges, of course, with their golden juice and high vitamin content. There are grapefruits. There are lemons. There are tangerines and kumquats and limes. Tangerines and kumquats are minor members of the citrus family, but they are fun to use occasionally in marmalades. Limes are not plentiful during this blustery season, but they make delicious summer marmalade.

Of course, citrus fruit is "in season" all the year around, but it is during these winter months that citrus comes into its own, when the fruits of summer—the peaches and pears, the berries and the melons we all love so well—are not available to us.

One of the pleasant things about all of the citrus fruits is that they combine well with each other and also with fruits and vegetables which are in season at the same time. Cranberries or apples may be added to citrus fruit to make colorful jellies or fragrant conserves to be served with poultry. Oddly enough, colorful yellow carrots—that humble and inexpensive winter favorite—take on an almost unbelievable glamor when they are part of a citrus marmalade.

There are only a few secrets in jelly making. Glasses should be sterilized. A "full rolling boil" means one which cannot be stirred down with a spoon. The bubbles in "a gentle simmer" disappear when the pot is stirred. Be sure to use a kettle that is large enough. Nothing makes more of a mess than boiled-over jelly!

Happy jelly-making! You will have a marvelous feeling of accomplishment when you see the glowing jars lined neatly on the shelf.

23

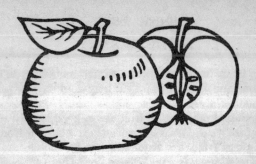

APPLES

AVAILABILITY AND USES

There are a great many varieties of applies; we shall discuss the most popular varieties here.

DELICIOUS

A medium to large size apple, striped deep red to solid red. Flesh is crisp, juicy, low acid; an excellent table apple and good in salads, but not generally used for cooking. Season: Sept.—June.

GOLDEN DELICIOUS

A medium to large size apple, yellow or golden skin. Flesh is white often with a yellowish tinge, crisp, juicy, low acid; ideal for salads because flesh does not turn brown, good cooker and a fine eating apple. Season: Oct.—June.

McINTOSH

Size is above medium, with a bright deep red skin, striped with carmine. Flesh is white, crisp, very juicy, medium acid becoming mild and nearly sweet when ripe. Excellent for dessert and salad; good for cooking and baking, requiring less cooking time than most other varieties. Season: Oct.—May.

ROME BEAUTY

Size is medium to very large; skin is yellow or greenish, mottled with bright red. Flesh is nearly white, crisp, juicy, mildly acid. Excellent for baking because it holds its shape; good for pie, sauce and all cooking purposes—not generally eaten raw, but good raw when fully ripe. Season: Oct.—April.

JONATHAN

Usually small to medium size; skin is deep red. Flesh is whitish, crisp and juicy, medium acid. Excellent for dessert or cooking; fine for baking. Season: Sept.—May.

YORK IMPERIAL

Size is medium to large; skin is light red or pinkish-red. Flesh is yellowish, a bit coarse, moderately juicy, medium acid. Good for eating fresh and a fine cooking apple, holding its shape and flavor under heat. This apple has a lopsided kind of shape. Season: Oct.—March.

STAYMAN

Size is medium to large; skin is a dull striped red. Flesh is whitish, tinged with yellow, rather coarse, juicy, medium acid; a fine all-purpose apple. Season: Oct.—April.

WINESAP

Size medium to small; skin is bright red. Flesh is yellowish, rather coarse, very juicy, medium acid. A fine all-purpose apple, keeps very well. Season: Nov. 15—July.

NEWTOWN PIPPIN

Size medium to very large; skin is greenish-yellow to bright yellow. Flesh is tinged with yellow, crisp, juicy, medium acid. Excellent for dessert, good cooker, one of the best keepers. Season: Oct.—June.

GRAVENSTEIN

Size above medium to large; skin is greenish-yellow to orange-yellow with red striping. Flesh is whitish-yellow, crisp and juicy, medium acid. Good for table use, cooking and salads. Should be used quickly, summer apples do not keep well. Season: July 15—Sept. 15.

GRIMES GOLDEN

Medium to large in size; skin is deep yellow. Flesh is yellow, very firm, moderately juicy, medium acid. Good for cooking or dessert. Season: Sept.—Dec.

CORTLAND

Size is medium to large; skin is shiny deep red. Flesh is snow white, tender mildly acid. This apple does not turn brown on exposure to the air; excellent for eating fresh, salads and fruit cocktails; fine for all cooking purposes. Season: Oct.—Jan.

NORTHERN SPY

Size is usually large to very large; skin is bright red or striped red. Flesh is yellowish, very tender, very juicy, medium acid. Excellent for dessert or cooking. Season: Oct.—May.

RHODE ISLAND GREENING

Size ranges from medium to very large; skin is green or yellowish. Flesh is yellowish, firm, juicy, medium acid. Not generally used for dessert or salad; extra good for pie, sauce and good for baking. Season: Oct.—Feb.

HOW TO BUY

Select firm, crisp, bright, well-colored apples. Flavor depends upon the variety and is also influenced by the stage of maturity at which the fruit is picked and the conditions under which it is kept. Apples that are well-colored for the variety usually have the full flavor of that variety, if they are in good condition. Larger apples are more likely to be overripe, especially toward the end of the season, than smaller fruit. Apples which have been picked at the immature stage often lack color and flavor.

NUTRITIONAL VALUE

Apples are relatively low in calories. A medium apple (2½ inches in diameter, 150 grams) provides 66 Calories. Apples are low in sodium—1 milligram per 100 grams, and therefore are suitable for use in a low-sodium diet.

STORAGE TIPS

Recently harvested unripe apples can be stored for several weeks in a cool, dark, airy place. Apples can be kept in the refrigerator for one or two weeks.

SHREDDED UNCOOKED APPLE SAUCE

2 cups shredded fresh apples
1 tablespoon fresh lemon
   juice

3 tablespoons sugar

Combine apples, lemon juice and sugar. Mix well. Serve at once since raw apple sauce does not have the keeping qualities of cooked apple sauce. Makes 2 cups.

MERINGUE-TOPPED FRESH APPLES

6 large baking apples
½ cup graham cracker
   crumbs
¼ cup walnuts, finely
   chopped
2 tablespoons butter or
   margarine, melted
1 tablespoon sugar
1 teaspoon ground
   cinnamon

1 cup sugar
⅓ cup water
1 tablespoon butter or
   margarine
Dash of salt
2 tablespoons fresh lemon
   juice
2 egg whites
¼ cup sugar
Dash of salt

Peel a 1-inch strip around stem end of apples. Core, being careful not to cut through to blossom end. Place in 12 x 8 x 2-inch baking dish. Mix together graham cracker crumbs, nuts, butter, sugar and cinnamon. Spoon into center of each apple. Combine 1 cup sugar, ⅓ cup water, 1 tablespoon butter, 2 tablespoons lemon juice and salt in small saucepan. Heat to boiling; pour over apples. Cover. Bake in preheated moderate oven (375°F.) basting several times during baking, for about 45 minutes. Cool. Beat egg whites until foamy. Beat in sugar and salt. Frost top of each apple with meringue. Bake in preheated hot oven (425°F.) for 5 minutes or until brown. Makes 6 servings.

MOLDED SHREDDED APPLE AND ORANGE SALAD

1 envelope unflavored
    gelatin
½ cup cold water
1 cup fresh orange juice
3 tablespoons fresh lemon
    juice

¼ cup sugar
1 cup shredded fresh apple
Fresh apple slices
Fresh orange sections

Soften gelatin in cold water. Place over hot water (not boiling) to melt. Add to orange juice, 2 tablespoons of the lemon juice and sugar. Chill until the mixture begins to thicken. Shred apples into the remaining 1 tablespoon fresh lemon juice and fold into the gelatin. Turn into an oiled 1-pt. mold. Chill until firm and ready to serve. Turn out onto a serving plate. Garnish with apple slices and fresh orange sections. Serve with mayonnaise. Makes 6 servings.

BAKED FRESH APPLES STUFFED WITH HAM

6 large baking apples
1 cup finely diced cooked
    ham
2 tablespoons seedless
    raisins

1 tablespoon butter or
    margarine
$\frac{1}{16}$ teaspoon black pepper
½ cup sweet apple cider or
    apple juice

Wash and core apples. Scoop out insides and chop fine. Mix with ham, raisins, butter and pepper. Pack stuffing firmly in cavities. Place in baking pan. Heat cider or juice and pour over tops. Cover. Bake in preheated moderate oven (375°F.) 45 minutes to 1 hour or until tender. Baste with apple cider or juice at 15-minute intervals. Serve as main dish for supper or lunch. Makes 6 servings.

SAUSAGE BAKED APPLES

6 medium-sized cooking apples
½ pound bulk pork sausage
½ cup light corn syrup
2 tablespoons water
1 tablespoon butter

Wash, core and pare apples ⅓ way down from stem. Place in shallow baking pan. Sauté sausage until light brown; pour off drippings. Fill apple centers with sausage. Combine corn syrup, water and butter in small saucepan; heat and stir until butter dissolves. Pour evenly over apples. Bake in moderate oven (350°F.) about 45 minutes, or until tender, basting occasionally. Serve with scrambled eggs or omelets, as desired. Makes 6 servings.

CURRIED APPLES

2 tablespoons butter or margarine
1½ teaspoons curry powder
⅛ teaspoon cinnamon
⅛ teaspoon ground ginger
¼ teaspoon salt
2 tablespoons diced onion
¼ cup diced celery
1 tablespoon flour
½ cup chicken stock
3 medium baking apples
½ teaspoon sugar or sugar to taste

Melt butter or margarine in a small saucepan. Stir in spices, salt, onion and celery. Cook until vegetables are tender. Blend in flour. Add chicken stock and cook until slightly thickened. Wash unpeeled apples, quarter and core. Place in a 1-quart casserole. Sprinkle with sugar. Pour curry sauce over apples and bake, covered, in a preheated moderate oven (350°F.) for 45 minutes or until fork tender. Remove cover 5 minutes before cooking time is up. Allow to cool slightly before serving. Use as an accompaniment to pork, veal or poultry. Makes 6 servings.

SKILLET BAKED CINNAMON
FRESH APPLES

6 baking apples	⅓ cup grenadine syrup
¼ cup fine bread crumbs	1½ cups boiling water
2 tablespoons butter, melted	¾ cup sugar
2 tablespoons raisins	½ cup small red hot cinnamon candies
2 tablespoons sugar	1 stick cinnamon
1 teaspoon ground cinnamon	2 teaspoons fresh lemon juice
1 teaspoon ground nutmeg	

Wash and core apples and peel 1-inch strip from top of apple. Arrange in electric skillet. Prepare stuffing for apples by mixing together bread crumbs, butter, raisins, sugar, cinnamon and nutmeg. Fill center of each apple. Combine in skillet grenadine, water, sugar, cinnamon candies, stick cinnamon and lemon juice. When syrup boils, cover skillet, set temperature dial at 250°F. and open vent. During baking, baste several times with syrup. Bake about 15 to 25 minutes or until apples are tender. If electric skillet is not available, apples may be cooked in covered skillet over low heat following same method. To serve, pour some of syrup over apples. Makes 6 servings.

SPICED APPLE AND ORANGE SAUCE

4 large tart cooking apples	½ cup sugar
2 large oranges	⅛ teaspoon salt
½ cup water	⅛ teaspoon ground cloves

Peel, core and slice apples. Place in a saucepan. Peel oranges, cut into sections and add along with water. Cover and cook over medium heat until tender, about 10 minutes. Remove from heat and stir in remaining ingredients. Serve for breakfast or for lunch or dinner, as a dessert, meat accompaniment or as a relish. Makes 5 to 6 servings.

CANDIED APPLE BLOSSOMS

4 baking apples, cored
½ cup packed light brown
   sugar
½ cup granulated sugar
½ cup water

3 tablespoons fresh lemon
   juice (juice of 1
   lemon)
Vanilla ice cream

In medium skillet combine sugars, water and lemon juice. Bring mixture to a boil; add apples, reduce heat, cover and cook 15 minutes. Uncover, turn apples, and simmer uncovered for 30 minutes or until apples are tender. Chill, reserving sauce. Cut apples into 6 wedges "petal fashion," but do not cut all the way through. Put a scoop of vanilla ice cream in the center of each, and top with sauce. Makes 4 servings.

DEEP-DISH APPLE AND PEAR PIE

4 large tart cooking apples
4 large firm ripe pears
1 cup sugar
¼ teaspoon salt
½ teaspoon ground
   cinnamon

¼ teaspoon ground nutmeg
3 tablespoons flour
2 tablespoons butter or
   margarine
Pastry, using 2 cups flour

Peel, core and slice apples and pears into ½-inch slices. Combine sugar, salt, spices and flour and mix with the fruit. Turn into a 2-quart oblong baking dish, lined with one half the pastry dough rolled ⅛-inch thick. Dot fruit with butter or margarine. Roll remaining pastry dough ⅛-inch thick and cut into six 3¼-inch squares. Place squares in 2 horizontal rows over fruit. Bake in a preheated hot oven (425°F.) 10 minutes. Reduce heat to moderate (350°F.) and bake 35 minutes longer—or until done. Serve warm or cold. Make 6 to 8 servings.

APRICOTS

AVAILABILITY

June and July.
Varieties include Royal, Tilton, Blenheim, Perfection, Moorpark, Riland and others.

The Royal is orange-yellow often with a red blush; medium to large; roundish ovate; flesh deep orange, rich and sweet. Tilton is orange to light yellow, often blushed; large; oval with a compressed flat appearance; flesh lighter in color than Royal. Moorpark orange to brownish red; large; roundish ovate with a distinct suture and halves often uneven; flesh bright orange, rich, juicy and sweet.

HOW TO BUY

Apricots should be mature, plump, orange-yellow, and relatively soft though not damaged. Pass up immature apricots, greenish in color. Hold at room temperature until apricots yield to gentle pressure when squeezed. After ripening use immediately or refrigerate.

PREPARATION AND SERVING SUGGESTIONS

Fresh apricots are eaten out of the hand; are fine stewed or baked, either by themselves or with meat; are excellent in pies, puddings, cakes and compotes; in or on ice cream and sherbet; and in molded deserts. Or try broiled apricots brushed before broiling with margarine and brown sugar. Rolling a thin strip of boiled ham around a fresh apricot wedge makes an interesting hors d'oeuvre. Apricots make excellent preserves.

NUTRITIONAL VALUE

Apricots are rich in vitamin A. Apricots are relatively low in calories. A 100-gram portion, which is about the edible part of three medium fruits, provides only 51 Calories. They can be used in low-sodium diets.

FROZEN FRESH APRICOT SALAD

2 tablespoons mayonnaise
1 package (8-ounces)
    creamcheese, softened
2 cups chopped
    fresh apricots

½ cup chopped walnuts
2 tablespoons fresh
    lemon juice
1 cup heavy cream,
    whipped
    Fresh apricot halves

Gradually blend mayonnaise into cream cheese. Add chopped apricots, walnuts and lemon juice; mix well. Fold whipped cream into apricot mixture. Turn into an 8-inch square pan. Cover tightly with heavy duty aluminum foil. Freeze. Let stand at room temperature about 1 or 2 hours before serving or until salad can be cut easily. Cut into squares and serve each topped with an apricot half. Garnish with fresh mint, if desired. Makes 8 to 10 servings.

AVOCADOS AVAILABILITY

Don't be confused by avocados of varied skin colors! Avocado skin color signifies different varieties, but all varieties have the same delectable, butter-smooth flavor and texture.

Avocados come in several different varieties. Primarily, some are pear shaped, some are oval. Skin color ranges from bright green to dark black-green, while skin textures may be relatively smooth and thin or rough, leathery and pebbled.

HOW TO BUY

Avocados are harvested mature, but not ripe, so expect to find firm, hard avocados in the produce department, in addition to those that are ready-to-eat. If you don't plan to use avocados for a few days, select fruit that is hard to the touch. Keep at room temperature for several days until soft and ready to eat. If you don't plan to use ripe avocados immediately, refrigerate them to slow down the ripening process and use as soon as possible. As avocados ripen, they darken.

If you're looking for avocados to serve the same day as purchase, use this test to select ripe fruit. Hold the avocado in the palm of your hand and **gently** squeeze. If the fruit gives, it's ready to eat!

PREPARATION AND SERVING SUGGESTIONS

Medium to large avocados are preferred when cutting them for use in salads and fruit cups because there are fewer fruits to be peeled for the same weight of fruit. If fruit is to be cut in Parisienne balls for garnish, larger size fruit gives best yield.

When serving avocados either in halves or smaller pieces which are to be peeled, cut them before peeling. For halves, run the point of the knife lengthwise all the way around, then twist the two halves to free the seed; then peel. Waste is avoided if the handle of a tablespoon or a table knife is used for peeling, rather than a sharp knife. After cutting through the skin, work the dull blade along the cut between skin and meat until the skin will come away easily. Peeled pieces of avocado can be dipped in lemon juice immediately to prevent darkening.

Devotees of the avocado claim its use as a food is limited only by the user's imagination. Beginning with breakfast, avocados are used to enhance the flavor and nourishment of scrambled eggs (cubed or mashed avocado is blended in just as the eggs begin to "set"). Mashed avocado spread on toast is another breakfast treat. For lunch, an avocado sandwich is attractive, filling and good. Or, avocado cubes can be added to soup or made into a cream of avocado soup. The fruit also goes well in almost every salad. Some like just the thinly sliced avocado with a sprinkling of salt and pepper and lemon or lime juice . . . or it can be served with lettuce, watercress, bean sprouts, tomatoes, litchi nuts, cashew nuts, or as a mousse. The avocado is the basic ingredient of a popular Mexican and American dish, guacamole. There are an infinite number of guacamole recipes governed mostly by the consumer's tolerance for highly seasoned food. Avocados are served with fish, they can be baked, they are made into soufflés, sauces, cream pies, whips and even ice cream.

NUTRITIONAL VALUE

Avocados are rich in vitamins and minerals, especially B vitamins. They also contain fruit oil (amounts differing among varieties) which is largely unsaturated. Avocados contain **no cholesterol**! They are low in sodium and are easily digestible, too. Depending on the variety, the sizes of avocados will differ. Therefore, the calorie count will too. Percentage-wise, the caloric content differs depending on the avocado variety.

AVOCADO AND FRESH CITRUS MOLD

1 pkg. unflavored gelatin

¼ cup cold water

1 cup boiling water

2 cups (2 large) mashed fresh avocado

2 tablespoons finely minced fresh parsley

2 tablespoons fresh lemon or lime juice

1 teaspoon salt

1½ teaspoons sugar

⅛ teaspoon ground ginger

¼ cup mayonnaise

1 cup small curd cottage cheese

½ cup coarsely chopped walnuts

2 cups fresh orange sections

2 cups fresh grapefruit sections

2 cups sour cream

3 tablespoons honey

1 teaspoon fresh lemon or lime juice

1½ tablespoons chopped candied ginger

Dissolve gelatin in cold water. Add boiling water and stir until gelatin is dissolved. Chill until slightly thickened. Combine avocado, parsley, lemon or lime juice, salt, sugar, ginger, mayonnaise, cottage cheese and walnuts. Add gelatin mixture. Pour into a greased 2-quart mold. Refrigerate until set. Unmold on serving platter. Serve with orange and grapefruit sections and sour cream dressing. To make dressing, combine sour cream, honey, lemon or lime juice and candied ginger. Makes 8 to 10 servings.

AVOCADO RINGS

2 envelopes unflavored
    gelatin
½ cup water
3 cups mashed avocado

½ cup mayonnaise
¼ cup fresh lemon juice
1 teaspoon salt
¼ teaspoon pepper

Soften gelatin in cold water; dissolve over boiling water. Combine avocado, mayonnaise, lemon juice, salt and pepper; stir in dissolved gelatin. Pour into 4 individual ring molds (about 1 cup capacity each). Chill about 2 hours or until firm. Just before serving, unmold on individual plates. Garnish with salad greens, radish roses and carrot curls, as desired. Makes 4 servings.

AVOCADO FRUIT SALAD

2 medium-sized avocados
    Lemon juice
    Salad greens
2 cups seedless grapes
2 cups fresh cantaloupe
    balls
3 tablespoons fresh lemon
    juice

½ cup salad oil
1 teaspoon honey
½ teaspoon salt
    Dash pepper
2 tablespoons chopped
    fresh mint

Peel avocados; cut into wedges. Brush avocado wedges with lemon juice. Arrange avocado wedges in 4 sections on salad greens on a large platter. Combine grapes and cantaloupe; place between avocado sections on platter. Shake 3 tablespoons lemon juice and remaining ingredients together in a jar with tight-fitting cover. Serve with salad. Makes 4 servings.

STUFFED AVOCADO BUFFET SALAD

Wash ripe avocados, cut in half and remove seeds. Brush inside of cavities and around the edge with fresh lemon juice to prevent discoloration. Fill with one or as many of the following mixtures as desired. Arrange on a large serving plate or tray. Let the guests help themselves to the ones they prefer. Garnish the tray as desired with fresh parsley, radish roses or carrot curls.

CRAB SALAD

2 cups cooked crab meat
1¼ cups diced celery
¼ cup diced green pepper
1 teaspoon salt or salt to taste
¼ teaspoon black pepper
1 tablespoon fresh lemon juice
3 tablespoons mayonnaise
Green pepper sticks
3 avocados, halved

Flake crab meat and mix with celery, diced green pepper, salt, black pepper, lemon juice and mayonnaise. Pile into avocado cavities. Garnish with green pepper sticks. Makes 6 servings.

SHRIMP SALAD

2 cups cooked deveined shrimp
1 cup diced celery
1 tablespoon fresh lemon juice
3 avocados, halved
1 teaspoon finely chopped fresh onion
1 teaspoon salt or salt to taste
¼ teaspoon pepper
3 tablespoons mayonnaise

Reserve a whole shrimp for use as a garnish. Mix remaining shrimp with rest of the ingredients. Pile into avocado cavities. Garnish each with a whole cooked shrimp. Makes 6 servings.

LOBSTER SALAD

2 cups cooked lobster
  meat
1 cup fresh pineapple
  wedges
1 cup diced celery
3 avocados, halved

1 teaspoon salt or salt to
  taste
¼ teaspoon pepper
Dash cayenne pepper
¼ teaspoon soy sauce
¼ cup mayonnaise

Reserve attractive red pieces of lobster for use as a garnish. Combine remaining ingredients. Pile into avocado cavities. Garnish each with red lobster pieces saved for that purpose. Makes 6 servings.

CHICKEN SALAD

2 cups cold diced cooked
  chicken
1 cup diced celery
1 tablespoon fresh lemon
  juice
3 tablespoons mayonnaise

¾ teaspoon salt or salt to
  taste
¼ teaspoon pepper
½ teaspoon curry powder,
  optional
Unpeeled diced apples

3 avocados, halved

Combine chicken, celery, lemon juice, mayonnaise, salt, black pepper and curry powder if used. Pile into avocado cavities. Garnish each with a few pieces of unpeeled diced apples. Makes 6 servings.

FRESH ORANGE AND GRAPEFRUIT SALAD

3 large fresh navel oranges
1 large fresh grapefruit
½ cup diced peeled apples

¼ cup diced celery
French dressing
3 avocados, halved

Peel oranges and grapefruit and cut into sections, being careful not to break them. Reserve one whole section of each, grapefruit and orange to use as a garnish. Combine remaining oranges and grapefruit with apples and celery. Moisten with French dressing to taste. Pile into avocado cavities. Garnish each with a whole grapefruit and orange section. Makes 6 servings.

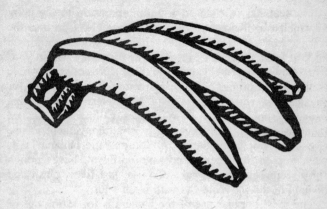

BANANAS

AVAILABILITY

Bananas are available all year long. There are two main varieties—the Gros Michel, and the Cavendish. The Gros Michel has more taper at the end, while the Cavendish, the major variety in quantity, is blunter. PLANTAINS: a species of banana not suited to eating raw but excellent for cooking. This fruit is extra large and has salmon colored pulp when ripe; available in large cities.

HOW TO BUY

Good quality bananas at retail may be anything from partly green to all yellow with brown spots. If you purchase bananas too green for immediate use, they can easily be ripened by leaving them at room temperature. If in a film bag, open the bag. Avoid fruit that is bruised or split.

PREPARATION AND SERVING SUGGESTIONS

Allow bananas to ripen at room temperature to the point at which you like to eat them. Bananas CAN go into the refrigerator (after they have ripened) where they will keep at least a couple of days longer than they will in your fruit bowl. Green-tip fruit is best for cooking whole (sauteing, broiling, baking); for eating raw on cereals, or in salads a riper banana may be preferred. Very ripe bananas should be used in recipes calling for mashed bananas for full, rich flavor. If it is not convenient to use over-ripe fruit immediately, plastic bag the banana in its peel, pop in the freezer and save until you have enough for a recipe or time to bake. To use, just thaw, mash and include in the the recipe as with fresh fruit.

The most popular use of the banana is for eating out of hand; however, bananas have a very wide use in menus, as sliced in salads; for banana cream pie; banana cake; banana pudding; fried or baked banana slices; banana ice cream; and of course the banana split sundae. And how about banana chunks in a gelatin mold . . . banana cookies or muffins . . . a sponge cake with bananas and lemon sauce; banana custard. Roasted loin of pork takes on new glamour when ringed with broiled banana, and roast chicken is sparked by the addition of bananas that have been delicately sautéed in butter. Bananas sliced in cream is a favorite . . . and for a simple frosting for a plain cake mash ripe bananas, adding a teaspoon or so of fresh lemon juice, and sugar to taste. A favorite dessert for children is a banana whip. Just whip mashed ripe bananas into stiffly beaten egg white (sweetened) and serve.

For a tropical fruit medley, combine slices of banana with wedges of papaya, mango, fresh pineapple, fresh orange sections and fresh sliced strawberries. Sprinkle with fresh lime juice and a little wine, chill and serve in sherbet glasses.

NUTRITIONAL VALUE

In a perfect package. Naturally sweet, mellow bananas are nutritionally valuable with a contribution of many nutrients. medium banana (120 grams edible portion) provides about 26 percent of the Recommended Dietary Allowance of vitamin C and 25 percent of the vitamin B_6, is a good source of potassium and offers its quota of other minerals and vitamins. Bananas are low in sodium, virtually fat free and have only about 100 calories in an average fruit. They are easily digestible for bland diets, wonderful for babies and contain fiber pectin useful in promoting regularity.

BANANA TEA MUFFINS

1¾ cups sifted flour
2 teaspoons baking powder
¼ teaspoon baking soda
¾ teaspoon salt

¼ cup butter or margarine
⅓ cup sugar
1 egg
1 cup mashed bananas (2 to 3 bananas)

Sift together flour, baking powder, baking soda, and salt. Cream butter or margarine; gradually beat in sugar and egg. Add flour mixture to creamed mixture alternately with banana, beating well after each addition. Fill greased muffin pans ⅔ full. Bake in hot oven (400°F.) 15–20 minutes. Makes 12 2½-inch muffins.

FRESH BANANA WHIP

3 medium-sized bananas,
   peeled
3 egg whites, unbeaten
2 tablespoons sugar
¼ teaspoon salt
1 teaspoon vanilla extract

½ cup heavy cream,
   whipped
18 lady fingers
Grated nutmeg for
   garnish

Place banana, egg whites, sugar, salt and vanilla in small bowl of electric mixer. Beat with electric beater until stiff. Fold in whipped cream. Stand 3 lady fingers around sides of each deep sherbet glass. Add banana whip. Garnish with grated nutmeg. Chill before serving. Makes 6 servings.

ORANGE GLAZED BANANAS

4 medium-sized bananas*
2 tablespoons fresh orange
   juice
2 tablespoons honey

1 tablespoon melted butter
   or margarine
½ teaspoon grated orange
   rind

Peel bananas and place in lightly buttered 8 x 8 inch baking pan. Combine remaining ingredients; pour over bananas coating well. Bake in hot oven (450°F.) 10 minutes. Remove from oven. Arrange bananas on serving plate. Spoon syrup in pan over bananas. Makes 4 servings.

* Use slightly green-tipped or all yellow firm bananas.

FRESH FRUIT

FRESH BANANAS IN SOUR CREAM

2 large bananas, sliced
½ pint (1 cup) sour cream
¼ cup diced fresh
  oranges

2½ tablespoons light
  brown sugar
¼ teaspoon vanilla extract
  Grated orange peel for
  garnish

Place all ingredients except orange peel in mixing bowl.
Toss lightly. Serve, as dessert, in sherbet glasses. Garnish
with grated orange peel. Makes 4 servings.

TROPICAL CHIFFON PIE

1 envelope unflavored
  gelatin
¼ cup cold water
3 eggs, separated
1 cup mashed bananas
  (fully ripe bananas)
1 tablespoon fresh lemon
  juice

¼ teaspoon grated lemon
  rind
⅓ cup sugar
¼ teaspoon salt
½ cup heavy cream
⅓ cup finely grated coconut
  9-inch baked pie shell

Soften gelatin in cold water. Slightly beat egg yolks in
top of double boiler; stir in bananas, lemon juice, and rind,
sugar and salt. Cook over boiling water, stirring constantly,
until slightly thickened. Remove from heat. Stir softened
gelatin into banana mixture until dissolved. Chill until mixture is slightly thickened. Beat egg whites until stiff but
not dry. Beat cream until stiff. Fold egg whites, cream and
coconut into banana mixture. Pile into 9-inch pie shell.
Chill until firm. Garnish with additional whipped cream,
shaved chocolate and banana slices, if desired. Makes 6–8
servings.

BAKED FRESH COCONUT CUSTARD

½ cup fresh coconut milk   ½ cup sugar
½ cup grated fresh coconut   ⅛ teaspoon salt
 4 eggs   1½ cups milk

Pierce eyes of coconut and drain milk into measuring cup; reserve. Place coconut in a 350°F. oven for 15 minutes. Remove from oven. Crack shell with hammer and remove meat. Peel brown outer rind with vegetable peeler and grate coconut meat. Beat eggs until light and lemon colored. Add sugar and salt and beat until thick. Gradually add coconut milk and milk. Pour into 6 buttered custard cups or 1-quart baking dish. Sprinkle grated coconut over top. Place in pan of water and bake in 325°F. oven 45 minutes for individual cups or 1¼ to 1½ hours for large dish, until a knife inserted in center comes out clean. Serve warm or chilled.
Makes: 6 servings.

BANANA BLENDER MILK SHAKE

3 cups milk   ¼ teaspoon nutmeg
2 ripe bananas, cut in pieces

Place all ingredients in container of electric blender. Cover and blend at high speed about 30 seconds until smooth. Serve immediately. Makes about 4½ cups; 4 servings.

FRESH FRUIT
BANANA FROSTING

1 stick butter or margarine
(½ cup)
1 cup mashed bananas (2
bananas)
1 teaspoon fresh lemon
juice

5 cup sifted confectioners'
sugar
¼ cup nonfat dry milk
½ teaspoon vanilla extract

Combine butter or margarine, bananas, and lemon juice. Mix until creamy. Gradually stir in the confectioners' sugar and nonfat dry milk. Add vanilla extract and beat until fluffy. Makes sufficient frosting for inside and outside of a sponge roll.

BANANA SAUTÉ

4 bananas
¼ cup fresh lemon juice
½ cup sugar

¼ cup butter or margarine
1 tablespoon grated fresh
orange rind

Peel bananas and cut in half lengthwise. Roll in lemon juice and then in sugar. Melt butter in large skillet. Add orange rind. Place bananas in butter mixture and cook over low heat, turning once, just until barely tender, 5 to 10 minutes. Makes 4 servings.

BLACKBERRIES

AVAILABILITY

Fresh blackberries are available May through August.
Blackberries, dewberries, boysenberries, olallieberries,
loganberries and youngberries are similar and for practical
purposes can be considered together.

HOW TO BUY

Look for bright, black (or characteristic) color, fresh
clean appearance and dryness. Loganberries are dark red
and youngberries deep wine color. Large, plump berries
are more desirable than small ones. Check for any staining
of the containers, indicating crushed and leaky fruit. The
berries should be free from dirt, trash or adhering caps.
Overripe berries can be spotted by their very dull color as
well as softness. On the other hand, unripe fruit will show
drupelets that are green or off color. There should be no
mold or decay.

PREPARATION AND SERVING SUGGESTIONS

Use fresh blackberries as toppings for cereal, in tarts, pies and salads. When they start to go soft, mash them and cook briefly in a simple sugar syrup. This makes a delicious ice cream topping or sauce for day old cake. It holds fine under refrigeration. Blackberries can also be canned in plain water or in syrup; frozen with sugar; and made into wines, cordials and brandies.

NUTRITIONAL VALUE

Blackberries, though not considered an important source of nutrients, contain a fair amount of vitamins and minerals; 100 grams (uncooked) contains 58 Calories.

BLUEBERRIES

AVAILABILITY

The main season is May through August.

HOW TO BUY

Blueberries should be plump, fresh in appearance, fairly uniform in size, clean, dry, free from trash, with good blue color. They may be covered with more or less bloom (a natural waxy protective coating) depending on variety. Berries that are held too long after picking have a dull lifeless appearance, and may be shrivelled.

FRESH FRUIT

PREPARATION AND SERVING SUGGESTIONS

As with other seasonal berries, fresh blueberries are a real menu star. Served simply with cream or over cereals, they are excellent. Fresh blueberry pie always proves to be a top dessert attraction, as do blueberry muffins and pancakes. For a delicious syrup or topping, place fresh blueberries in a pot with only enough water to be visible (not to cover), flavor with lemon juice and sugar and bring the berries to a boil. They can be kept under refrigeration for a long time and thickened with starch later if needed.

NUTRITIONAL VALUE

Blueberries contain moderate amounts of important vitamins and minerals; 100 grams contain 62 Calories when raw.

FRESH BLUEBERRY BANANA BREAD

1 cup fresh blueberries
1¾ cups sifted flour
2 teaspoons baking powder
¼ teaspoon baking soda
½ teaspoon salt
⅓ cup butter or margarine
⅔ cup sugar
2 eggs
1 cup mashed ripe bananas

Wash and thoroughly drain blueberries; toss berries with 2 tablespoons flour. Sift together remaining flour, baking powder and soda and salt. Cream butter or margarine; gradually beat in sugar until light and fluffy. Beat in eggs, one at a time. Add flour mixture and bananas alternately, in three parts. Stir in blueberries. Spoon into greased loaf pan (9x5x3-inches). Bake in 350°F. oven about 50 minutes or until done. Makes 1 loaf.

FRESH BLUEBERRY PINWHEEL BISCUITS

2 cups biscuit mix
⅔ cup milk

1 cup fresh blueberries
1 teaspoon sugar

Stir biscuit mix and milk to make a soft dough. Beat about 20 strokes until stiff but not sticky. Roll out dough on lightly floured surface into rectangle measuring about 14 x 6-inches. Meanwhile, wash and thoroughly drain blueberries; sprinkle sugar over dough. Sprinkle blueberries evenly over dough. Roll up tightly from long end. Cut into 12 slices. Place each slice in greased 2½-inch muffin cup. Bake in 450°F. oven 12–14 minutes. Makes 1 dozen.

FRESH BLUEBERRY REFRIGERATOR CAKE

1 envelope unflavored
   gelatin
½ cup fresh orange juice
½ cup hot water
1 tablespoon fresh lemon
   juice
½ cup sugar
¼ teaspoon salt
1 cup fresh blueberries

2 egg whites, beaten
½ cup heavy cream,
   whipped
Lady fingers
½ cup heavy cream,
   whipped
1 tablespoon sugar
Blueberries

Soften gelatin in orange juice. Stir in hot water. Add lemon juice, sugar and salt. Wash and crush blueberries and add. Chill until mixture begins to thicken. Fold in beaten egg whites along with whipped cream. Line bottom and sides of an 8-inch spring-form pan with lady fingers. Pour in half the mixture and cover with a layer of lady fingers. Repeat, using remaining blueberry mixture and lady fingers. Chill until firm and ready to serve. Garnish as desired with remaining whipped cream, sweetened with the 1 tablespoon sugar. Top with blueberries. Makes 8 servings.

FRESH FRUIT

QUICK FRESH BLUEBERRY PUDDING

4 cups fresh blueberries	Butter or margarine
¾ cup sugar	2 teaspoons fresh lemon
1 tablespoon flour	juice
¼ teaspoon salt	⅓ cup heavy cream,
8 slices close-textured	whipped
bread	

Wash and drain blueberries. Mix sugar, flour and salt and mix with berries. Set aside. Spread both sides of each slice of bread with softened butter or margarine. Place 2½ slices in the bottom of a 5x9x3-inch loaf pan. Top with sugared berries. Sprinkle with 1 teaspoon lemon juice. Repeat, using remaining bread and berry mixture, having bread as the top layer. Bake in a preheated moderate oven (375°F.) 60 minutes or until berries are cooked and bread is brown. Serve warm with whipped cream. Makes 6 servings.

FRESH BLUEBERRY RICH MUFFINS

1¾ cups sifted all-purpose flour	⅔ cup sugar
	1 large egg, beaten
½ teaspoon salt	⅔ cup milk
2½ teaspoons double-acting baking powder	¼ cup shortening, melted
	1 teaspoon vanilla extract
	1 cup fresh blueberries

Sift together flour, salt, baking powder and sugar into a mixing bowl. Add egg, milk, shortening and vanilla extract. Mix *only* until all ingredients are blended, using about 28 strokes. Stir in dry washed blueberries. Drop batter into well-greased, lightly floured muffin pans, filling them ¾ full. Bake in a preheated moderate oven (375°F.) 20 to 25 minutes. Serve hot. Makes 14 muffins.

FRESH BLUEBERRY JAM

4 cups sugar
1½ quarts fresh blueberries
2 tablespoons fresh
    lemon juice

1¾ ounce package,
    powdered pectin

Measure sugar into a bowl and set aside to use later. Wash blueberries and turn into a 6 or 8 quart saucepan. Crush and add lemon juice. Add powdered pectin and mix well. Place over high heat, stir and cook until the mixture comes to a hard boil. Boil 1 minute, Stir in sugar at once. Bring to a full rolling boil and boil hard 1 minute, stirring constantly. (A full rolling boil cannot be stirred down.) Remove from heat. Then stir and skim off foam with a metal spoon. Stir and cool about 5 minutes. Pour into hot sterilized jars. Seal at once. Makes 7–8-ounce jars.

FRESH BLUEBERRY CREAM

1 pint (2 cups) fresh
    blueberries
⅛ teaspoon salt
1 large egg white
1 cup diced large
    marshmallows

1 cup heavy cream,
    whipped
½ teaspoon pure vanilla
    extract
3 tablespoons sugar

Wash and drain blueberries. Add salt to egg whites and beat them until stiff. Fold in marshmallows, 1½ cups of the blueberries, whipped cream and vanilla extract. Chill until ready to serve. Just before serving, crush remaining ½ cup blueberries and fold into the mixture. Serve as dessert. Makes 4 cups.

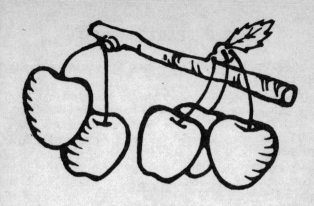

CHERRIES

AVAILABILITY

Sweet cherries are available May through August. Sour cherries have their peak season July-August.

Sweet cherries are the larger of the two types and are slightly heart shaped, colored bright to deep red, white or golden. Sour (tart) cherries are red to nearly black in color and are usually used for cooking.

SWEET CHERRIES

BING—extra large, heart shaped, deep maroon to black in color.

TARTARIAN (or BLACK TARTARIAN)—large, heart shaped, mahogany to black in color.

ROYAL ANN (or NAPOLEON)—large, heart shaped, amber to yellow with a red blush. Used primarily for canning.

LAMBERT—large to extra large, roundish, red to dark red.

REPUBLICAN (BLACK REPUBLICAN or LEWELLING)—small to medium in size, heart shaped, purplish-black in color.

CHAPMAN (or EARLY CHAPMAN)—very large, roundish, purplish-black in color.

SOUR OR TART CHERRIES

EARLY RICHMOND—first on the market, roundish, light to dark red.

ENGLISH MORELLO—roundish, very dark red; good for cooking purposes, but cannot be eaten out of hand.

MONTMORENCY—very similar to Richmond, juicy, good for eating out of hand, but best for pies, jellies, tarts, all cooking.

HOW TO BUY

Good quality in cherries is indicated by bright, fresh appearance and color. They should be fairly firm, juicy and have a well-developed flavor. Immature cherries are of small size, poor color and lacking in juice. Over-mature or stale fruits are generally soft, dull in appearance and may be shriveled or leaky. Decay is indicated by small circular brown spots.

PREPARATION AND SERVING SUGGESTIONS

Sort and throw away any spoiled cherries and then store in the refrigerator without washing; they will keep for up to two weeks. Cherries are eaten out of hand, in salads, and cooked in pies, tarts, cakes. They are also used for making jellies, jams, preserves, sauces and candies. Some varieties of both sweet and sour cherries are preserved and often added to drinks and ices, as much for ornament as to give flavor.

NUTRITIONAL VALUE

Although cherries contain essential nutrients (vitamins and minerals) they are not considered important for their nutritional value. A 3½-ounce serving of sweet fresh cherries contains only 70 Calories.

MOLDED FRESH CHERRY
AND LIME SALAD

4 envelopes unflavored gelatin	¼ teaspoon salt
1 cup cold water	Few drops red food coloring
2 cups boiling water	¾ cup fresh lime juice
¾ cup sugar	1¾ cups honeydew balls
2 cups pitted fresh cherries	Salad greens

Soften gelatin in cold water. Add boiling water, sugar, cherries and salt. Mix well. Add food coloring until desired color is reached. Stir in lime juice. Chill until the mixture begins to thicken. Fold in melon balls. Turn into an 8-cup mold. Chill until firm and ready to serve. Unmold onto a serving plate. Garnish as desired with salad greens and honeydew melon. Serve with mayonnaise or your favorite fruit salad dressing. Makes 10 servings.

MOLDED FRESH CHERRY
CREAM CHEESE SALAD

4 envelopes unflavored gelatin	¼ teaspoon salt
1 cup cold water	½ cup fresh lemon juice
2 cups hot water	4-oz. package cream cheese, softened
¾ cup sugar	1 cup seedless or seeded grapes
2 cups pitted sweet cherries	Salad greens

Soften gelatin in cold water. Stir in hot water, sugar, cherries and salt. Add lemon juice. Arrange a pattern of cherry halves in bottom of mold and cover with a little of the gelatin mixture. Chill until firm. Chill remaining mixture until it begins to thicken. Beat cream cheese with a little of the gelatin mixture, and fold into gelatin along with grapes. Turn into a lightly oiled 2-quart mold. Chill until firm and ready to serve. Turn out onto a serving plate and garnish with salad greens and additional cherries. Makes 12 servings.

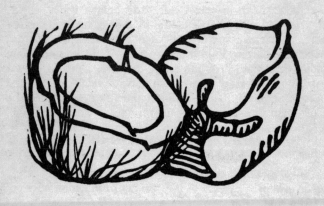

COCONUTS

AVAILABILITY

Available all year but mostly September through December.

HOW TO BUY

Look for coconuts that are heavy for their size and full of milk. The milk should slosh around when the nut is shaken. Coconuts without milk are spoiled and should be rejected. Those with moldy or wet "eyes" are unsound.

PREPARATION AND SERVING SUGGESTIONS

Coconuts are easily shelled in either of two simple ways. After draining the milk, place them in the freezer for approximately an hour or put them in a moderate oven (350 degrees F.) briefly, then rap them sharply with a hammer or cleaver, and the shell will shatter. The meat will also come away from the shell easier after one of these treatments.

The milky juice of the coconut is a nutritious and refreshing drink. The delicious meat of the coconut can be eaten with a spoon, or grated and used to sprinkle on desserts, toppings, and pastries.

NUTRITIONAL VALUE

The meat of the coconut is a source of food energy—100 grams contains 346 Calories and an assortment of other nutrients. The liquid (milk) of the coconut is also nutritious, but contains only 22 Calories per 100 grams.

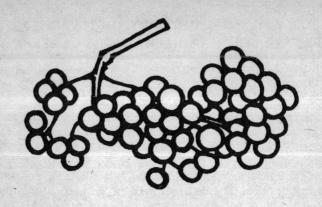

CRANBERRIES

AVAILABILITY

In good supply late September through December. Cranberries vary in size and color according to variety and maturity.

HOW TO BUY

Cranberries generally are of good quality, so buying is not much of a problem. Look for fresh, plump, lustrous, firm berries. Poor quality is indicated by shrivelling, dull appearance, softness or stickiness.

PREPARATION AND SERVING SUGGESTIONS

The Thanksgiving season is when cranberries are especially popular. When brought home from the store, place, unwashed, in your refrigerator and they will keep for one to four weeks. Wash before using.

Cranberries are flavorsome, tart and tempting and so its worth noting that they can be easily frozen for use at a later date. Buy extra when they are in season and freeze in the unopened package.

FRESH FRUIT

Cranberries have a wide variety of uses, from an ingredient of turkey stuffing to a juice cocktail spicy with cloves and cinnamon. Of course, cranberry sauce and jelly are old reliables. But cranberries are also used in relishes, ices, fruit salads, fruit molds and in many combinations with apples, oranges and other fruits . . . For a raw cranberry relish that's mighty good for serving with any kind of meat, poultry or fish, USDA's Food Facts gives the following ingredients: one pound of fresh cranberries, one orange and one cup of sugar. Quarter the orange and take out the seeds, but use both pulp and skin. Grind the raw berries and orange peel, mix and place in covered jar in the refrigerator. It will keep for two or three weeks. . . . Fresh cranberry nut bread is excellent. . . . A baked fresh cranberry and apple compote is mouth watering . . . Cranberries make fine pies, pudding and tarts. . . . There is a recipe for fluffy cranberry custard . . . And a fresh cranberry and apple cobbler is deluxe.

NUTRITIONAL VALUE

Fresh cranberries are low in calories—$\frac{1}{2}$ cup fresh cranberries has only 25 calories. That amount uncooked has over 10 percent of the recommended daily allowance of vitamin C. They are also low in sodium-perfect for those on sodium restricted diets.

The creative cook can find endless ways to capitalize on the cranberry's unique flavor charms—particularly in salads. Cranberry sauce, either raw or cooked is an old standby. But for variety, mold the sauce into a gelatin salad joining it perhaps with other fresh fruits in season. Avocado halves filled with a fresh cranberry and grapefruit relish is an alluring company treat. Incidentally, be sure to use the relish as an accompaniment to poultry. For holiday dinners try filling the centers of fresh pear halves with cranberry sauce and serve it as a side-dish salad.

CRANBERRY CRUNCH

1½ cups uncooked
    rolled oats
½ cup all-purpose flour
¾ cup brown sugar
⅓ cup butter or margarine

1½ cups 10-MINUTE
    CRANBERRY
    SAUCE, cooled
1 tablespoon cornstarch

Preheat oven to 350°. In a bowl, mix together oats, flour and brown sugar. Cut in butter until crumbly. Press half of crumb mixture in a greased 8 inch square pan. In a small bowl mix together cranberry sauce and cornstarch; spread onto crumb base. Top with remaining crumb mixture. Bake 45 minutes. Cool, cut into squares. Makes 9 squares.

10-MINUTE CRANBERRY SAUCE

1½ cups sugar
1 cup water

1 pound (4 cups) fresh or
    fresh frozen cranberries

Combine sugar and water in saucepan; stir to dissolve sugar. Bring to boil; add cranberries; cook till skins pop, about 5 minutes longer. Remove from heat. Serve sauce warm or chilled. Makes 4 cups of sauce.

FRESH CRANBERRY SAUCE HAS MANY DELICIOUS USES

Cook fresh cranberries only until they burst, advise the experts. Additional cooking tends to make them a little bitter.

To make the traditional fresh cranberry sauce, combine 2 cups sugar, 1 cup water and a few grains of salt in a saucepan. Bring to boiling point. Add 1 pound (4 cups) fresh cranberries. Cover and cook until the skins pop, about 5 to 8 minutes.

This basic cranberry sauce can be used in dozens of ways. Combined with whipped cream and mayonnaise it makes a delectable fruit salad dressing. It could not be easier: Combine ¾ cup heavy cream, whipped; ¼ cup mayonnaise and ⅓ cup strained cranberry sauce. Serve over fresh pear halves, orange sections or a salad of mixed fresh fruits.

CRANBERRY STEWED APPLES: DESSERT OR MEAT ACCOMPANIMENT

This recipe for Cranberry Stewed Apples is a useful one. You can serve half a batch as a meat accompaniment at one meal, then stir an additional tablespoon or two of sugar into the remainder and serve it another day as a dessert with cream cheese and crackers. Either way, it's a lovely red and easy to prepare.

Select 6 medium tart apples that hold their shape when cooked. Peel, cut into quarters and remove cores. Place in a saucepan with 2 cups fresh whole cranberries, 1 cup sugar, ½ cup water and ¼ teaspoon salt. If desired, add ½ teaspoon ground cinnamon, ½ teaspoon ground ginger, ½ teaspoon ground allspice and ¼ teaspoon ground cloves. Cover and bring to boiling point. Cook 15 minutes, or until apples are tender and skins of cranberries have burst. Cool. Serve with poultry, ham, pork or veal. Or add an additional ¼ cup sugar and serve as a dessert. Makes 1 quart.

CRANBERRY LEMON SAUCE

¾ cup sugar
2 teaspoons unflavored
  gelatin
⅓ cup water

2 cups fresh or fresh frozen
  cranberries
2 tablespoons lemon juice
1 teaspoon lemon peel

In a saucepan, mix together sugar and gelatin. Gradually add water; stir to dissolve sugar. Bring to a boil over medium heat, stirring occasionally. Add cranberries, lemon peel and juice. Cook, stirring until skins pop. Chill until thickened. Serve as a topping for cheesecake, crepes or ice cream. Makes 2 cups sauce.

CRANBERRIES JUBILEE

1 cup sugar
1½ cups water
2 cups fresh or frozen
  cranberries

¼ cup brandy
Vanilla ice cream

Combine sugar and water in saucepan, stirring to dissolve sugar. Bring to boiling; boil 5 minutes. Add cranberries and bring to boiling again; cook 5 minutes. Turn into heat-proof bowl or blazer pan of chafing dish. Heat brandy. Ignite brandy and pour over cranberry mixture. Blend into sauce and serve immediately over ice cream. Makes 2½ cups sauce.

FRESH FRUIT

CRANBERRY CHEESECAKE TOPPING

To prepare topping:

1 teaspoon cornstarch
2 tablespoons water

⅓ cup reserved ground
cranberry mixture

Stir cornstarch with water to make a smooth paste. Mix in cranberry mixture. Cook over medium heat, stirring constantly, until mixture thickens and reaches boiling point. Cool to room temperature. Remove sides of cake pan. Drizzle topping over surface of cake. Makes 8 to 10 servings.

CRANBERRY CHIFFON PIE

2 cups fresh cranberries
½ cup sugar
½ cup water
1 envelope unflavored
gelatin
¼ cup water
3 egg yolks

Few grains salt
1 teaspoon fresh lemon
juice
3 egg whites
½ cup sugar
9-inch baked pastry shell

Combine cranberries, sugar and ½ cup water in saucepan. Cook over medium heat, stirring constantly, until cranberry skins pop. Put cranberry mixture through a strainer or food mill. Soften gelatin in ¼ cup water. Beat egg yolks in top of double boiler. Mix in cranberry puree and salt. Cook over hot water, stirring constantly, until mixture thickens. Stir in gelatin and lemon juice. Stir until gelatin is dissolved. Chill until mixture mounds when dropped from a spoon. Beat egg whites until soft peaks form. Gradually beat in ½ cup sugar until stiff peaks form. Fold into cranberry mixture. Turn into pastry shell. Chill at least 2–3 hours, or until firm. Garnish with whipped cream, if desired, just before serving. Makes 1 9-inch pie.

CRANBERRY BONBONS

Bonbon shells:

1 jumbo package or 2
    regular packages (2
    cups) semi-sweet
    chocolate pieces
¼ cup butter or margarine

6 dozen tea-size paper
    baking cups (2 inches
    in diameter at top and
    1¾ inches across
    bottom)

Melt chocolate and butter in saucepan over very low heat. Have ready 24 double baking cups, made double by placing one inside another. Using back of spoon, spread melted chocolate over inside of baking cup to cover completely. Place in refrigerator 30 minutes, until firm. Carefully peel baking cups from chocolate and slip chocolate shells into clean baking cups. Return to refrigerator.

Cranberry filling:

1 envelope unflavored
    gelatin
¾ cup fresh orange juice,
    divided
1 pound (1 quart) fresh
    cranberries

1½ cups sugar
2 teaspoons grated
    orange rind
1 cup heavy cream

Sprinkle gelatin over ½ cup orange juice in small saucepan. Place over low heat; stir constantly until gelatin dissolves, about 3 minutes. Remove from heat. Place cranberries in medium saucepan with remaining ¼ cup orange juice, sugar and orange rind. Cook over medium heat, stirring occasionally, until cranberry skins pop, about 10 minutes. Remove from heat; stir in gelatin mixture. Chill until mixture is completely cooled and slightly thickened. Whip cream; fold into cooled cranberry mixture. Spoon into chilled chocolate shells and refrigerate until set. Makes 24 bonbons.

FRESH CRANBERRY MARMALADE SAUCE

4 cups raw cranberries   ¼ cup sugar
1 cup thick orange
     marmalade

Wash cranberries and put through a food chopper, using the large blade. Combine chopped cranberries with remaining ingredients; mix well. Chill thoroughly before serving. Makes approximately 3½ cups.

FRESH CRANBERRY SWEETPOTATO STUFFING

1 cup mashed
     sweetpotato
3½ cups toasted bread
     cubes
½ cup finely chopped
     celery
½ cup onion
1 cup fresh cranberries

3 tablespoons sugar
1 teaspoon salt
⅛ teaspoon black pepper
1 teaspoon poultry
     seasoning
1½ lbs. (7) sausage links
2 tablespoons butter or
     margarine

Combine sweetpotatoes, bread cubes and celery. Put onion and cranberries through food chopper, using coarse blade. Add sugar. Stir in salt, black pepper and poultry seasoning. Cut sausage links into ½-inch pieces, brown and add to the mixture. Discard fat. Melt butter or margarine, toss lightly to mix well. Stuff loosely into crop and body cavity of a 10 to 12 lb. turkey. Close openings with skewers and lacings. Makes sufficient stuffing for a 10 to 12 lb. turkey.

FRESH CRANBERRY CHEESE TARTS

4 pkgs. (3 oz. each) soft
   cream cheese
3 large eggs
½ cup sugar
1 teaspoon vanilla extract
½ teaspoon grated lemon
   peel

12 unbaked tart shells, each
   3 inches in diameter
2 cups fresh cranberries
½ cup water
¾ cup sugar
⅛ teaspoon salt

Beat cream cheese until light. Add eggs, the ½ cup sugar, vanilla extract and lemon peel; beat until blended. Do not overbeat. Pour into unbaked tart shells. Bake in a preheated slow oven (325°F.) 40 minutes. Place on racks and cool. In the meantime wash cranberries and set aside. Place water, remaining sugar and salt in a saucepan. Bring to a boil and boil one minute. Add cranberries; cover and cook 5 to 8 minutes or until skins pop. Cool. Remove cool cheese tarts from pans; spoon cool cranberry mixture on tarts. Refrigerate. Makes 12 tarts.

GRAPEFRUIT

AVAILABILITY

Available all year, with largest supplies November through April and smallest July through August. Grapefruit are either pink, red or white. Suppliers are from Florida, California, Arizona and Texas.

The major types of grapefruit include:

DUNCAN - seeded, medium to large with yellowish skin; excellent flavor.

MARSH - available in red, pink and white varieties; seedless and medium to large.

RUBY RED AND STAR RED - seedless, golden skin with areas of red blushes, deep red flesh, sweet flavor, small to large.

HOW TO BUY

Good grapefruit is firm, spring to the touch. Avoid fruit that is soft and fruit that is wilted or flabby. They should be well shaped and heavy for their size. Heavy fruit usually is thin-skinned and contains more juice than fruit that is coarse-skinned and puffy. Color does not affect the quality nor do small spots on the skin.

PREPARATION AND SERVING SUGGESTIONS

Grapefruit is ready to eat when you bring it home, since only "ripe" fruit is allowed to be shipped. You may keep grapefruit a day or two at room temperature; however, it is best to refrigerate in order to avoid drying and wrinkling; grapefruit can be kept one to four weeks in the refrigerator. You can start breakfast with grapefruit . . . or end a meal with it; its tartly sweet flavor stimulates the taste buds.

A grapefruit spoon makes it especially easy to section a grapefruit. However, a grapefruit spoon is not necessary for full enjoyment of the fruit. The usual way to serve grapefruit is to cut it in half, cut around a section to loosen it, and if necessary, sweeten. Other serving suggestions include: segments in various salad combinations; and they are also good broiled with brown sugar, spices and other toppings. The juice of the grapefruit is used with other juices in punch; the segments and juice go into a variety of jellied molds; a grapefruit cake with grapefruit icing is unique—but delicious! The fruit makes a nice stuffing for poultry; and grapefruit marinated in French dressing is a good accompaniment for any meat course. Grapefruit peel is used in making candied strips.

NUTRITIONAL VALUE

Grapefruit offers a variety of good nutrients and is especially known for its vitamin C content. One half a medium size grapefruit (4½ inches in diameter) adds only 55 Calories to the energy intake.

GRAPEFRUIT PORK CHOP CASSEROLE

1 tablespoon salad oil
1 onion, chopped
6 loin pork chops, about ¾ inch thick
1 green cabbage, shredded (about 6 cups)
2 teaspoons caraway seeds
1½ teaspoons salt
1 tablespoon brown sugar
1½ cups fresh grapefruit juice
2 apples, cored, pared and diced
2 grapefruits, sectioned (2 cups sections)*

Heat oil in skillet, add onion and cook until tender. Add chops and slowly brown on both sides, about 20 minutes. Remove to 3- or 4-quart casserole. Add cabbage. Sprinkle with caraway seeds, salt, sugar and juice. Cover and bake in a 350°F. oven 30 minutes. Add apple, cover and bake 25 minutes longer. Add grapefruit sections and bake an additional 5 minutes. Makes 6 servings.

FRESH GRAPEFRUIT AND BANANA FLUFF

2 envelopes unflavored gelatin
1½ cups fresh grapefruit juice
1 cup hot water
¼ teaspoon salt
½ cup sugar
½ cup fresh lemon juice
¼ teaspoon ground nutmeg
1 cup grapefruit sections, cut in bite-size pieces
1 cup diced banana

Sprinkle gelatin over grapefruit juice. Stir to dissolve. Add next 5 ingredients. Chill until as thick as fresh egg whites. To hasten process, set bowl in a larger bowl of ice cubes. Stir frequently. Beat with a rotary beater until frothy. Combine grapefruit sections and diced banana. Toss gently and add to gelatin mixture. Spoon into individual sherbet glasses. Chill until set. Makes 8 servings.

* To section grapefruit, cut slice from top, then cut off peel in strips from top to bottom, cutting deep enough to remove white membrane, then cut slice from bottom. Or cut off peel round and round spiral fashion. Go over fruit again, removing any remaining white membrane. Cut along side of each dividing membrane from outside to middle of core. Remove section by section over bowl to retain juice from fruit.

FRESH GRAPEFRUIT SHRIMP SALAD IN HALF SHELL

2 medium-sized fresh grapefruit	Lettuce leaves
1 cup cooked shrimp	Cherry tomatoes for garnish
¾ cup diced fresh celery	Cooked whole shrimp for garnish
⅓ cup diced fresh green pepper	Grapefruit Salad Dressing
⅛ teaspoon salt	

Cut grapefruit in half crosswise and remove seeds. With sharp knife cut out sections and remove pulp. Reserve shells. Cut grapefruit sections into pieces and combine with shrimp, celery, green pepper and salt. Toss lightly. Line grapefruit shells with lettuce leaves. Fill with grapefruit mixture. Garnish with cherry tomato and whole shrimp. Serve with chilled Grapefruit Salad Dressing.

FRESH GRAPEFRUIT PINWHEELS

3 tablespoons cream cheese, softened	1 tablespoon finely chopped hazelnuts
1 teaspoon sour cream	12 large pitted dates
½ teaspoon sugar	3 cups fresh grapefruit sections
⅛ teaspoon salt	Salad greens

Combine first 5 ingredients. Blend well. Cut a slit, lengthwise, in each date and stuff with approximately 1 teaspoon cheese mixture. For each serving, arrange ½ cup grapefruit sections on salad greens in pinwheel shape on plate, centering 2 stuffed dates in each. Serve chilled. YIELD: 6 servings.

TOSSED FRESH GRAPEFRUIT AND GREEN SALAD

½ head lettuce
½ head curly endive
½ head romaine
1 cup fresh grapefruit
  sections
½ cup sliced cucumbers
½ cup diced green peppers

¼ cup onion rings
1 teaspoon salt
¼ cup salad oil
2 tablespoons fresh
  lemon juice
Fresh grapefruit sections
Cucumbers and onion
  rings

Wash and dry salad greens. Combine with grapefruit, cucumbers, green pepper, onion rings, salt, salad oil and lemon juice. Toss lightly. Garnish as desired with fresh grapefruit sections, cucumbers and onion rings.
YIELD: 8 to 10 servings

FRESH GRAPEFRUIT PIE

1 9 inch baked pie shell
32 marshmallows, regular
  size
½ cup grapefruit juice

1 cup heavy cream
2½ cups fresh grapefruit
  sections
¼ cups coconut, shredded

Cut marshmallows in quarters and melt them in ¼ cup grapefruit juice. Cool to room temperature. Add remaining ¼ cup juice to sections. Whip cream. Fold cooled marshmallows, grapefruit and cream together. Pour into cooled pie shell. Allow to set about 3 hours. Sprinkle coconut over pie just before serving.

GRAPES

AVAILABILITY

Since there is a large variety of grapes, we shall list the availability under each important variety.

European types (grown in U.S.A.)

THOMPSON SEEDLESS—medium size, green-white to gold, sweet. Season: June–November

EMPEROR—normally seeded, light red to red-purple, large, neutral flavor. Season: October–April

TOKAY—normally seeded, large, brilliant to dark red, neutral flavor. Season: August–December

RIBIER—normally seeded, very large, purple-black, neutral flavor. Season: July–February

CARDINAL—few seeds, very large, cherry red to red-purple, sweet flavor. Season: June–August

PERLETTE—seedless, white with waxy appearance, neutral flavor. Season: June–July

RED MALAGA—normally seeded, large, pink to reddish purple, neutral flavor. Season: July–September

ALMERIA—normally seeded, large, green-white, neutral flavor. Season: October–April

CALMERIA—normally seeded, large, cylindrical, green-white, neutral flavor. Season: October–April

ITALIA MUSCAT—very large, green, heavy sweet flavor. Season: August–November

FRESH FRUIT

There are four major American-type grapes.

CONCORD—seeded, large, round, purple, sour flavor. Season: September–October

NIAGARA—seeded, large, amber with heavy gray bloom, sweet flavor. Season: September–November

CATAWBA—seeded, large, purplish-red, sweet distinctive flavor. September–November

DELAWARE—seeded, small, pink skin, sweet flavor. Season: August–September

HOW TO BUY

Look for grapes that are firmly attached to the stem. Gentle shaking of a bunch will reveal the condition. Grapes should appear fresh, smooth, plump, not sticky, well colored for the variety. Usually green grapes are at their best for flavor and sweetness when they are yellow-green in color.

PREPARATION AND SERVING SUGGESTIONS

Grapes for commerce are divided by use into four major groups and one minor group. These are: *table* grapes, *raisin* grapes, *wine* grapes, *juice* grapes, and the minor group—*canning* grapes. However, the same grape may be in more than one or even in all groups. Thompson Seedless, for example, is suitable for all five types of uses. The mature fruit of all grape varieties that have been named, some 8,000 or more, will ferment into a kind of wine when crushed, and most of them can be dried or eaten fresh. However, only a limited number of varieties produce wines of good quality, and the raisins of commerce are produced mainly from three varieties.

Fewer than a dozen varieties are grown extensively for table grapes. Most of the sweet juice produced in America is from one variety (Concord). Only one or two varieties are used for canning. Concord grapes are used extensively for juice and also for jams, jellies, puddings and pies. Table grapes, such as Emperor, Thompson Seedless, Tokay, Cardinal, Ribier and others are mostly eaten out of hand but are also used in salads, fruit cups, pies, puddings, cakes, stewed fruit, and as meat accompaniments.

NUTRITIONAL VALUE

Grapes provide a good quota of vitamins and minerals, though not outstanding for any one kind. An average 100 grams of European-type grapes contain 67 Calories; grapes are low in sodium and can be used in most low-sodium diets.

GRAPE STUFFED CHICKEN

1 broiling chicken, split in half (2-2½ pounds)	2 tablespoons chopped fresh onion
Salt	1½ cups coarsely crumbled cheese crackers
3 tablespoons butter or margarine	1 cup seedless grapes
	Few grains pepper
	1 egg, well beaten

Sprinkle chicken lightly with salt. Place on rack, skin side up, in shallow baking pan; dot with 2 tablespoons butter or margarine. Bake in 375°F. oven 30 minutes. While chicken is baking, sauté onion in remaining butter or margarine until golden. Remove from heat. Mix onion and drippings lightly with remaining ingredients. Remove chicken from oven; turn over. Pile grape stuffiing into chicken. Remove rack from baking pan; place chicken in baking pan. Bake 45 minutes longer, basting occasionally with drippings. Makes 2 generous servings. SPECIAL NOTE: To serve four, double amounts of all ingredients.

CHILLED GRAPE SOUFFLÉ

1 envelope unflavored gelatin	2 tablespoons grated lemon rind
¼ cup cold water	½ cup fresh lemon juice
2 cups sour cream	2 cups halved pitted grapes
¾ cup sugar	

Fold a 30-inch piece of waxed paper in half lengthwise. Tie around outside of 4-cup soufflé as a collar. Soften gelatin in cold water. Beat sour cream in small electric mixer bowl until fluffy (consistency of soft whipped cream). Add sugar, a little at a time, beating well after each addition. Mix in lemon rind and juice. Dissolve gelatin over hot water; beat into lemon mixture. Chill until mixture mounds when dropped from a spoon. Fold in grapes. Pour into prepared soufflé dish. Chill overnight. Remove waxed paper before serving. Makes about 6 servings.

GRAPE FLAMBÉ

1½ pounds fresh grapes (4 cups)	2 strips lemon rind (remove with vegetable parer)
¼ cup sugar	
2 tablespoons butter or margarine	2 tablespoons chopped candied ginger
¼ cup fresh orange juice	2 tablespoons cognac
1 tablespoon fresh lemon juice	

Halve grapes and remove seeds. In large skillet or crepe pan heat sugar, stirring constantly, until it melts and turns pale golden brown. Add butter, orange juice, lemon juice, lemon rind and ginger; heat until mixture is smooth. Add grapes and heat. Pour cognac over grapes and ignite. Shake pan or stir until flames die. Serve with ice cream or pound cake. Makes about 6 to 8 servings.

RECIPE FOR GRAPE PARFAITS

Prepare one package (the 3¾-ounce size) of instant vanilla pudding mix according to package directions. Fold in 1½ cups halved seeded grapes and one teaspoon grated lemon rind. Whip one-half cup of heavy cream. Fold the cream into the grape mixture. Spoon into desert glasses. Chill about thirty minutes before serving. This makes about six servings.

LEMONS

AVAILABILITY

Lemons are available all year long.

HOW TO BUY

Select fresh-looking fruit. The best lemons have a fine textured, all-yellow skin. They should be firm and heavy for their size.

PREPARATION AND SERVING SUGGESTIONS

While the principal use of lemons is in making drinks, large quantities are used in other ways. Lemon juice is a popular ingredient of salad dressings, and the juice is also used as the main dressing. The juice is excellent on meat and is a popular seasoning for seafoods of all kinds. Slices of lemon are an accepted part of a vegetable or combination vegetable and meat or fish salad. No tall glass of iced tea is complete without a generous wedge of lemon. Lemon pies, tarts, cakes and cookies are highly popular. Lemon is used to add flavor to salt-free diets, and frequently is used to replace oil in dressings used by those seeking to reduce their weight. A squeeze of lemon accents the flavor of soups and juices, such as tomato juice. Lemon adds zest to many kinds of cooked vegetables, such as green beans, asparagus or spinach. Hot lemonade is a pleasant way to get the necessary fluid when you have a cold. Lemon rubbed on lamb, fish or poultry before cooking helps tenderize the meat as well as to add flavor.
Fresh lemon juice helps to keep cut apples, pears, bananas and avocados from turning brown. Lemon is also a mild bleaching agent, useful for keeping white vegetables white. For example, a little lemon can be used in the water when cooking potatoes to retain the natural coloring. Celery dipped in "lemonated" water is guarded against browning. Refrigeration is desirable. However, lemons can be kept at room temperature.

NUTRITIONAL VALUE

Lemons, like other citrus fruits, are of special value for vitamin C content. They are low-carbohydrate fruit and can be used in a low sodium diets. A tablespoon of fresh lemon juice is less than 4 calories. One medium lemon provides almost twice the recommended U.S. daily allowance for an adult.

FRESH LEMON MERINGUE PIE

1 cup sugar	3 egg yolks
1/3 cup cornstarch	1/3 cup fresh lemon juice
1/2 teaspoon salt	1 teaspoon grated lemon
1/4 cup cold water	rind
1 1/4 cups hot water	2 teaspoons pure vanilla
2 tablespoons butter or	extract
margarine	9-inch baked pie shell
	Meringue

Combine 1/2 cup of the sugar, cornstarch, salt and cold water in the top of a double boiler. Mix well. Stor in boiling water. Cook over boiling water 3 to 5 minutes or until thick, stirring constantly. Cover and continue cooking over boiling water 8 minutes or until very thick, stirring occasionally. Add butter or margarine. Beat egg yolks lightly and blend with remaining 1/2 cup sugar to which add a little of the hot mixture. Then stir into the remaining hot mixture. Cook, uncovered, over hot water (not boiling) 10 minutes or until very thick, stirring frequently. Stir in lemon juice and rind. Cool. Add pure vanilla extract and turn into a baked 9-inch pie shell. Top as desired with Meringue. Bake in a preheated slow oven (300° F.) 20 minutes or until lightly browned. Cool before serving.

YIELD: 6 servings.

LEMON PARMESAN DRESSING

¼ cup grated Parmesan
   cheese
½ cup salad oil
2 teaspoons grated lemon
   peel
½ cup freshly squeezed
   lemon juice

¾ to 1 teaspoon salt
¼ teaspoon sweet basil,
   crushed
⅛ teaspoon coarsely ground
   black pepper

Combine all ingredients in covered container. Chill thoroughly. Shake well before using. Excellent on seafood salads. Makes 1 cup.

FRESH LEMON MARSHMALLOW FROSTING

2 egg whites
1½ cups sugar
⅛ teaspoon salt
¼ cup cold water
2 tablespoons fresh
   lemon juice

1 cup small
   marshmallows
1½ teaspoons vanilla
   extract
Few drops red food
   coloring

Place in top of double boiler egg whites, sugar, salt, water and lemon juice. Mix well. Place over hot water and beat with an electric beater about 7 minutes or until the frosting thickens and stands in peaks. Remove from heat, add marshmallows and vanilla extract. Continue beating until frosting stands in very stiff peaks. Add desired amount of food coloring. Makes sufficient frosting for two 9-inch square cake layers.

LIMES

AVAILABILITY

Limes are available year round, mainly Florida, Mexico, and California. Heaviest shipments occur June through September.

HOW TO BUY

Domestically produced limes are bright green and juicy, and are of the Age or Tahiti variety. They are seedless. Exposure to light causes deterioration of color. The Mexican, or key lime, has limited availability. It is yellow when mature and contains seeds.

PREPARATION AND SERVING SUGGESTIONS

Refrigerate limes and keep out of sunlight to retain peak of flavor juiciness. Limes will keep fresh this way 6-8 weeks.

Fresh lime juice is used in the preparation of beverages such as limeade and lime rickey. It is used as flavoring for jellies, jams, and marmalades. Slices of fresh limes make attractive garnishes for meat and fish dishes. They dress up iced tea. The flavor peps up salad dressings, or the juice alone may be used on salads. Lime juice is popular in sherbets, ices, pies and ice-box cakes. It is a natural base for fruit punches and supplies a spicy fresh fruit flavor for beverages. It blends well with other citrus juices.

NUTRITIONAL VALUE

Limes contain a good amount of vitamin C, although not nearly as much as lemons do; 100 grams contain 28 calories.

FLORIDA FRESH LIME PIE

1 cup sugar
⅓ cup cornstarch
½ teaspoon salt
¼ cup cold water
1¼ cups hot water
2 tablespoons butter or
   margarine
3 large egg yolks

⅓ cup fresh lime juice
1 teaspoon grated lime
   peel
1 teaspoon vanilla extract
9-inch baked pie shell
½ cup heavy cream
1 tablespoon sugar

Combine ½ cup of the sugar, cornstarch, salt and cold water in the top of a double boiler. Mix well. Gradually add boiling water. Cook 5 minutes over rapidly boiling water or over very low heat, stirring constantly. Cover and cook 8 to 10 minutes over rapidly boiling water, stirring occasionally. Add butter or margarine. Beat egg yolks and blend with the remaining ½ cup sugar, to which add a little of the hot mixture. Then stir into the rest of the hot mixture. Cook, uncovered, over hot water (not boiling) 10 minutes or until very thick, stirring frequently. Gradually stir in lime juice and peel. (To prevent the pie from being bitter, grate only the green portion of the peel.) Remove from heat. Cool. Add vanilla extract and turn into a cold, baked 9-inch pie shell. Top as desired with the heavy cream sweetened with the 1 tablespoon sugar. Garnish with a little grated lime peel, if desired.

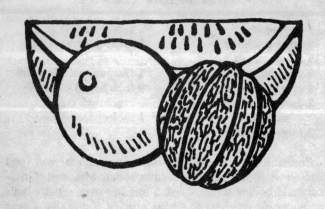

MELONS

AVAILABILITY

There are several varieties in the melon family: CANTALOUPES, CASABAS, CRENSHAWS, HONEY DEWS, PERSIANS, and WATERMELONS.

CANTALOUPES—small, oval-shaped, rind is coarse with a netting-type of ridging, grayish in color; has pungent aroma, sweet when ripe. Peak season: May–September.

CASABAS—large, globe-shaped, rind is rough, but without netting of cantaloupe, yellow, sweet. Season: July–November.

CRENSHAWS—as big as Casabas, but with a more pointed stem end, smooth rind, green-gold color, spicy taste. Season: July–October.

HONEY DEWS—large, round or football-shaped, rind is generally velvety smooth, creamy white to creamy yellow when ripe, sweet and has little or no fragrance. Peak season: June–October.

FRESH FRUIT
AVAILABILITY

HONEYBALL—similar to Honey Dews but much smaller, round, netted surface. Season: June–October.

PERSIANS—large (same size as cantaloupe or larger), deep green with fine netting overall, moderately sweet, pleasant aroma. Season: July–October.

WATERMELONS—largest variety of melon (25–40 pounds), smooth skin, deep green to grayish-green, sweet and very juicy. Many varieties. Flesh bright red. Season: April–September.

HOW TO BUY

CANTALOUPES—look for a smooth, rounded, depressed scar at the stem end. This indicates melon was picked at full maturity and separated easily from the stem. Avoid bruised or damaged fruit.

CASABAS—The deeper the yellow, the riper the melon.

CRENSHAWS—Fully ripe when blossom end is very soft and the rind dark.

HONEY DEWS (HONEYBALLS)—when fully mature, color is whitish, no aroma, blossom end hard to slightly springy.

PERSIANS—when ripe, blossom end is soft and rind color lightens.

WATERMELONS—ripeness difficult to determine, should have good color, lower side should be yellowish, should also be firm. Thumping a melon is not considered an accurate test. Immature melons are usually very hard.

PREPARATION AND SERVING SUGGESTIONS
CANTALOUPES

Serve plain or squeeze fresh lemon or lime juice over the melon. Serve in combination with other fruits, berries or ice cream. Cantaloupes fit into any meal as an appetizer, salad or dessert. Half of a cantaloupe makes a natural bowl for berries or ice cream. Wrap when storing in your refrigerator to prevent their pungent odor from spreading in the refrigerator.

PREPARATION AND SERVING SUGGESTIONS

HONEY DEWS
(and Casabas, Crenshaws, Persians, Honeyballs)

For breakfast melons are quick and tasty. For luncheon, try this idea: peel a chilled melon and slice the center in inch-thick slices. Dice the ends. Fill the rings with cottage cheese and sprinkle with the diced melon. Garnish with sliced peaches or other fruit, and serve with favorite dressing.

You can do some very special and artistic things with melons. For example, make fresh melon boats cutting the melon in half crosswise, remove seeds and stringy portion; then cut each half into three wedges; place each boat on a serving plate and place a mixture of grapes, orange sections, fresh lemon juice and sugar on each boat, garnish with mint leaves. Or use fresh melon balls in a fruit sauce made of orange juice, lemon juice, currant jelly and vanilla extract. And how about melon rings, 1 to 1½ inches thick served on lettuce beds and filled with shrimp salad? Diced fresh melon with fresh blueberries and some lime ice or sherbet makes a mighty fine dessert. Yes, there are endless ways to serve melons—with dressings such as bleu cheese french dressing.

Be sure to hold your melons at room temperature until well ripened, then store in your refrigerator.

WATERMELONS

On torrid days, nothing beats icy cold watermelon for instant refreshment. Cut it anyway you like—into juicy wedges, chunks or rosy cubes. Watermelon is ideal for gelatin molds and fruit cups; watermelon juice is a colorful base for fruit beverages, ices and molded jellies.

NUTRITIONAL VALUE

Cantaloupes (and other melons) are a good source of vitamin A and C and an assortment of other valuable nutrients. Melons are all low in calories; cantaloupes have 30 calories per 100 grams, honey dews have 33 calories and watermelons, 26 calories per 100 grams.

CANTALOUPE FRUIT BOWL

3 small cantaloupes
1 cup fresh blueberries
1½ cups green seedless
    grapes or seeded
    grapes in season

2 cups fresh strawberries
2 tablespoons sugar
2 teaspoons fresh lemon
    juice

Wash cantaloupes, cut in half and remove seeds. Combine blueberries and grapes. Spoon into cantaloupe cavities. Wash strawberries. Remove caps and push through a coarse sieve. Add sugar and lemon juice. Spoon over blueberries and grapes. Chill 2 to 3 hours. Garnish each with a whole fresh strawberry and a fresh mint leaf. Makes 6 servings.

CANTALOUPE FRUIT SALAD

1 cup diced cantaloupe
½ cup seeded grapes
½ cup sliced fresh
    strawberries
½ cup sliced bananas
½ cup diced fresh oranges

½ cup diced celery
½ teaspoon grated lemon
    rind
3 tablespoons sour cream
Head lettuce

Chill fruit, drain and combine with celery, lemon rind and sour cream. Serve on lettuce. Garnish with cantaloupe balls. Makes 6 servings.

MELON FIESTA

Wash small cantaloupe, cut in half, crosswise and remove seeds. Cut out melon balls from each half, leaving the holes intact. Fill holes with cantaloupe, honey dew and watermelon balls. Sprinkle each with a tablespoon of anisette, white wine or grenadine. Serve as appetizer or dessert course. Allow ½ cantaloupe per serving.

FRESH CANTALOUPE SNOW PUDDING

1 envelope unflavored gelatin
¼ cup water
1 cup hot water
¾ cup sugar
¼ cup fresh lemon juice
1 large egg white
¹⁄₁₆ teaspoon salt
½ teaspoon vanilla extract
2 cups finely diced ripe cantaloupe
Custard Sauce, optional
Whipped cream, optional

Soften gelatin in the ¼ cup water. Add hot water and stir until gelatin has melted. Add sugar and lemon juice and chill over ice water until the mixture begins to thicken. Add egg white, salt and vanilla. Beat with an electric or rotary beater until the mixture is fluffy. Fold in cantaloupe. Chill until ready to serve. Serve in tall sherbet glasses with or without Custard Sauce and whipped cream.

CUSTARD SAUCE

¼ cup sugar
⅛ teaspoon salt
2 large eggs
2 cups milk
½ teaspoon vanilla
¼ teaspoon grated lemon peel

Combine sugar and salt in a 1-quart saucepan or in the top of a double boiler. Beat in eggs and ¼ cup of the milk. Heat the remaining milk and add to mixture. Stir and cook over low heat or hot water until the custard coats metal spoon. Remove from heat and stir in vanilla and lemon peel. Cool and chill. Makes 8 servings.

FRUIT FILLED CANTALOUPE

Ripe cantaloupe Sugar
Blueberries Fresh lemon juice
Seedless grapes Fresh orange juice

Wash cantaloupe, cut in half and remove seeds and stringy portion. Fill cavities with fresh blueberries and grapes, using equal parts of each. For each serving mix 1 teaspoon sugar, ½ teaspoon fresh lemon juice and 2 tablespoons fresh orange juice. Pour over fruit. Serve as dessert or as an appetizer. Allow ½ cantaloupe per serving.

FRESH CANTALOUPE BAVARIAN

2 medium-sized ½ cup sugar
  cantaloupes 1 teaspoon vanilla
2 envelopes unflavored 1 cup heavy cream,
  gelatin   whipped
1 tablespoon fresh lemon Fresh Strawberry Sauce
  juice

Cut cantaloupes in half, remove seeds; remove pulp and cut into small dice. (There should be about 4 cups.) Turn shells upside down on paper towel to drain. Reserve. Drain diced cantaloupe; reserve ½ cup liquid. Soften gelatin in the ½ cup cantaloupe liquid in a custard cup. Place in pan of simmering water until gelatin dissolves. Combine diced cantaloupe, gelatin, sugar, lemon juice and vanilla extract. Mix well. Chill until slightly thickened. Fold in whipped cream. Turn into cantaloupe shells and refrigerate until set. Cut shells in half and serve with Fresh Strawberry Sauce. (See next page for recipe.)

FRESH STRAWBERRY SAUCE

1 pint fresh strawberries
½ to ¾ cup sugar

Dash salt
½ teaspoon vanilla

Hull and slice berries. Add remaining ingredients; mix well. Refrigerate 1 hour. Makes 8 servings.

FRESH MELON PIE

1 package (3 ounces)
lemon-flavored gelatin
½ cup heavy cream,
whipped

1 cup cubed honey dew
melon, well drained
1 cup cubed cantaloupe,
well drained
1 cup cubed watermelon,
well drained
9-inch baked pastry shell

Prepare gelatin according to package directions, using only 1½ cups water. Chill until mixture is slightly thickened. Fold in whipped cream and melons. Turn into pastry shell. Chill several hours or until firm. Makes 6 servings.

FRESH HONEY DEW BOATS

1 cup grapes, seeds removed
1 cup fresh orange sections
2 tablespoons sugar

1 tablespoon fresh lemon
juice
1 large honey dew melon
Fresh mint leaves

Combine grapes, orange sections, sugar, and lemon juice. Chill about 1 hour. Just before serving, cut honey dew in half, crosswise and remove seeds and stringy portion. Cut each half into 3 wedges of equal size. Place each boat on a serving plate and spoon grapes and orange sections in the center. Garnish with fresh mint leaves. Serve for dessert. Makes 6 servings.

FRESH FRUIT

FRESH HONEY DEW MELON IN FRUIT SAUCE

¼ cup sugar
¼ cup fresh lemon juice
¾ cup fresh orange juice
½ cup currant jelly
1 teaspoon vanilla

3 cups fresh honey dew balls
Fresh orange sections
Honey dew Balls

Combine sugar, lemon and orange juices and jelly. Mix well. Bring to boiling point and boil 2 to 3 minutes. Add vanilla. Chill and pour over cold honey dew balls. Serve in sherbet glasses. Garnish with fresh orange sections and honey dew balls. Serve for dessert. Makes 6 servings.

WATERMELON FRUIT SALAD

2 fresh oranges, cut into segments
2 fresh peaches, sliced
1 cup green seedless grapes

½ cup fresh blueberries
Head lettuce
2 cups watermelon balls
Fruit salad dressing

Combine first 4 fruits. Place in a circle on a bed of salad greens. Pile watermelon balls in the center. Serve with FRUIT SALAD DRESSING. Makes 5 to 6 servings.

FRUIT SALAD DRESSING

Fold ½ cup whipped cream into ½ cup mayonnaise. Add 1 tablespoon confectioners' sugar and ½ teaspoon grated lemon or orange rind. Chill. Makes 1 cup.

NECTARINES

AVAILABILITY

Available June through September, with peak in July and August.

HOW TO BUY

Like the peach, the nectarine does not gain sugar after harvest, and if not well matured when picked it will be unsatisfactory. In addition to maturity, points to check in buying are general plumpness, firmness, smooth unblemished skin and good color. The flesh may be red, white or yellow.

FRESH FRUIT
PREPARATION AND SERVING SUGGESTIONS

The nectarine can be used in any recipe that calls for peaches. Obviously, a main use is eating out of the hand. Other uses are in compotes with a variety of other fruits; in salads of many kinds; as a garnish with meat or poultry; a cereal topping; sliced and topped with cream or ice cream; for shortcake; in frozen desserts such as ice cream, sherbets and parfaits; in tarts; in a variety of puddings; and how about a deep-dish fresh nectarine pie? Fresh nectarine ambrosia calls for nectarines, orange sections, sliced bananas, sugar, fresh lemon juice, vanilla extract and shredded coconut. The combinations are limitless. In addition to fresh uses, nectarines are canned.

NUTRITIONAL VALUE

Nectarines provide a valuable amount of vitamin A and some vitamin C. They are low in Calories, 64 in 100 grams, and low in sodium, therefore suitable as desserts in low sodium diets.

FRESH NECTARINE SANGRIA

3 cups chilled Rose wine
3 cups fresh orange juice
1 cup thinly sliced fresh
   strawberries

2 cups thinly sliced fresh
   nectarines (about 3-4
   medium-sized

Combine wine, orange juice, strawberries and nectarines in a large mixing bowl or pitcher. Chill about 1 hour. If desired, sweeten to taste. Makes about 2 quarts.

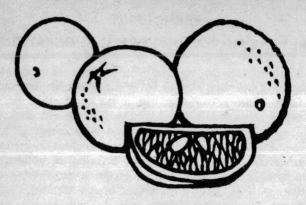

ORANGES
AVAILABILITY

Oranges are on the market all year, with largest supplies December through April.

Valencias, the most important variety, are marketed from February through November. *Navels* are available mainly November through February; *Temples* mostly late November through March. The Early varieties include *Hamlin,* a smooth-skinned seedless kind, of very good quality; seedy *Parson Brown;* and *Pineapple.*

HOW TO BUY

Oranges of the best quality are firm, heavy, have a fine textured skin, varying, however, according to variety. Color at destination is of no value in judging the maturity of an orange. All fruit, as required by law, is picked mature, depending on color and their sugar, acid and soluble solids contents. *Green fruit is as ripe as golden fruit,* and in fact sometimes fruit picked all golden later turns green. Florida oranges may have color added to satisfy the public view that an orange is supposed to be orange-colored. Such fruit is stamped "color added." California fruit is of natural color. Oranges which are russeted are just as good as the brightly colored fruit of the same variety. Avoid oranges that are light, puffy and spongy, since they lack juice.

FRESH FRUIT

PREPARATION AND SERVING SUGGESTIONS

Any way you slice them fresh oranges can be used in many ways. Freshly squeezed, sectioned, cut into cartwheels or orange smiles, fresh oranges are simply delicious. They can be used in salads and fruit cocktails, for flavoring in meats, poultry and seafoods, in cakes, pies, puddings and sauces or wherever a tangy taste is desired. Don't forget to include them in lunch boxes or as snacks for quick out of hand eating.

NUTRITIONAL VALUE

Oranges are famed for their vitamin C (an eight-ounce glass of fresh orange juice contains 124 mg of vitamin C, three times the U.S. Recommended Daily Allowance) and also contribute part of the daily body needs for vitamins A, B complex factors, essential minerals and amino acids. And that's not all—oranges are low in sodium and in calories, too. A whole peeled medium orange (2⅝ inch diameter) has only 64 Calories. There is fiber also, to aid in the digestive process.

FRESH AMBROSIA

3 cups fresh orange cart-
   wheels or half slices
2 tablespoons
   confectioners' sugar

½ cup grated fresh
   coconut

In glass serving bowl, or in individual cups or dessert dishes, layer the orange cartwheels or half-slices, confectioners' sugar and coconut; begin with the oranges and end with the coconut. Makes 4 servings.

FRESH ORANGE GLAZE FOR HAM

3½ tablespoons coarsely
   grated orange peel
   (2 oranges)
½ cup freshly squeezed
   orange juice

1 cup firmly packed
   brown sugar
2 teaspoons dry mustard
2 tablespoons prepared
   mustard

In small saucepan, thoroughly combine all ingredients; boil hard 5 minutes, stirring constantly. *Cool* to room temperature. Follow glazing instructions above. Remaining glaze from pan may be used over sweet potatoes. Makes about 1 cup.

FRESH FRUIT
GOLDEN ORANGE SAUCE

½ cup sugar
3 tablespoons cornstarch
¼ teaspoon salt
1 cup freshly squeezed
   orange juice
1 cup boiling water

2 tablespoons grated orange
   peel
2 oranges, peeled, cut into
   small bite-size pieces,
   well drained

In saucepan, thoroughly combine sugar, cornstarch and salt; blend in orange juice until very smooth. Stir in boiling water; bring to a boil over medium heat, stirring constantly. Boil 2 to 3 minutes; stir in orange peel and bite-size pieces. Serve warm or cool. Makes 2½ cups.

FRESH ORANGE CAKE

3 cups sifted all-purpose
   flour
3 teaspoons double-acting
   baking powder
½ teaspoon salt
1 cup shortening
2 cups sugar

1 tablespoon grated orange
   rind
1 teaspoon grated lemon
   rind
3 egg yolks
2 whole eggs
1 cup fresh orange juice

Sift together first 3 ingredients. Set aside for later use. Blend shortening with sugar, orange and lemon rinds. Beat in eggs, one at a time. Add flour mixture alternately with orange juice. Pour batter into 3 well-greased lightly floured 9-inch layer-cake pans. Bake in preheated moderate oven (350°F.) 30 minutes or until a toothpick or cake tester inserted in center comes out clean. Cool cake in pan 10 minutes. Cool. Frost with Fresh Orange Seven-Minute Frosting. Garnish plate with orange sections, if desired. Makes 10 to 12 servings.

FRESH ORANGE SEVEN-MINUTE FROSTING

1 unbeaten egg white
¾ cup sugar
2 tablespoons fresh
orange juice
⅟₁₆ teaspoon salt
1 teaspoon grated
orange rind

⅛ teaspoon grated lemon
rind
Few drops yellow
food coloring
Few drops red food
coloring

Combine first 4 ingredients in top part of a double boiler. Place over boiling water and beat with a rotary or electric beater until mixture stands in stiff peaks. Beat in grated orange and lemon rinds. Add few drops red and yellow food coloring to tint frosting pale orange. Frost top and sides of Fresh Orange Cake. Makes sufficient frosting for three 8- or 9-inch layers.

ORANGE-DILLED CARROTS

2 cups sliced pared carrots
1 teaspoon salt, divided
2 tablespoons butter or
margarine
½ teaspoon dried dill weed

1 cup fresh orange sections
or bite-size pieces
(2 medium oranges)
½ teaspoon grated fresh
orange rind

Place carrots in medium saucepan with 1 cup water and ½ teaspoon salt. Bring to boil, cover and simmer for 15 minutes, or until tender. Drain. Add remaining ½ teaspoon salt, butter and remaining ingredients. Stir over low heat for 1 or 2 minutes. Makes 4 servings.

FRESH ORANGE CHICKEN, GOURMET

2 broiler-fryers (3 pounds each), cut into serving pieces
Salt and pepper
½ cup butter or margarine
1 cup chopped onion
2 tablespoons grated orange peel
1 cup freshly squeezed orange juice
½ cup dry white wine or canned chicken consomme
2 tablespoons sugar
2 tablespoons freshly squeezed lemon juice
3 oranges, peeled, sliced into cartwheels

Season chicken well with salt and pepper. Saute in butter over medium heat until golden brown on all sides. Add onions; saute until soft. Transfer to shallow baking pan; pour over mixture of orange peel juice and wine. Bake uncovered at 375 degrees F. for 45 minutes, or until tender. Turn once during baking. Place chicken on serving platter; keep warm. Strain pan drippings; reserve. In small saucepan, melt sugar over medium heat just until golden. Remove from heat; immediately stir in lemon juice, then strained drippings. Bring to a boil, stirring until syrupy. Add orange cartwheels; heat until warm. Pour over chicken; serve at once. Makes 6 servings.

FRESH ORANGE SHAKE

2 egg whites
½ cup crushed ice
⅓ cup fresh lemon juice
3 cups fresh orange juice
½ cup sugar

Combine all ingredients in an electric blender or fruit jar and blend ½ minute in blender or shake well in tightly-capped fruit jar. Serve in tall glasses with ice cubes in each. Makes 8 servings.

ORANGE FRUITED CHICKEN SALAD

2 cups cut-up cooked
chicken
1 cup chopped celery
1½ cups fresh orange sec-
tions or bite-size pieces

1 cup halved, seeded red
grapes
2 tablespoons toasted
slivered almonds
Salad greens

Combine all ingredients except greens and toss lightly
with Citrus Dressing* Chill. Turn into bowl lined with
salad greens. Makes 6 servings.

*CITRUS DRESSING

¼ cup mayonnaise
¼ cup sour cream
3 tablespoons fresh
orange juice

1 teaspoon grated fresh
orange rind
1 teaspoon sugar
¼ teaspoon salt

(Reserved from sections)

Mix all ingredients in small bowl.

FRESH ORANGE AND SWEETPOTATO CASSEROLE

3 cups mashed cooked
  sweetpotatoes
2 eggs, separated
3 tablespoons sugar

½ teaspoon salt
½ cup fresh orange juice
1 teaspoon grated orange
  rind

Combine sweetpotatoes with egg yolks and beat well. Stir in sugar, salt, orange juice and rind. Beat egg whites until they stand in soft peaks. Gently fold into the mixture. Turn into a buttered 1½-quart casserole. Bake in a preheated moderate oven (375°F.) 45 to 50 minutes or until puffed and lightly browned. Serve at once. Makes 6 to 8 servings.

FRESH ORANGES AND COCONUT IN SYRUP

1 cup fresh orange juice
¼ cup fresh lemon juice
½ cup sugar
1/16 teaspoon salt

2 cups fresh orange
  sections
½ cup grated fresh coconut

Combine first 4 ingredients. Bring to boiling point and boil 5 minutes. Add orange sections and cook 1 minute. Remove from heat and chill. Just before serving turn into a serving dish and sprinkle with grated fresh coconut. Makes 6 servings.

PEACHES

AVAILABILITY

Peaches are generally available from May through September.

HOW TO BUY

The first rule in peach buying is—insist on mature peaches only, no green ones. A red blush doesn't indicate ripeness. A more reliable guide is provided by a yellowish background color. A deep uniform yellow is a good sign of ripeness. Select peaches that are firm but give a little when squeezed gently. Peaches often require additional ripening. To ripen hold peaches a few days at room temperature. Once fully ripened they are ready to eat or can be refrigerated for later use.

FRESH FRUIT

PREPARATION AND SERVING SUGGESTIONS

The peach is a popular fruit. Not only is it eaten fresh out of hand but is canned in great quantities and is used in appetizers, garnishes, salads, desserts and baked goods, jellies, preserves, nectar, and pickles. The delicious flavor of this fruit is reflected in the slang expressions, "sweet as a peach" "just peachy" . . . "everything's peaches and cream" (terrific).

Let's review some serving suggestions:

As appetizer, use with other fruits, such as blueberries, for a compote. The hollowed, shell-like shape of the halved peach lends itself to a variety of fillings, from single jellies to flaming sugar cubes. Use finely diced peaches and chopped walnuts with chicken salad. *For other salads,* use fresh peaches with grapes and cottage cheese; halve and top with other fruit and sour cream; or combine with other fruit and serve plain or set in gelatin. *Use as garnish,* such as broiled with lamb chops, grilled with barbecue chicken, glazed with baked ham, or filled with cranberries to accompany turkey; and *sliced for cereal topping. For dessert,* serve whole or sliced, plain or topped with sweet, sour, or whipped cream; in baked desserts, puddings, pies, cobblers, dumplings, or shortcake; or *in frozen desserts,* such as ice cream, sherbets, and parfaits. Substitute peaches for cherries in Cherries Jubilee or for strawberries in Baked Alaska.

Peaches will turn brown when cut, so sprinkle them with a little lemon juice to prevent this from happening.

NUTRITIONAL VALUE

Peaches contain many nutrients; they are an important source of vitamin A. They are low in calories, 100 grams contain 38 Calories.

SUN BLUSHED PEACH CHEESE CAKE

To prepare crumb mixture:

1 cup graham cracker crumbs

¼ cup sugar

¼ cup softened butter or margarine

Blend together all ingredients; press firmly into an even layer over bottom of 9-inch springform pan.

To prepare filling:

3 envelopes unflavored gelatin

¾ cup water

2 pounds peaches (6 medium-sized)

1 tablespoon fresh lemon juice

2 egg yolks

¾ cup sugar

1 pound cream cheese, softened

2 egg whites

½ teaspoon salt

¼ cup sugar

1 cup heavy cream

Soften gelatin in water. Peel, pit and thoroughly crush or puree peaches (you should have 3 cups). Stir in lemon juice. Beat egg yolks slightly in top of double boiler; stir in ½ cup crushed peaches and ¾ cup sugar. Cook and stir over hot water until mixture thickens; mix in softened gelatin; remove from heat. Combine cream cheese and remaining peaches; stir in gelatin mixture. Chill until mixture mounds. Beat egg whites and salt until foamy. Gradually beat in ¼ cup sugar until stiff peaks form. Whip cream stiff. Fold egg whites and cream into cheese mixture. Pour into prepared pan. Chill at least 4 hours, or until firm. Serve with Crushed Peach Sauce.* Makes 12 servings. See next page for recipe.

CRUSHED PEACH SAUCE

6 medium-sized peaches   ⅓ cup sugar
   (about 2 pounds)

Peel, pit and slightly crush peaches; stir in sugar. Makes about 2¼ cups.

PEACH PARFAIT

1 package (3⅝ ounces)   ½ cup sour cream
   vanilla pudding mix   2 cups diced peeled fresh
1½ cups milk   peaches

Combine pudding mix and milk in medium saucepan. Cook over medium heat, stirring constantly, until mixture reaches boiling point. Remove from heat; blend in sour cream. Cool thoroughly, stirring frequently. Arrange alternate layers of peaches and pudding in parfait glasses ending with pudding layer. Chill until serving time. Makes about 4 servings.

FRESH PEACH JELLY

3½ pounds fresh peaches   7½ cups sugar
  ½ cup water   1 bottle (6-ounces) liquid
  ¼ cup fresh lemon juice   fruit pectin

Pit peaches. Crush thoroughly. Add water. Heat to boiling point and simmer, covered, 5 minutes. Place a large square of cheesecloth, several layers thick, in colander. Pour peach mixture into cheesecloth. Bring corners together and press tightly to extract liquid. (You should have about 3½ cups.) Place juice in large saucepan. Mix in lemon juice and sugar. Heat to boiling point, stirring constantly. Stir in pectin immediately. Heat to full rolling boil and boil hard for 1 minute, stirring constantly. Remove from heat. Skim off foam. Pour quickly into prepared glasses or jars.* Seal at once. Makes about 2 quarts.

* Rinse with boiling water before filling.

HAM STEAK WITH A VARIETY OF BROILED PEACH ACCOMPANIMENTS

To serve six, cut three large peaches in half and remove pits. Drizzle two tablespoons melted butter or margarine over cut surfaces of peaches. Place peaches in broiler with ham steak for the last five to ten minutes of broiling. To serve, fill peach centers, as suits your mood, with chutney, pineapple preserves, currant jelly, shredded coconut, chopped nuts or crystallized ginger.

FRESH PEACH "UPS 'N DOWN" CAKE

¼ cup butter or margarine
6 tablespoons brown sugar
6 fresh peaches
2 cups sugar
1 cup water
2½ cups sifted all-purpose flour

4 teaspoons double-acting baking powder
½ teaspoon salt
⅔ cup shortening
3 eggs
1½ teaspoons vanilla extract
1 cup milk

Melt butter or margarine in bottom of a 9 x 9 x 2-inch baking pan. Blend in brown sugar, spreading it evenly over the bottom. Peel peaches and slice into eighths. Boil 1 cup sugar with water for 5 minutes. Add peaches and cook, covered, 3 to 5 minutes or until almost tender. Drain and arrange in rows over brown sugar mixture. Sift together flour, baking powder and salt. Set aside. Cream shortening with the remaining sugar until fluffy. Beat in eggs, one at a time. Add vanilla. Stir in the flour mixture alternately with the milk, beating well after each addition. Pour batter over peaches. Bake in a preheated moderate oven (375°F.) 45 to 55 minutes or until done. Cool in pan 15 minutes on wire rack. Invert on wire rack, peach side up. Serve, topped with whipped cream or ice cream if desired. Makes 8 servings.

FRESH FRUIT

FRESH PEACH TARTS

4 cups sliced fresh peaches	1 tablespoon cornstarch
¾ cup sugar	4 baked 5-inch tart shells
2 teaspoons fresh lemon juice	Dark grapes for garnish

Combine peaches, sugar and lemon juice. Let stand 20 minutes. Drain off juice into a measuring cup. There should be 1 cup of liquid. If not, finish filling cup with water. Combine with cornstarch. Cook until transparent. Cool. Divide fruit equally among the 4 baked tart shells. Spoon the cold syrup over each to form a glaze. Chill until the glaze is set. Garnish with clusters of grapes. Makes 4 tarts.

FRESH PEACH MOUSSE

¾ cup sweetened condensed milk	2 teaspoons vanilla extract
½ cup sugar	1 cup crushed fresh peaches
½ cup water	1 cup heavy cream, whipped
¼ teaspoon salt	

Combine milk, sugar and water in a saucepan. Heat and mix until well blended. Chill. Add salt and vanilla extract. Turn into an ice cube tray and freeze to a mush. Remove from freezer and turn mixture into a bowl. Beat until light and fluffy, about 2 minutes. Fold in peaches and whipped cream. Return to freezing tray and freeze until firm. Makes 8 servings.

PEACH CREAM PIE

1 cup diced peeled
   peaches
2/3 cup sugar, divided
1 tablespoon fresh lemon
   juice
1 envelope unflavored
   gelatin
1/8 teaspoon salt
1/2 cup milk

3/4 teaspoon vanilla
1/4 teaspoon almond extract
2 egg whites
1 cup heavy cream,
   whipped
1 baked 9-inch pastry
   shell
Additional peaches for
   garnish

Sprinkle diced peaches with 2 tablespoons sugar and lemon juice; set aside. Reserve 4 tablespoons sugar. Mix remaining sugar, gelatin and salt in small saucepan. Stir in milk and cook over low heat, stirring constantly, until gelatin dissolves, about 5 minutes. Remove from heat; add vanilla and almond extract. Chill, stirring occasionally, until mixture is the consistency of unbeaten egg white. Beat egg whites until soft peaks form. Add reserved 4 tablespoons sugar gradually, continuing to beat until stiff. Drain peaches and add to gelatin mixture. Fold in beaten egg whites, then whipped cream; turn into baked pastry shell. Chill until set, several hours. Garnish with additional peaches, peeled and sliced, just before serving. Makes 6 to 8 servings.

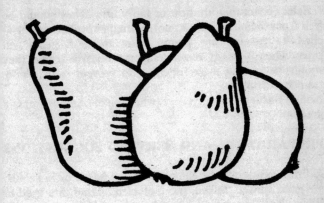

PEARS

AVAILABILITY

The domestic pear season starts in July (California Bartletts) and runs through November. The winter pear season starts in October (Anjou, Bosc, Comice) and runs into May.

The main varieties include:

BARTLETT—the most popular variety, medium in size, yellow with blush, sweet. Season: July—October.

ANJOU—large, green or yellowish-green skin, sometimes crimson, spicy sweet flavor. Season: October—May.

BOSC—has long tapering neck, dark greenish-yellow to brownish-yellow, overlaid with cinnamon-colored russeting, a bit acid tasting. Season: October—March.

COMICE—large, roundish, greenish-yellow to yellow-red skin, sweet, rich flavor. Season: October—January.

SECKEL—very small, brownish-yellow to blushed dull red, sweet, spicy flavor. Season: September—December.

HOW TO BUY

Select pears that are firm or fairly firm. They should be free from blemishes, clean, not misshapen, wilted or shrivelled. In general, big, plump pears are best. Pears will ripen when kept at room temperature; when ripe they should be kept in the refrigerator to prevent overripening from occurring.

Note: Bartletts turn yellow when ripe, Anjous remain green.

PREPARATION AND SERVING SUGGESTIONS

Fresh pears may be eaten out of the hand; or in salads; are good stewed, baked, fried, pickled, glazed; are used in jellies, jams, marmalades and baked goods; are canned in great quantities; and some are dried. . . . *To bake pears,* core and peel about 1-inch strip at the top, fill with fruit and place in oven, serving hot. . . . *For a sundae,* place one scoop of mint chocolate ice cream in a sherbet glass, top with fresh pear slices and garnish with fresh mint. . . . *Serve* whole pears in a bowl and let each guest select his own, cutting the pear as he likes and eating it with selected cheese and crackers. . . . For a pear salad, peel, halve and core pears, fill center with cream cheese, place on a bed of lettuce. . . . *Fresh pears and apples poached* together in a syrup made with equal parts of sugar and water and fresh lemon juice to taste makes a delightful dessert or meat accompaniment. . . . *Dip fresh pear cubes* in a mixture of 2 tablespoons fresh orange and 2 tablespoons fresh lemon juice, place on toothpicks and alternate with cheese cubes. . . . *For fresh pear and shrimp appetizer* toss diced fresh pears (unpeeled), cooked shrimp and chopped celery with a lemony fresh dressing and spoon into cocktail glasses lined with crisp greens. . . . *Try combining* diced pears with nuts and celery in a crunchy flavorful salad. . . . *Another salad* is fresh pear balls in clear aspic, ringed with fresh cucumber slices and centered with cottage cheese.

PREPARATION AND SERVING SUGGESTIONS

. . . *Fresh pears* make a delightful addition to Waldorf salad. Replace half of the diced apples with diced fresh pears. Add the usual amounts of diced celery and chopped walnuts. Season well and bind together with mayonnaise or salad dressing. . . . Try the French custom of serving a plump pear with a wedge of a fragrant cheese. . . . *Serve pears* cool but not icy. When they are too cold, they lack some of their bouquet, while if too warm, they are not as refreshing as when cool. . . . *A famous, easily prepared* continental dessert is poached fresh pear halves filled with vanilla ice cream and bathed in a warm, bittersweet chocolate sauce. . . . *For fresh pear ambrosia,* wash, core and dice fresh pears, sprinkle with fresh orange juice and arrange in sherbet glasses with shredded moist coconut.

NUTRITIONAL VALUE

Pears contain a good spectrum of nutrients in useful amounts; pear juice has been found to contain all of the B vitamins. A 100-gram portion of pears (3½-ounces) contains 61 Calories.

DUCKLING WITH FRESH PEARS

1½ teaspoons salt
½ teaspoon grated orange rind
1 duckling (4½ to 5 pounds)
1½ cups fresh orange juice
2 tablespoons butter or margarine

1 tablespoon sugar
½ teaspoon grated orange rind
4 fresh pears
2 teaspoons cornstarch
2 tablespoons water
2 tablespoons chopped pecans

Combine salt and ½ teaspoon orange rind; rub over outside and inside of duckling. Place on rack in shallow baking pan. Roast in 350°F. oven 2 hours. About ½ hour before duck is done, combine orange juice, butter or margarine, sugar and ½ teaspoon orange rind in large skillet; simmer 3 minutes. Meanwhile, halve, pare and core pears. Add pears to orange juice mixture. Simmer 5 minutes, basting pears often with orange juice mixture. Remove pears to shallow baking pan; keep warm. Combine cornstarch and water to make a smooth paste; stir into juice mixture. Cook until mixture boils, stirring constantly. Remove duckling from pan. Drain all drippings from baking pan. Pour juice mixture into roasting pan. Add pecans. Return duckling to baking pan. Spoon sauce over duck. Return to oven for 5 minutes. Place duckling on platter. Serve with pears and orange sauce. Makes 4 servings.

FRESH FRUIT

FRESH PEAR SALAD

1 package (8 ounces) cream
  cheese, softened
1 can (4½ ounces) deviled
  ham
Few grains powdered
  cloves

2 tablespoons chopped
  walnuts
4 fresh pears
Lemon juice

Combine cream cheese, deviled ham, cloves and walnuts. Cut pears in half lengthwise. Core and peel pears. Brush surfaces lightly with lemon juice. Fill pears generously with cheese-nut mixture. Arrange on salad plates. Garnish with lettuce, as desired. Makes 4 servings.

PEAR-CRANBERRY COMPOTE

2 cups fresh cranberries
1 cup fresh orange juice

1 cup sugar
4 large fresh pears

Combine cranberries, orange juice and sugar in saucepan. Cook over medium heat, stirring constantly, until berries start to pop. Simmer 3 minutes. Pour into shallow baking pan. Halve, pare and core pears. Place in orange cranberry mixture. Cover and bake in 350°F. oven about 30 minutes or until pears are just tender, turning once. Serve warm or cold as an accompaniment for poultry. Makes 8 servings.

PINEAPPLES

AVAILABILITY

Pineapples are available in all months. The period of relative abundance is March through June.

Red Spanish (Pina Morada) is an extensively grown variety in Puerto Rico, and some are grown in Florida. This is a thick fruit, pale red when ripe, weight 2 to 5 pounds. Mexico and Hawaii grow the Smooth Cayenne (Cayena) for export. This is a large yellow-orange fruit of good quality.

HOW TO BUY

Color and odor are the factors indicating quality in pineapples. A ripe pineapple in good condition has a fresh, clean appearance and has characteristic color combined with a decidedly fragrant odor. The eyes then are flat and almost hollow. Usually the heavier the fruit is in proportion to its size, the better the quality, provided the fruit is mature. Pineapples picked when immature will not ripen properly. If picked too early, the fruit has a dull yellowish appearance and the flavor will be very acid. The eyes are then poorly developed and often somewhat pointed. How the spikes pull out is of no value as a test for ripeness. Pineapples cannot be ripened at home. Refrigerate and use as soon as possible.

FRESH FRUIT

PREPARATION AND SERVING SUGGESTIONS

Pineapples are used in salads and desserts, sliced, crushed, cubed, grated, eaten plain or dipped in sugar. They make a natural ingredient for cakes, cookies, pies and sundaes. Pineapple makes tasty jam, garnish for beverages, is good pickled, and traditionally goes with ham. Special recipes include layers of pineapple sprinkled with sugar and alternated with vanilla ice cream; chicken salad with pineapple; seafood and pineapple, and fresh fruit salad. If pineapple is harvested sufficiently ripe, no sugar is needed. Such a stage would be with one-eighth of its shell yellow.

For slicing or dicing pineapple, wash it and slice it crosswise with a large sharp knife into one-inch thick slices. With a paring knife, peel each slice. Make the peeling thick enough to remove the eyes, or thinner, removing the eyes with the tip of a vegetable peeler or apple corer. Then cut into desired shapes.

For serving in the shell, wash the pineapple and with a large sharp knife, start at the center of the crown and saw gently down the spikes cutting it in half lengthwise. Cut each half into two pieces. With a paring knife, cut about ¼ inch from the skin, loosening the wedge completely. Cut the fruit into chunks and remove, leaving shell. The shell may then be used as an attractive container in which to serve the pineapple, or one of the many salads containing pineapple.

For serving in the shell, there is a special knife which cuts pineapple into six sections while coring it. This is similar to a pear cutter.

For serving luau style, there is a special barrel-type knife on the market which sections the fruit into spears and leaves the shell intact. The shell can be used for drinks or in the case of small pineapples, as salad or appetizer cups.

For serving in the half shell: slice pineapple in half longitudinally through the crown. Using curved knife, scoop out core and flesh. Refill with fruit salad topped with sherbet or cottage cheese.

For pineapple snacks, wash the pineapple and then cut around each section with a sharp paring knife. Cut deeply enough to reach the core. Leave a row of uncut sections at the top and bottom. Guests may then serve themselves by pulling out a section at a time.

To prepare a pineapple luau style, cut a thick slice from the top and the bottom of a fresh ripe pineapple, saving the bottom slice. Run a sharp, thin, long knife blade around the pineapple between the rind and the meat, leaving an intact shell ⅜ inches thick. To do this, cut the pineapple from either end to the half-way point keeping the knife blade pointed toward the rind. Push the cylinder of pineapple out the big end by pressing from the small end. Cut the cylinder in half lengthwise, then cut each half into quarters. Cut away and discard the core adhering to the quarters. Cut the quarters into lengthwise strips, place the bottom on a plate, over which rests the pineapple shell. Fill with the pineapple strips.

NUTRITIONAL VALUE

Pineapples are a good source of vitamin C; they contain many other nutrients and are low in sodium content, hence suitable for low-sodium diets. A 100-gram portion of pineapple (3½ ounces) contains a moderate 52 Calories.

PINEAPPLE-BACON ROLL UPS

1 small pineapple　　　**½ pound bacon**

Cut off crown and stem end of pineapple. Stand pineapple upright and cut off rind in lengthwise strips. Remove eyes with pointed knife. Cut into lengthwise quarters and cut away the core. Cut pineapple into large chunks. Cut bacon slices in half. Wrap piece of bacon around each pineapple chunk, fasten with wooden pick. Place on broiler rack set 5 inches from heat. Broil until browned, 5 to 8 minutes; turn and broil until second side is brown and crisp, 2 to 3 minutes. Makes about 32 hors d'oeuvre servings.

PINEAPPLE LOBSTER SALAD

2 cups lobster, diced　　　**⅛ teaspoon black pepper**
1½ cups fresh pineapple　　　**Dash of ground**
　　wedges　　　　　　　　　**cayenne pepper**
1½ cups diced celery　　　**½ teaspoon soy sauce**
1 teaspoon salt　　　　　**⅓ cup mayonnaise**
　　　　　　　　　　　　　　Head Lettuce

Place first 8 ingredients in a mixing bowl. Toss lightly. Serve on beds of crisp lettuce. If desired, serve this salad from fresh pineapple shells. Makes 6 servings.

PINEAPPLE KABOBS

1 small pineapple	½ teaspoon salt
½ cup salad oil	Cherry tomatoes, halved
¼ cup lemon juice	Ham cubes
½ teaspoon dry mustard	Cheese cubes
1 teaspoon dried leaf rosemary	

Cut off crown and stem end of pineapple. Stand pineapple upright and cut off rind in lengthwise strips. Remove eyes with pointed knife. Cut into lengthwise quarters and cut away the core. Cut pineapple into large chunks and place in bowl. Mix together oil, lemon juice, dry mustard, rosemary and salt. Pour over pineapple and refrigerate several hours or overnight. When ready to serve, drain and place on skewers, alternating with tomatoes, ham and cheese. Makes 10 to 12 kabobs.

STUFFED PINEAPPLE - WITH FRESH FRUITS

3 medium whole fresh pineapples	3 apples, unpeeled
6 fresh oranges	½ cup orange-flavored liqueur
3 fresh grapefruits	

Cut pineapples in half lengthwise through the fruit and green top (crown). With sharp pointed knife, make cut ½ inch wide around entire edge of meat. With a thin sharp knife, separate fruit from shell. Cut fruit into strips ⅓ inch wide and part of strips into triangles. Cut oranges and grapefruits into sections and apples into thin slices. Place sliced fruit in mixing bowl and sprinkle with liqueur. Refrigerate at least 1 hour. To fill pineapple, place layer of pineapple strips in bottom of each shell, cover alternating sections of apples, grapefruit and oranges. Stand pineapple triangles along outer edge of pineapple. Makes 6 servings.

PLUMS

AVAILABILITY

Fresh domestic plums are on the market June through September and prunes from August into October. Peak period for plums is July and August and for prunes September.

There are many kinds of plums and all may be eaten fresh. Only those with extra high sugar content can be dried into prunes without fermenting. Major types of plums are Japanese with yellow to crimson skins and European, purple to black, but some green or yellow.

HOW TO BUY

All plum varieties make good out-of-hand eating. However, some varieties are specially suited to particular uses. For example, Santa Rosa, Casselman and Queen Ann are excellent for jams and jellies; El Dorado, Nubiana, Santa Rosa and Queen Ann for canning and freezing; Kelsey, Nubiana. Laroda, Queen Ann, El Dorado and President for pies, cakes and tarts; Simka, Laroda and Santa Rosa for sundae toppings; Nubiana, El Dorado and Friar for compotes; and Laroda, Nubiana, Queen Ann and El Dorado for salads.

PREPARATION AND SERVING SUGGESTIONS

Plums and fresh prunes are excellent eaten out of hand. They make good pies and puddings, stewed fruit, preserves, jellies and jams. Plums also go well in cakes, tarts and other pastries. Stewed prunes and prune juice are well-known commodities. Plums may be stewed, scalloped, poached, or sliced into salads, served with ice cream, slaw, sherbet, Bavarian cream, or cake.

NUTRITIONAL VALUE

Plums and prunes contribute useful amounts of vitamins C and A, as well as other vitamins and minerals. Plums are low in sodium and suitable for use in a low-sodium diet. A 100-gram portion (3½-ounces) of plum (other than prune-type) contains only 48 Calories. The same portion of a prune-type plum contains 75 Calories.

DEEP-DISH FRESH PLUM PIE

2¼ lbs. pitted, sliced fresh
    plums
1¼ cups sugar
3 tablespoons tapioca
¾ teaspoon ground
    allspice
¼ teaspoon salt
2 tablespoons butter
Pastry, using 1 cup
    flour

Place plums in a 10 x 6 x 2-inch baking dish. Combine sugar, tapioca, allspice and salt. Sprinkle over plums. Shake dish to distribute mixture uniformly. Dot top with butter. Cover with pastry rolled to ⅛-inch thickness cut 2 inches larger than the diameter of the dish. Trim, turn under and flute edge. Cut a gash in the top to allow for the escape of steam. Bake in a preheated very hot oven (450° F.) 10 minutes. Reduce heat to moderate (350°F.) and continue baking 30 to 40 minutes or until crust is brown. Serve warm or cold. It is advisable to put a square of foil in the bottom of oven to catch any of the juice that might boil out. Makes 6 to 8 servings.

SCALLOPED FRESH PLUMS

2 lbs. fresh plums
3 cups soft bread crumbs
¾ cup sugar
1 teaspoon grated lemon
    peel
¼ cup butter, melted

Cut plums in half and remove pits. There should be 3 cups. Combine bread crumbs, sugar, lemon peel and butter. Fill a buttered 1-quart casserole with alternating layers of plums and crumb mixture, with plums on bottom and crumbs over top. Cover. Bake in a preheated hot oven (400°F.) 30 minutes or until plums are tender. Remove cover and bake 10 minutes or until crumbs are brown. Serve as dessert. Makes 4 to 5 servings.

RASPBERRIES

AVAILABILITY

Available June through November, but June-July is peak season. There are three kinds of raspberries: red, purple, and black.

HOW TO BUY

Raspberries should have a bright, clean appearance with solid, full color. They should be plump, free from caps and moisture. Overripe berries are usually dull in color, soft and sometimes leaky.

PREPARATION AND SERVING SUGGESTIONS

Raspberries are an extremely perishable fruit and should be bought for immediate use only. Keep them cold and covered until ready for use.

Raspberries are excellent to eat as is or add cream and sugar. They can be used in a wide variety of dessert dishes such as: bavarian cream, chiffon pie, ice or ice cream, mousse, preserves, pudding, punch, in cakes and tarts, and as syrup for pancakes.

If they are mashed, sugared and brought to a boil the resulting sauce keeps well. When berries show any sign of deterioration they should be made into sauce at once.

NUTRITIONAL VALUE

Raspberries are a good source of vitamin C and supply useful amounts of other vitamins and minerals. They are low in sodium and suitable for use in low-sodium diet; 100 grams contain only 57 Calories.

FRESH RASPBERRY WHIP

2 cups fresh raspberries	1 envelope unflavored gelatine
1 egg white, unbeaten	1/4 cup cold water
1/3 cup sugar	1/2 cup heavy cream, whipped
1/16 teaspoon salt	1 cup fresh whole raspberries
1/4 cup cold water	

Combine raspberries, egg white, sugar and salt in bowl. Beat with an electric beater, until fluffy and berries are mashed. Add 1/4 cup cold water. Soften gelatine in the remaining 1/4 cup water. Dissolve over hot water and add to berry mixture. Chill until mixture begins to thicken. Beat 1 minute with electric beater. Fold in whipped cream and the remaining 1 cup berries. Serve in sherbert glasses. Serves 6.

RHUBARB

AVAILABILITY

Rhubarb is on the market all year but mainly January into July, with peak in April and May, and very little August through December.

Variety is not important, but red color is sometimes indicated in names used, and it is often offered by length, as extra-long or special-long.

HOW TO BUY

Good quality rhubarb is fresh, firm, crisp, tender, and bright in appearance. Stalks should not be excessively thin. Well colored rhubarb is usually well flavored but some varieties from some soils may be desirable with little color. The younger stems having immature leaves are usually the most tender and delicate in flavor. Wilted or flabby stalks may indicate stringiness, lack of freshness and poor flavor. Oversize stalks may be tough. Tenderness and crispness can be tested by puncturing the stalk.

PREPARATION AND SERVING SUGGESTIONS

Rhubarb is used as a fruit because of its high acidity and flavor. It has long been popular in pies and is frequently referred to as "pieplant." It is also used in tarts, sauces, puddings, punch, jams and jellies. It is easily prepared and preserved and readily adapts to freezing. Rhubarb may be baked or stewed and eaten as a breakfast food, side dish with other meals, or as a dessert. The cooked juice, with a sweetener added, and chilled, makes a refreshing drink. Rhubarb has also been used for making homemade wines.

NUTRITIONAL VALUE

Rhubarb has a fair amount of nutritional value but is not noted for possessing any particular nutrient in outstanding quantity. A 3½-ounce serving of cooked rhubarb contains 141 Calories, but most of these calories result from the addition of sugar during the cooking.

FRESH RHUBARB BETTY

6 cups diced fresh
  rhubard
1¼ cups sugar
2½ tablespoons quick-
  cooking tapioca
1 teaspoon grated
  lemon rind

1 tablespoon grated
  orange rind
¼ teaspoon salt
2⅔ cups soft bread crumbs
1/3 cup melted butter or
  margarine
1 teaspoon vanilla

Combine the first 6 ingredients and set aside. Mix bread crumbs with melted butter or margarine and vanilla. Fill a 1½ quart casserole with alternate layers or rhubarb and bread crumbs, having rhubarb as the bottom layer and bread crumbs as the top layer. Cover and bake in a preteated hot oven (400°F.) 25 minutes. Remove cover and bake until crumbs are brown, 10 minutes. Serve warm. YIELD: 6 to 8 servings.

BAKED RHUBARB AND ORANGE SAUCE

4 cups diced fresh rhubarb
2 fresh oranges, diced
1 cup sugar
⅛ teaspoon salt

2 sticks whole cinnamon,
    2 inches long
12 whole cloves, tied in a
    bag

Place all ingredients in a 1-quart casserole. Cover and bake in a preheated oven (350°F.) 1 hour or until rhubarb is tender. Remove cinnamon and cloves. Serve warm or chilled for breakfast, lunch or dinner. Makes 6 to 8 servings.

FRESH RHUBARB AND STRAWBERRY LEMONADE

1 pound fresh rhubarb
2 cups water
1¼ cups sugar
1 cup fresh strawberries
½ cup fresh lemon juice

1 cup water
Whole fresh
    strawberries for
    garnish

Wash rhubarb and cut into 1-inch pieces. Add 2 cups water. Cover and simmer 10 minutes. Strain and add sugar. Stir until dissolved. Cool. Crush strawberries, strain and add. Add lemon juice and water. Serve in tall glasses over ice. Garnish with whole fresh strawberries. Makes 6 servings.

STRAWBERRIES

AVAILABILITY

Strawberries are available all year, but peak period of supply is April-June. There are many varieties and sizes range from small to very large.

HOW TO BUY

Strawberries should be fresh, clean, bright and have full solid red color. They should be free from moisture and dirt. Caps should be attached—a bright green color in the caps indicates good quality. Avoid very small, misshapen berries, they are usually of poor texture and flavor. Watch out for leaky berries, indicated by stained containers.

PREPARATION AND SERVING SUGGESTIONS

Strawberries are highly perishable, use them within a day or two or freeze for later use.

Fresh strawberries can be eaten uncooked or cooked, with or without cream or milk and sugar. Strawberry short-cake is a favorite American dish. Strawberries are excellent on ice cream, in sauces and syrups, in pies and tarts, jams, jellies, custard, creams, compotes and salads. A novel way to serve them is in the French manner, in wine and sugar.

NUTRITIONAL VALUE

Strawberries are an excellent source of vitamin C and also contain useful amounts of vitamin A as well as other vitamins and minerals. One cup of strawberries or 149 grams, contains only 54 calories (without any sugar added).

GLORIOUS STRAWBERRY CAKE

3 envelopes unflavored
  gelatin
¾ cup cold water
3 pints fresh strawberries,
  washed and hulled
2 tablespoons fresh lemon
  juice

3 eggs
⅛ teaspoon salt
1 cup sugar
1 pint heavy cream
Pound cake

Soften gelatin in cold water; dissolve over boiling water; cool. Crush strawberries until smooth. Stir in lemon juice. Stir strawberries into gelatin. Beat eggs and salt until frothy; add sugar and continue beating until very light and lemon-colored. Beat cream until stiff. Fold strawberry mixture and egg mixture into cream until evenly blended.

Meanwhile, line sides of 9-inch springform pan with slices of pound cake, sliced about ½-inch thick. Pour strawberry mixture into pan. Refrigerate overnight. Just before serving, place on platter and remo.e sides of pan. Garnish with whipped cream and strawberries, if desired. Makes 12 servings.

STRAWBERRY COTTAGE CHEESE MOLD

1 package (3-ounces)
   strawberry-flavored
   gelatin
1 cup boiling water
1 cup cold water

1 pint strawberries, hulled
   and halved
½ pint cottage cheese
⅛ teaspoon salt

Dissolve gelatin in boiling water; stir in cold water. Chill half of mixture until consistency of unbeaten egg whites; fold in strawberries. Pour into 4-cup mold which has been rinsed in cold water; refrigerate. Chill remaining gelatin until slightly thickened; fold in cottage cheese and salt. Carefully pour over strawberry mixture in mold. Chill at least 3 hours. Unmold onto serving plate just before serving. Makes 4–6 servings.

FRESH STRAWBERRY BAKED ALASKA

9-inch square yellow or
   white cake
About 2 cups sliced
   fresh strawberries
1 quart vanilla ice cream,
   frozen very hard

7 egg whites
⅛ teaspoon salt
¾ cup sugar
1 teaspoon vanilla extract
9 whole uncapped fresh
   strawberries

Have all ingredients ready before you start this cake for best results. Be sure the strawberries are chilled, the ice cream is very hard, the meringue is made and the oven preheated to 450°F. (very hot). Place the layer of cake on a baking sheet over which spread half of the strawberries. Top with ice cream. Spread with remaining berries. Cover the entire cake with meringue made by combining egg whites and salt and beating until they stand in soft peaks. Gradually add sugar and vanilla extract. Continue beating until they stand in stiff peaks. Place cake in very hot oven 1 to 2 minutes or until brown. Watch closely to prevent browning too much. Lift to a serving plate with 2 wide spatulas and garnish with whole, uncapped fresh strawberries. Serve at once. Makes 9 servings.

FRESH STRAWBERRY LEMONADE

To prepare syrup:

1 pint fresh strawberries   2½ cups sugar
1½ cups fresh lemon juice

Wash, hull and crush strawberries. Add lemon juice and sugar to strawberries. Stir until sugar dissolves. Store in covered jar in refrigerator until ready to prepare lemonade. Makes 4½ cups syrup.

To make lemonade:

Place 3 or 4 ice cubes in a tall glass. Add ¼ cup syrup for each serving. Fill each glass with club soda. Stir well.

FRESH STRAWBERRY TARTS

1½ teaspoons unflavored gelatin

2 tablespoons cold water

3 cups washed, capped fresh strawberries

½ cup sugar

2½ teaspoons cornstarch

1½ teaspoons fresh lemon juice

1/16 teaspoon salt

6 baked 5-inch tart shells

½ cup heavy cream, whipped

6 whole strawberries

Soften gelatin in cold water and set aside for later use. Crush half of the berries in a saucepan. Mix sugar with cornstarch and add to crushed berries. Stir in lemon juice and salt. Cook over low heat stirring constantly, until mixture is transparent and of medium thickness. Stir in softened gelatin. Cool. Cut one cup of the remaining berries in half and gently fold into the cooked mixture. Pour into 6 cold baked tart shells. Chill. Just before serving, cut the remaining berries in half and arrange over the top, cut side up. Garnish with whipped cream and a whole berry. Makes 6 tarts.

OLD FASHIONED STRAWBERRY SHORTCAKE

2 cups sifted all-purpose
   flour
3 teaspoons double-acting
   baking powder
½ teaspoon salt

⅓ cup butter or margarine
1 large egg, beaten
½ cup milk (about)
3 pints fresh strawberries
¾ cup sugar

Heat oven to 450°F. (very hot). Sift the first 3 ingredients together. Cut in butter or margarine with a pastry blender or 2 knives until the mixture resembles coarse meal. Pour beaten egg into a measuring cup and add milk to make ¾ cup. Gradually stir into the flour mixture. Knead about 20 seconds. Pat half the dough into a greased, round, 8-inch layer-cake pan. Brush with melted butter or margarine. Pat out the remaining half of the dough on top. Bake 12 to 15 minutes or until done. Turn out on cooling rack. When cold, split layers apart and place on large serving plate. Wash, hull and slice strawberries. Add sugar and let stand 30 minutes. Spoon between and on top of shortcake. Serve with whipped cream, if desired. Makes 6 servings.

FLAMEE STRAWBERRY FRUIT CUP

2 cups sliced fresh
   strawberries
1 cup diced fresh pineapple
1 cup fresh orange sections

2 tablespoons sugar
⅓ cup brandy or
   Cointreau, heated

Combine first 4 ingredients. Allow to stand at least 1 hour. Add hot brandy. Ignite and serve at once. Yield: 6 servings. (109 calories per serving.)

FRESH FRUIT

FRESH STRAWBERRY ANGEL FOOD CAKE

⅔ cup sifted cake flour
¾ cup sugar
¼ teaspoon salt
¾ teaspoon cream of tartar
6 large egg whites
½ teaspoon vanilla extract

¼ teaspoon almond extract
3 cups sliced fresh
  strawberries
3 tablespoons sugar
Whipped cream
  (optional)

Sift flour with sugar 6 times and set aside. Add salt to egg whites and beat until they are foamy. Add cream of tartar and beat until they stand in soft, stiff peaks. (DO NOT OVERBEAT.) Carefully fold in sugar and flour about 2 tablespoons at a time, using as few strokes as is necessary to blend ingredients. Fold in vanilla and almond extracts. Turn into an 9x3-inch tube cake pan which has been rinsed in cold water. (DO NOT GREASE PAN.) Run a spatula through the batter to cut air bubbles. Bake in a preheated slow oven (325°F.) 1 hour or until cake springs back with a light touch. Remove from oven. Invert on a wire rack to cool. (Cake will shrink if removed from pan while warm.) To serve, cut cake into 1½-inch slices and top with sliced strawberries which have been sweetened with the 3 tablespoons sugar. Garnish with whipped cream, if desired. Makes 10 to 12 servings.

FRESH STRAWBERRY-BANANA SAUCE

1 pint fresh strawberries
⅓ cup sugar
1 teaspoon fresh lemon
  juice

1/16 teaspoon salt
1 medium-size banana,
  sliced

Hull strawberries and mash. Add sugar, lemon juice, salt and banana. Mix well. Serve over ice cream, pudding or cake.
Makes: 2 cups

TANGERINES

AVAILABILITY

Tangerines are available from October through January with the peak supply in November. The tangerine is a form of the species known popularly as mandarins.

HOW TO BUY

Tangerines should be heavy for their size indicating ample juice content. They should have a deep orange or almost red coloring. A puffy appearance and feel is normal but there should be no soft, water-soaked areas or mold.

There are many different varieties commonly sold as "tangerines." Retailers are increasingly using the correct names for each type of "Tangerine". These common varieties found in the supermarket:

Tangelo - (MINNEOLA) bright red-orange, slightly elongated with a knob-like formation at the stem end;

Temple - slightly rough, red-orange rind, spherical to slightly flattened, very juicy with many seeds.

FRESH FRUIT

Murcott - (recently renamed the Honey Tangerine) thin skinned, fairly easy to peel, very sweet.

Mandarin - light orange, with smooth skin and few seeds.

PREPARATION AND SERVING SUGGESTIONS

Tangerines are very perishable. They should be kept cold and used as soon as possible. They are loose-skinned for easy peeling and segmented for bite-sized convenience.

They are excellent for garnishing fruit cups and salads. An ambrosia made with tangerine sections and shredded fresh coconut can be a tasty appetizer or dessert. Many other recipes indicate use in seafood cocktails, puddings and sauces for cakes and puddings. Tangerine sherbet makes a light and tasty dessert.

NUTRITIONAL VALUE

Tangerines are a good source of vitamin C; they also contain a variety of other vitamins and minerals. A 100-gram portion (3½-ounces) contains only 46 Calories.

TANGERINE CREAM PUDDING

2 tablespoons cornstarch
3 tablespoons sugar
⅛ teaspoon salt
2 cups milk

1 teaspoon grated fresh tangerine rind
1½ cups halved, seeded tangerine sections

Mix together cornstarch, sugar and salt in saucepan. Gradually stir in milk. Place over moderate heat, stirring constantly, until mixture thickens and comes to a boil; boil 1 minute. Remove from heat; stir in tangerine rind. Cool, stirring occasionally. Fold in tangerine sections. Chill. Makes 4 to 6 servings.

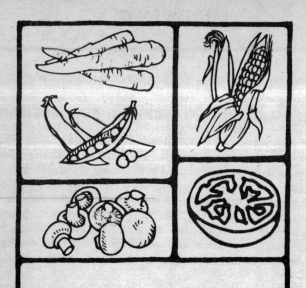

PREPARATION &
SERVING SUGGESTIONS
FOR
FRESH VEGETABLES

FRESH VEGETABLES

BUDGET COOKING WITH FRESH VEGETABLES

Fresh vegetables are one of the most economical food purchases you can make. This is especially true when you use your good judgment in making your purchases. Here are some important tips to keep in mind when shopping at your local produce department.

HOW TO BUY FRESH VEGETABLES

1. Select the varieties that are "in season"—the time of year when certain vegetables are most plentiful locally.
2. Choose vegetables that are firm, crisp, bright in color and free from decay.
3. Don't buy dirty vegetables; they are difficult to clean and you may have to throw away portions that you find to hard to clean.
4. Buy vegetables that are kept in a cool place; vegetables that are kept in a hot or sunny location wilt rapidly and lose some of their nutritive values.
5. Be very careful about buying vegetables that are marked down. Examine them for bruises, wilting or overripeness. Vegetables that are not in good condition are frequently high in waste and low in food value.
6. Learn what to look for in each variety and type of vegetable you are planning to buy (this information appears in this book under the alphabetical listing of each vegetable).

   Selecting the proper vegetables for purchase is only half of your job, the other half entails the proper cooking of these vegetables to insure that you will retain the full food value and flavor of these vegetables. The best recipe in the world is worthless if your vegetables lose their flavor, color and most of their nutritional value through improper cooking technique.

PREPARATION

First remove any bruised, wilted, discolored or tough portions from fresh vegetables. Trim very sparingly to avoid loss of food and nutrients. Make your paring thin when preparing potatoes and root vegetables. Remember, the dark-green outer leaves of cabbage, lettuce and other leafy green vegetables are high in food value so don't throw them away unless they are tough or wilted.

Wash vegetables thoroughly before cooking. Lift leafy greens from the water and let any sand and grit settle. Avoid long soaking of most vegetables as it is undesirable because some nutrients disolve in the water.

MICROWAVE COOKING

Be sure to check your oven's manual for specific instructions for cooking vegetables. Here are a few general tips to keep in mind when cooking vegetables in this manner.

• Prepare vegetables as you would for conventional cooking, but don't add salt until just before serving. Salt toughens vegetables cooked in this way if added before cooking.

• When cooking whole vegetables in their skins, pierce them before cooking. Leave a space of one inch between vegetables and arrange in a circle rather than rows for more even cooking.

• Cover vegetables with a glass lid or plastic wrap. They cook quicker and more evenly. Plastic wrap coverings should be pierced before cooking.

• Do not overcook vegetables. Vegetables continue to cook after they are removed from the oven, so make allowances in cooking time if serving will be delayed.

METHODS OF COOKING
FRESH VEGETABLES

"Experiment" is the by-word of every good cook! Vegetables are versatile . . . but to explore their true versatility you should use a variety of different cooking techniques.

First, however, you should take note of these basic rules of vegetable cookery:

1. *Guard against overcooking!* Fresh vegetables should be served crisp-tender to be at their best.
2. *Use as little water as possible.* If cooking method calls for water, remember that minerals, certain vitamins, and natural vegetable sugars essential to flavor dissolve in water . . . when you throw away the water some of these nutrients and flavoring materials go with it.
3. Pare or cut fresh vegetables just before cooking, this helps preserve essential nutrients.
4. Use a sharp knife to cut vegetables—a dull knife bruises the vegetables and thus hastens the loss of valuable nutrients.
5. Do not add soda to vegetables, it is apt to make them mushy and impair flavor.
6. Serve vegetables immediately after cooking.

OTHER TIPS

HOW TO PREVENT COLOR CHANGES

Of the green, yellow, white and red vegetables, only the yellow ones retain their color regardless of cooking methods. Green vegetables, on the other hand, are the most easily discolored and can turn to an unappetizing olive green during cooking. This is caused by "overcooking" or "excessive heat" during cooking.

Another cause of discoloration is the mild acids which all vegetables contain. If you leave your pan uncovered or only partially covered some of these acids will "go off" in the steam and thus you can help avoid any discoloration from this source.

In parts of the country where water is alkaline, it is easier to preserve green color, but white and red vegetables discolor in that kind of water. Just add a teaspoon of fresh lemon juice or white vinegar to the cooking water for potatoes, cauliflower and other white vegetables. This bit of acid will also keep red cabbage from acquiring an unappetizing bluish cast. Tomatoes keep their red color because tomato juice itself is acid.

HOW TO PREVENT STRONG FLAVORS

Some vegetables such as cabbage, broccoli, cauliflower, Brussels sprouts and turnips have strong flavors and strong odors. They can develop disagreeable flavors if overcooked. Therefore, cook these vegetables in an *uncovered* pan to allow the substances which cause strong flavors to go off in the steam. Remember, however, to add additional water to compensate for the water that goes off as steam and thus prevent burning.

FRESH VEGETABLES

VEGETABLE COOKERY

BOILING VEGETABLES

Here are some tips that will enable you to get the best flavor, food value, color and texture in the vegetables that you boil.

1. Cook only until tender.
2. Use very little water.
3. Two ways to cut cooking time: one, bring water to a boil before you add the vegetables (unless you are using so little water that no time at all would be saved by doing this), two, cut, slice, dice or coarsely shred vegetables.
4. Salt the water, allowing ½ to 1 teaspoon salt for each six servings of vegetable.
5. Use a tight-fitting lid that will keep the steam in the pan. Since you are using little water, most of the vegetable will cook in steam.
6. Keep heat low so that the water boils gently. Vigorous boiling will cause steam to escape around the edges of the lid.
7. If you have used too much water and find some liquid left when you have finished boiling vegetables try to use this liquid as it contains vitamins and minerals that have dissolved in it.

HOW TO STEAM VEGETABLES

Steaming vegetables is more satisfactory for white, yellow, and red vegetables than for green vegetables, which may turn olive-green or brown. Steamed vegetables are prepared by placing them on a rack over boiling water and cooking with a tight cover. Since vegetables are cooked entirely by steam, the required cooking time may be longer than for boiling.

BOILING GUIDE FOR FRESH VEGETABLES

Vegetable	Cooking time after water returns to boil	Approximate amount as purchased for six servings (about ½ cup each)
	Minutes	*Pounds*
Asparagus	10 to 20 (whole spears)	2½ for spears.
	5 to 15 (cuts and tips)	1¾ for cuts and tips.
Beans, lima	25 to 30	2¾ in pods.
Bean, snap	12 to 16 (1-inch pieces)	1.
Beets	30 to 45 (young, whole)	2½ with tops or
	45 to 90 (older, whole)	1½ without tops.
	15 to 25 (sliced or diced)	
Broccoli	10 to 15 (heavy stalks split)	1¾.
Brussels sprouts	15 to 20	1¼.
Cabbage	3 to 10 (shredded)	1¼.
	10 to 15 (wedges)	1½.
Carrots	15 to 20 (young, whole)	
	20 to 30 (older, whole)	1½ without tops.
	10 to 20 (sliced or diced)	
Cauliflower	8 to 15 (separated)	2.
	15 to 25 (whole)	
Celery	15 to 18 (cut up)	1½.
Corn	5 to 15 (on cob)	3 in husks.
Kale	10 to 15	1¼ untrimmed.
Okra	10 to 15	1¼.
Onions, mature	15 to 30	1¾.
Parsnips	20 to 40 (whole)	1½.
	8 to 15 (quartered)	
Peas	12 to 16	3 in pods.
Potatoes	25 to 40 (whole, medium)	
	20 to 25 (quartered)	1½.
	10 to 15 (diced)	
Spinach	3 to 10	2 untrimmed or 1½ prepackaged.
Squash, summer	8 to 15 (sliced)	1½.
Squash, winter	15 to 20 (cut up)	3.
Sweetpotatoes	35 to 55 (whole)	1½.
Tomatoes	7 to 15 (cut up)	1¼.
Turnip greens	10 to 30	2¾ untrimmed.
Turnips	20 to 30 (whole)	1¾ without tops.
	10 to 20 (cut up)	

FRESH VEGETABLES
HOW TO BAKE VEGETABLES

Baking is a slower method of cooking than boiling. It is an excellent method for cooking certain vegetables because it helps retain vitamins, minerals and flavor. Potatoes, tomatoes, squash and onions can be baked in the skin and corn in the husks. The steam is held in so that the vegetable stays moist while it cooks. Vegetables such as sliced or whole potatoes, onions, carrots, beets and squash can be baked in a casserole from the raw or partially cooked state. Carrots and beets are especially good if shredded for baking. Be sure to prick the skin of potatoes and sweet potatoes before baking to allow the steam to escape.

TO BAKE: Add seasonings and a small amount of water to the vegetables. Cover tightly to hold in the steam and keep the vegetables moist. Bake in a hot oven, 400°F., until tender.

HOW TO BROIL VEGETABLES

Broiling is a quick, easy method to use for both leftover vegetables and for raw sliced ones such as potatoes, onions, eggplant, and tomatoes.

Preheat your broiler. Place the vegetable on the greased broiler rack and brush with butter or other cooking oil. Place the rack about 3 inches below the source of heat and broil until the vegetable is tender. Usually, the vegetable must be turned once during the broiling period. Salt afterwards. Vegetables are especially good when broiled with meat.

HOW TO PAN VEGETABLES

Panning is a simple method of preparing fresh vegetables that are unusually flavorful. Carrots, beets, celery, cabbage, cauliflower, spinach, and other greens may be cooked this way.

DIRECTIONS FOR PANNING

- Slice, dice or shred the vegetable.
- Melt a small amount of fat (butter, margarine or drippings) in a heavy skillet or saucepan.
- Add vegetable and salt lightly.
- Add small amount of water and cover pan to hold in steam.
- Cook over low heat, stir the vegetable or shake the pan often to prevent burning; cook until tender.

PRESSURE COOKING VEGETABLES

Using a pressure cooker to cook vegetables can be desirable because it shortens the cooking time considerably and very little water is necessary, thus most of the vitamins and minerals are retained. Pressure cooking can be used for: artichokes, asparagus, beans, beets, broccoli, Brussels Sprouts, cabbage, carrots, cauliflower, celery, corn, onions, peas, potatoes, squash, sweetpotatoes and turnips.

DIRECTIONS FOR PRESSURE COOKING

- Follow the directions that came with your cooker.
- Bring pressure up quickly.
- Time the cooking period *exactly,* even one or two extra minutes of cooking can cause undesirable color, changes in texture, and loss of nutrients.
- Reduce pressure quickly as possible when time is up.
- Season vegetables in the same way as boiled vegetables.

STIR-FRYING

To stir-fry vegetables, heat about one to two tablespoons of cooking oil or butter in a heavy skillet or wok and add the vegetables. Stir over medium to high heat and cook until crisptender.

GIVE VEGETABLES A GOURMET TOUCH

Use spices and herbs to give your vegetable dishes a new and zesty flavor. Remember, however, that spices and herbs must be used sparingly or they overpower, rather than enhance, the natural flavor of vegetables. One-fourth to ½ teaspoon of most dried spices and herbs is enough for two cups of vegetables.

Herbs are leaves of aromatic plants grown in the Temperate Zone; spices come from aromatic plants grown in the Tropics. Dried herbs are more concentrated than fresh herbs. Use about ¼ teaspoon of a dried herb for 2 cups of vegetables and add it at the beginning of the cooking period. With fresh herbs, increase to about ¾ to 1 teaspoon for 2 cups of vegetables. Chop herbs very fine to allow some of the flavoring oils to escape. Heat chopped herbs in melted butter and add to vegetable after it has been cooked.

For suggestions on ways to successfully combine vegetables with spices and herbs, see pages 148–9.

Give Vegetables a Gourmet Touch with

SPICES AND HERBS

Vegetable	Spice or herb
Asparagus	Mustard seed, sesame seed, or tarragon.
Lima beans	Marjoram, oregano, sage, savory, tarragon, or thyme.
Snap beans	Basil, dill, marjoram, mint, mustard seed, oregano, savory, tarragon, or thyme.
Beets	Allspice, bay leaves, caraway seed, cloves, dill, ginger, mustard seed, savory, or thyme.
Broccoli	Caraway seed, dill, mustard seed, or tarragon.
Brussels sprouts	Basil, caraway seed, dill, mustard seed, sage, or thyme.
Cabbage	Caraway seed, celery seed, dill, mint, mustard seed, nutmeg, savory, or tarragon.
Carrots	Allspice, bay leaves, caraway seed, dill, fennel, ginger, mace, marjoram, mint, nutmeg, or thyme.
Cauliflower	Caraway seed, celery salt, dill, mace, or tarragon.
Cucumbers	Basil, dill, mint, or tarragon.
Eggplant	Marjoram or oregano.
Onions	Caraway seed, mustard seed, nutmeg, oregano, sage, or thyme.
Peas	Basil, dill, marjoram, mint, oregano, poppy seed, rosemary, sage, or savory.

Pepper and parsley may be added to any of the above vegetables. Curry powder is good with creamed vegetables.

FRESH VEGETABLES

Give Vegetables a Gourmet Touch with

SPICES AND HERBS

Vegetable	Spice or herb
Potatoes	Basil, bay leaves, caraway seed, celery seed, dill, chives, mustard seed, oregano, poppy seed, or thyme.
Spinach	Basil, mace, marjoram, nutmeg, or oregano.
Squash	Allspice, basil, cinnamon, cloves, fennel, ginger, mustard seed, nutmeg, or rosemary.
Sweetpotatoes	Allspice, cardamom, cinnamon, cloves, or nutmeg.
Tomatoes	Basil, bay leaves, celery seed, oregano, sage, sesame seed, tarragon, or thyme.
Green salads	Basil, chives, dill, or tarragon.

Pepper and parsley may be added to any of the above vegetables. Curry powder is good with creamed vegetables.

STORING VEGETABLES

Here are some important points to remember about storing fresh vegetables:

• Most fresh vegetables retain top quality for only a few days—even under ideal storage conditions.

• Green, leafy vegetables quickly wilt and change flavor as water evaporates from tissues.

• Keep corn, beans and peas cold. These commodities lose sweetness quickly as sugar converts to starch.

• If you wash lettuce, celery, and other leafy vegetables before storing, *drain thoroughly* because too much moisture can hasten decay.

• Always sort vegetables before storing. Use at once, or discard any bruised or soft vegetables; do not store them with sound, firm vegetables.

Most fresh green vegetables will keep well and stay crisp if you put them in covered containers or plastic bags and store them in the refrigerator. Use them within the time specified:

Asparagus—1 or 2 days; Beans, snap—3 to 5 days; Beets—1 or 2 weeks (remove tops); Broccoli, Brussels sprouts—1 or 2 days; Cabbage—1 or 2 weeks; Carrots—1 or 2 weeks (remove tops); Cauliflower, Celery—3 to 5 days; Cucumbers—3 to 5 days; Greens—spinach, kale, collards, chard, and beet, turnip and mustard greens—1 or 2 days; Lettuce and other salad greens—1 or 2 days; Mushrooms—1 or 2 days; Okra—3 to 5 days; Onions, green —1 or 2 days; Parsnips—1 or 2 weeks; Peppers—3 to 5 days; Radishes—1 or 2 weeks (remove tops); Squash, summer—3 to 5 days.

FRESH VEGETABLES
STORING VEGETABLES

Here are specific directions for storing other vegetables and the lengths of time they can be held:

BEANS, LIMA

Store in hydrator in pods in refrigerator—1 to 2 days.

CORN

Store in husk in hydrator or in plastic bag in refrigerator—1 or 2 days.

EGGPLANT

Store in the refrigerator in the hydrator or in a plastic bag—1 or 2 days.

ONIONS, MATURE

Store at room temperature or slightly cooler (60°F is best). Put into loosely woven or open-meshed containers with good circulation of air. Onions keep well for a week or two if kept dry.

PEAS, GREEN

Refrigerate in a plastic bag or hydrator—1 or 2 days.

POTATOES

Do not refrigerate. Long storage at room temperature is not practical but they can be kept for a couple of weeks.

STORING VEGETABLES

SQUASH

Store hard-rinded winter varieties in a cool, dry place (about 60°F.). Temperatures below 50°F. may cause chilling injury. Can be stored this way for a month or so.

TOMATOES

Tomatoes often require additional ripening at home. Store in cool place away from direct sunlight. Refrigerate only when fully ripe and use promptly. Ripe tomatoes should be used within 3 days. Never freeze raw tomatoes, only cooked ones.

RUTABAGAS

Refrigerate and keep them humid in a hydrator or plastic bag. They will keep well for weeks, especially if waxed.

SWEETPOTATOES

Do not refrigerate or they will spoil. They keep well at room temperature for a week or so if kept dry.

SALADS

The base of most salads is lettuce. There are many varieties to choose from. Try mixing varieties in different combinations; Iceberg, Bibb, Romaine, Boston and Endive. A few sprigs of celery tops and snipped spinach will add flavor and color to a salad. Carrots, grated or in curls, help to beautify salads. So do red onion rings, sliced radishes, cucumbers and green onion tops. Also don't overlook fresh vegetables which have been marinated in a well-flavored dressing.

SALAD MAKING POINTERS

• Use only the highest quality ingredients in making a salad.

• Fit the salad to the meal. A light one is usually better with a heavy dinner. A heartier salad with possibly a rich dressing is perfect for the main course of a meal.

• Keep salad greens in the refrigerator until you're ready to use them. If they are washed before refrigerating, dry them thoroughly first.

SALAD MAKING POINTERS

- Use a variety of greens in a tossed salad such as iceberg, romaine, bibb, Boston, spinach, and endive.
- Wash and dry salad greens thoroughly before using so that the dressing clings to the leaves and is not diluted.
- Make sure that the greens are cold and crisp before using them. Often a quick dip in a bath of ice water will restore crispness.
- Break greens into bite-sized pieces.
- If the greens are broken up before serving time, keep them in the refrigerator covered with a damp cloth.
- Use cooked fresh vegetables in tossed salads. To accent their flavors, marinate them in a tangy French dressing for an hour.
- Serve vegetable salads in a large wooden bowl which has been rubbed with a cut, unpeeled clove of garlic. Fruit salads are prettier if served in a cold glass bowl. Salad plates or bowls should always be well chilled.
- Add moist ingredients and dressing just before serving. Avoid adding more dressing than will just cling to the leaves.
- If you are using oil and fresh lemon juice for dressing, toss the leaves lightly first with the oil, and then add the seasoned lemon juice.
- Garnish salads artistically but simply with carrot curls, sliced fruit, radish roses, parsley, etc.

FRESH GARDEN SCALLOP

2 tablespoons butter or
    margarine
⅛ teaspoon finely chopped
    garlic
¼ cup coarsely chopped
    onion
¼ cup chopped green
    pepper
2 cups diced bread
1 lb. eggplant, cut in
    1-inch pieces
1 tablespoon salt
4 tablespoons butter or
    margarine
2 cups corn, cut-off-the-
    cob

½ teaspoon powdered
    mustard
½ teaspoon water
3 large eggs
½ teaspoon sugar
½ teaspoon Italian
    seasoning
¾ teaspoon salt
¼ teaspoon white pepper
1 cup milk
2 large ripe tomatoes, cut
    in wedges
1 tablespoon butter or
    margarine, melted

Melt the 2 tablespoons butter or margarine in a skillet. Add garlic and onion and cook over low heat until limp and transparent. Turn into a large mixing bowl; add green pepper and bread and toss gently. Sprinkle eggplant with the 1 tablespoon salt; drain. Melt the 4 tablespoons butter or margarine in a skillet. Add eggplant and cook until lightly browned. Add eggplant and corn to onion mixture; toss gently and turn into a buttered 2-quart casserole. Combine powdered mustard with water; let stand 10 minutes for flavor to develop. Lightly beat eggs with mustard, sugar, Italian seasoning, the ¾ teaspoon salt and white pepper. Blend in milk. Pour over casserole. Cover and bake in a preheated moderate oven (350°F) 45 minutes. Remove cover; arrange tomato wedges on top; brush with melted butter or margarine, and bake, uncovered, another 10 minutes. Makes 6 servings.

BUFFET FRESH VEGETABLE SALAD

1 cup shredded red
    cabbage
1 cup shredded green
    cabbage
1 cup curly endive
1 cup shredded lettuce
2 medium zucchini,
    sliced thin
1½ cups sliced
    cauliflowerets
1 small onion, sliced thin
6 anchovy fillets

3 tablespoons crumbled
    Roquefort cheese
1 teaspoon sugar
¼ teaspoon powdered
    mustard
¼ teaspoon black pepper
½ teaspoon paprika
3 tablespoons wine
    vinegar
6 tablespoons salad oil
½ cup sour cream

Combine first 7 ingredients and mix well. Cut anchovy fillets into small pieces and sprinkle along with crumbled cheese over salad. Mix in a small bowl sugar, mustard, black pepper, paprika and vinegar. Add oil slowly to sour cream and beat until smooth. Blend with vinegar mixture. Pour dressing over salad and toss lightly to mix well. Makes 8 servings.

GRECIAN TOSSED LETTUCE SALAD

1 head Iceberg lettuce
¼ cup sliced black olives
¼ cup sliced white onion
1 medium-size tomato,
    quartered
2 tablespoons red wine
    vinegar

2 tablespoons olive or
    salad oil
¼ teaspoon salt
¼ teaspoon ground
    black pepper
½ teaspoon sugar

Wash lettuce, drain, pat dry and tear into bite-size pieces. Add olives, onions and tomatoes. Combine vinegar, oil, salt, ground black pepper and sugar. Pour over salad just before serving. Toss lightly and serve at once. Makes 6 servings.

VEGETABLES, SOUPS, STEWS
AND CHOWDERS

The appetizing aroma of a delectable soup simmering on the back of the stove usually plays an important part in the nostalgic memories of early family, hearth and home.

Many a smart homemaker is well aware that a ready program of soups, hot or cold, hearty or delicate, provides the perfect solution for the immediate satisfaction of hunger pangs.

Today, appealing soup, rich in vitamins and minerals, combining fresh vegetables and beef broth, can be achieved without all those hours of cooking grandmother endured. What's more, in addition to time—the vegetables are also saved! Modern cooking methods result in better tasting vegetables.

A traditional favorite is a hearty vegetable soup made with fresh carrots, shredded cabbage, diced potatoes and tomatoes, sliced celery and mushrooms, onion rings and perhaps green peas or snap beans.

When making the stock, use a soup bone with a good amount of meat still clinging to it and cook, starting in cold water, with pieces of celery. Include the flavor packed celery tops, as well as parsley, sliced carrots, onion and perhaps turnip. About a half hour before the cooking time is up, add a generous amount of fresh vegetables cut in different shapes. When served, it's easy to understand why hearty fresh vegetables are cut in different shapes.

Fresh vegetable soups should look as good as they taste and garnishes can help in this department. Snipped chives and chopped parsley are commonly used but why not try some radish circles, thin slices of celery, cucumber or lemon? Or, perhaps you might try avocado balls or grated uncooked vegetables.

Even the serving of fresh vegetables can be done with a flair. Ladle them into heavy pottery mugs or pour them at the table from a pitcher or carafe.

Stews in one form or another can be found in almost every corner of the world. In all of them the meat, be it beef, veal or lamb, blended with a variety of fresh vegetables, turns into a dish fit for the simplest or most sumptuous fare.

Basically, in preparing a stew, the browned meat is simmered in a liquid with perhaps a few slices of carrots and celery, parsley and herbs. The main vegetables are added about a half hour before the meat is done so that they're still crisp-tender when served yet have taken on the rich meat flavor. Carrots, onions and potatoes are basic. In addition, try fresh turnips or squash, cubes of tomatoes and green peppers, snap beans, sliced mushrooms, or for that matter, any other vegetable that pleases your fancy. They all contribute a flavor bonus as well as vital nutrients and extra heartiness.

FRESH VEGETABLES

Try cooking stews not only on top of the range, but also in the oven. The long slow cooking develops a rich flavor that just can't be topped. Here again, the sliced fresh vegetables should be just crisp-tender when served so add them about 45 minutes before you expect the meat to be done.

Anything which tastes good with fish or other seafood is good in a chowder—fresh snap beans, asparagus chunks, cabbage, carrots, celery, corn, leeks, mushrooms, okra, green onions, parsley, green peppers, fresh green peas, shallots, spinach, tomatoes and/or turnips. Don't overlook any of these ingredients when making a chowder—neither the seafood nor the fresh vegetables. Vegetables should retain some of their pleasing texture—they shouldn't be boiled to a mush. To get the greatest benefits from cooked vegetables, cook only until tender, then use the cooking water—as you would be doing when preparing chowder.

FRESH VEGETABLE AND SEAFOOD STEW

4 medium carrots, peeled
5 ribs celery
4 cups boiling water
4½ teaspoon salt
1 cup finely chopped
  onion
1 medium clove garlic,
  minced
2 tablespoons butter or
  margarine
4 medium fresh
  tomatoes, diced
¾ teaspoon ground thyme

½ teaspoon crumbled
  saffron strands
  (optional)
¼ teaspoon ground ginger
¼ teaspoon pepper
2 teaspoons fresh lemon
  juice
4 lobster tails
12-ounce package peeled
  raw shrimp
1 pound package perch
  fillets
¼ cup flour
¼ cup cold water

Cut carrots and celery into 1-inch pieces. Place in a 2-quart saucepan with 2 cups of the water, 1 teaspoon of the salt. Cover and cook 15 minutes or until almost done. Sauté onion and garlic in butter or margarine until onions are limp. Add to vegetables along with tomatoes, remaining salt and water, seasonings and lemon juice. Cook lobster tails in boiling water according to package directions. Split underside of tails lengthwise, remove meat, cut into cubes and add. (Save lobster shells for a garnish.) Stir in shrimp and fish. Cover and cook 15 minutes or only until fish is flaky and shrimp is pink. Mix flour with the ¼ cup cold water to a smooth paste. Add and cook 1 minute or until slightly thickened. Garnish with lobster tail shells and parsley. Serve hot in soup plates as the main course. Makes 8 servings.

FRESH VEGETABLES

Old-fashioned vegetable stew, a timeless main dish, shines with luminaries from the world of fresh vegetables. Forever in style with good taste abounding, stew is thrifty to serve and eager to please. A glorious confusion of fresh vegetables in all their glory with lean chunks of meat, this sturdy dish gets a cordial reception from robust appetites of all ages. The cook relaxes as the pot simmers slowly, savoring the delight in store for those within eating distance. Make it for lunch, dinner, brunch or parties. Call it ragout if you're feeling fancy—it's the same healthful dish oblivious to fashion and always in vogue.

FRESH VEGETABLE STEW

1½ pounds beef chuck, cut in 1-inch cubes
Salt and pepper
2 tablespoons salad oil
2 medium-sized onions, sliced
3 medium-sized fresh tomatoes, peeled and quartered

1½ cups water
1 pound turnip, pared and quartered
6 medium-sized carrots, sliced
1 cup diced celery
2 sprigs parsley
¼ cup flour
Cold water

Season meat with salt and pepper. Brown meat cubes on all sides in heated salad oil. Add onions, tomatoes and 1½ cups water. Cover and simmer about 2 hours or until meat is almost tender. Add turnip, carrots, celery and parsley. Continue cooking about 30 minutes, or until vegetables are just tender. To thicken stew, blend flour with enough cold water to make a thin paste. Gradually stir into stew. Heat to boiling point. Stir constantly, until thickened. Makes about 6 servings.

THE CASSEROLE WAY OF COOKING— QUICK AND CONVENIENT

Casseroles or "one-pot cooking" is a convenient solution to many mealtime problems. Whether your favorite casserole recipe is a blend of beef or pasta or fish, adding a fresh fruit or vegetable makes for a delicious combination of flavor and nutrients. It becomes a nutrionally balanced meal in a dish, appealing to all members of the family.

FRUITS AND VEGETABLES IN MEAT MAIN DISHES

Fruits and vegetables add flavor and zest to many main dishes. Throughout the book, you will find many main dish recipes using fruits and vegetables. Here are some recipes that will give you a sampling of the interesting ways in which you can prepare vegetables along with main dish meats.

FRESH VEGETABLE AND HAMBURG CASSEROLE

½ cup diced onion
2 tablespoons butter or
   margarine or beef
   suet
1 pound lean hamburg
   meat
1 cup diced celery
1 cup sliced carrots

⅓ cup diced green
   peppers
1 beef bouillon cube
¾ cup hot water
1½ teaspoons salt
⅛ teaspoon pepper
2 tablespoons flour
¼ cup cold water
2 cups mashed potatoes

Saute onion in butter or margarine or beef suet. Add meat and cook until all the pink has disappeared. Add celery, carrots, green pepper, beef bouillon cube, water and seasonings. Cover and cook 5 minutes. Mix flour to a smooth paste with cold water and add to the mixture. Turn into a 1-quart casserole. Spoon fluffy mashed potatoes around the edge of casserole. Bake in a preheated moderate oven (350°F.) 45 minutes or until golden brown over the top. Makes 4 servings.

OVEN FRESH VEGETABLE AND BEEF FRICASSEE

4 minute cube steaks
   (about 1½ pounds)
¼ cup flour
2 tablespoons shortening
   or 4-ounces beef suet
2 cups diced potatoes
2 cups sliced carrots
1 cup sliced onions

1 cup sliced celery
1 cup hot water
2 tablespoons fresh
   lemon juice
1½ teaspoons salt
¼ teaspoon thyme leaves
¼ teaspoon pepper

Cut minute steaks in ½-inch strips. Roll in flour and brown in shortening or beef suet. Add remaining ingredients. Turn into 2½ cup casserole. Cover and bake in a preheated moderate oven (350°F.) 1 hour, stirring twice to mix well. Makes 6 to 8 servings.

CROWN LAMB ROAST WITH FRESH MUSHROOM STUFFING

12 to 15 crown lamb rib
   roast
¾ teaspoon salt
⅛ teaspoon pepper
   Fresh Mushroom
   Stuffing
12 to 15 small fresh
   mushrooms

1 teaspoon fresh lemon
   juice
¼ teaspoon salt
2 tablespoons melted
   butter or margarine
   Fresh parsley
   Lamb gravy

The crown of lamb roast is prepared by the butcher from the rack. It usually contains from 12 to 15 ribs. Wipe with a damp cloth and rub both sides with the ¾ teaspoon salt mixed with the ⅛ teaspoon pepper. Place on a rack in a shallow baking pan. Fill center with Fresh Mushroom Stuffing. Wrap ends of ribs separately with foil to prevent charring. Cover top of stuffing with foil. Bake 1 hour in a preheated slow oven (325°F.). Remove foil from stuffing and continue baking 1 more hour. Remove foil from rib ends. Wash and boil small mushrooms 1 minute in ½-inch boiling water, add lemon juice and the ¼ teaspoon salt. Dip each in melted butter or margarine and place one on each rib. Bake 15 minutes. Garnish with fresh parsley just before serving. Serve with Lamb Gravy. Makes 6 to 8 servings.

FRESH MUSHROOM STUFFING

¾ lbs. fresh small
   mushrooms
½ cups butter or margarine
1 teaspoon fresh lemon
   juice
½ cup chopped fresh onion
½ cup chopped celery
1 quart bread cubes
   (croutons)

½ cup chopped fresh
   parsley
1 teaspoon salt
¾ teaspoon poultry
   seasoning
⅛ teaspoon pepper
2 tablespoons water

Remove caps from mushrooms and save enough of the smallest ones to garnish each rib of the roast. Slice remaining mushrooms and sauté in butter or margarine and lemon juice along with chopped fresh onion and chopped celery. Combine with toasted bread cubes (measure after toasting), fresh parsley, salt, poultry seasoning, pepper and water. Mix lightly. Spoon into center of crown lamb roast. Makes sufficient stuffing for a 15 rib crown lamb roast.

LAMB GRAVY: Drain drippings from roasting pan and blend in 1 tablespoon flour. Stir in 1 cup cold water, ¼ teaspoon salt, ¹⁄₁₆ teaspoon each, pepper and garlic powder. Cook until slightly thickened. Makes approximately 1 cup.

PLANKED FRESH VEGETABLE
HAMBURGER STEAK

1 pound ground chuck
    steak
½ cup fine dry bread
    crumbs
1 egg, beaten
1 teaspoon salt
⅛ teaspoon pepper
1 tablespoon chopped
    parsley
⅓ cup finely chopped green
    pepper
⅔ cup finely chopped onion

¾ cup finely chopped fresh
    tomato
4 tablespoons melted
    butter or margarine
3 cups duchess potatoes
6 slices fresh tomatoes
12 small boiled white
    onions
¾ pound boiled whole
    fresh snap beans
1 small head cooked
    cauliflower

Thoroughly mix the first 9 ingredients. Pat onto a piece of aluminum foil, having the steak 10-inches long, 5-inches wide and 1-inch thick. Brush top with 2 tablespoons of the melted butter or margarine. Place under broiler 20 minutes or until brown, having the oven control set to 450°F. Have a steak plank dressed with a border of duchess potatoes put through a pastry bag. Place the steak in the center, cooked side down. Brush remaining melted butter or margarine over both, potatoes and steak. Place under broiler 15 minutes or until brown. Remove from broiler and arrange sliced tomatoes, boiled onions, cooked fresh snap beans and cauliflower around the steak as desired. Serve at once from the plank. Makes 6 servings.

CHICKEN AND FRESH VEGETABLE PIE

⅓ cup chicken fat, butter
   or margarine
1 cup sliced fresh
   mushrooms
⅓ cup chopped onion
⅓ cup flour
1½ cups chicken stock
2 cups diced tomatoes
½ cup celery
1½ cups diced chicken
½ cup chopped ripe olives
½ teaspoon salt
⅛ teaspoon pepper
Pastry, using 1 cup
   flour

Melt fat, butter or margarine in a saucepan. Add mushrooms and onion and cook until limp. Stir in flour. Add chicken stock, tomatoes and celery. Cook until slightly thickened. Add diced chicken, olives, salt and pepper. Place in a 1½ quart casserole. Cover with pastry rolled to ⅛-inch thickness. Trim, turn under and flute edges. Bake in a preheated hot oven (425°F.) 30 minutes or until brown. Makes 4 servings.

FRESH VEGETABLE POT ROAST AU JUS

3 pound pot roast
1 tablespoon shortening
   or a piece of beef
   suet
1¾ teaspoons salt
¼ teaspoon pepper
½ cup hot water
2 cups diced fresh
   tomatoes
1 cup diced potatoes
1 cup sliced carrots
1 cup chopped onion
½ cup chopped celery
½ cup chopped green
   pepper

Brown pot roast in shortening or beef suet, on all sides, in a Dutch oven or a heavy saucepan. Sprinkle with salt and pepper. Add water. Cover and cook over low heat 1½ to 2 hours or until meat is almost tender. Add vegetables. Cover. Cook 1 hour or until meat is tender. Slice meat and serve with the vegetables and juice spooned over it. Makes 6 to 8 servings.

FRESH VEGETABLES ORIENTAL

1 lb. boned pork, cut in
   1-inch squares
1 small clove garlic
½ teaspoon ground ginger
6 to 10 fresh medium
   mushrooms, halved
½ cup chopped onion
2 cups celery, sliced in
   ½-inch pieces

½ cup water
¾ cup fresh pineapple, cut
   in small wedges
¼ cup green pepper, cut in
   1-inch squares
¼ cup red pepper, cut in
   1-inch squares
Sweet and Sour Sauce

Brown pork in a large skillet. Add garlic and ground ginger while browning meat. Discard garlic when brown. Remove pork and set aside. Sauté mushrooms 5 minutes. Remove and set aside. Saute onions until transparent. Remove and set aside. In same skillet add celery and water. Cook, covered, until crisp-tender, about 15 minutes. Return pork, mushrooms, onion, pineapple, green pepper and red pepper to skillet. Bring to serving temperature. Pour Sweet and Sour Sauce over ingredients. Toss gently. Serve at once. Makes 4 servings.

SWEET AND SOUR SAUCE:

2 tablespoons cornstarch
1 tablespoon soy sauce
2½ tablespoons brown
   sugar

¼ cup cider vinegar
⅔ cup water

In small saucepan, mix cornstarch with soy sauce and enough water (1 to 2 tablespoons) to make smooth paste. Stir in brown sugar, vinegar and water. Blend. Cook, stirring constantly, over medium heat until mixture boils and becomes clear.

FRESH VEGETABLES
BARBECUES

Summer days are barbecue days whether it be on the porch, patio, picnic ground or in the backyard.

Although these old favorites are delicious, we're always looking for something new to serve—something that's not time consuming or difficult or tough on the budget. Here's where the wide choice of economical fresh fruits and vegetables available in the markets fills the bill perfectly.

For instance, there's hardly anything under the sun that tastes better than grilled shish kebabs. Onions, green pepper, tomatoes and lamb laced on long shiny shewers make a satisfying answer to outdoor appetites. For a new twist, cook the vegetables separately on skewers (choosing ones that take the same amount of time to do) and serve with lamb chops instead of the usual cubes of meat. This method solves the old problem of overcooked vegetables. and undercooked meat on kebabs because the foods are grilled only as long as necessary. Sweet corn is delicious grilled over an open fire. Strip off a layer or two of the husks, pull out the silk and re-smooth the husks, then give the ears about 20 to 25 minutes on the grill. Hot corn is much more manageable when you pull back the husks to make a sort of handle for the ear.

A crunchy tossed green salad makes a perfect accompaniment. If you're traveling to your picnic spot, wrap the prepared greens in foil and keep them cold to assure crispness. Just before you're ready to serve it toss lightly with just enough dressing to coat the leaves thoroughly.

And for dessert—something simple yet seasonable—a big bowlful of cantaloupe chunks and black grapes. Slices of juicy watermelon are always a hit, too. Fresh fruits make a wonderful and easily carried dessert. Just wash and pack!

STUFFED VEGETABLES

A wonderful way to vary the serving of vegetables is to stuff them with savory fillings. Almost any fine fresh vegetable which can be hollowed out—such as a tomato, pepper or eggplant—may be stuffed with some flavorful mixture of meat, rice, bread crumbs, seasonings and cooked as a thrifty luncheon or dinner dish. Cabbage leaves, slightly wilted by brief immersion in boiling water, are world famous as "wrappers" for such concoctions and are especially popular in Russia and the Scandinavian countries.

Tomato cups do not need any kind of pre-cooking, but green peppers should be parboiled about 5 minutes in an inch of boiling salted water. Eggplant should be scooped out, then half-cooked in a moderately hot oven for about 20 minutes before stuffing. Turn the hollowed-out shells upside down in a shallow baking dish containing about an inch of water. Butternut squash should be scooped out and pre-cooked the same way before being filled with some rich, meaty mixture.

FRESH VEGETABLES

Potatoes, baked until completely tender, can be scooped out and seasoned in dozens of delicious ways. Sour cream and fresh chives may either be mixed with the potato pulp, then piled back into the shell, or a well-chived sour cream can be brought to the table to be used on the steaming, newly-opened potato. Parsley, tomatoes, dill, minced green peppers, minced onion, sharp cheese, flaked fish, leftover ham bits, spiced sausage, all combine delectably with bland and mealy potatoes.

Yellow onions beckon from vegetable bins to urge you to use them in new ways such as "Stuffed Onions savory with bacon, ground beef and green pepper," a nourishing and different main dish to bring to your table.

A very good way to enjoy baked potatoes is with a stuffing that includes fresh onion, chopped carrot and a delightfully different seasoning of dill.

See Pgs. 39–40 for veg. fillers, omit avocados.

COOKING VEGETABLES CHINESE STYLE

Chinese vegetable cookery is an excellent example of how to cook vegetables. Cook vegetables only briefly, to that ideal point where they are just crisp-tender, never mushy and overcooked.

Oriental cooks braise or pan many of their vegetables. This is a method of cooking with very little water or with the steam formed from the vegetables' own juices. The liquid used becomes part of the flavorful sauce, which is served with the vegetable. Braising works well with a number of vegetables and is thrifty of color, flavor and food values. Shredded cabbage, kale, spinach, okra and snap beans are a few of the vegetables cooked successfully by this method. The vegetable is cut into small pieces and cooked in a heavy pan on top of the range. A little fat is added to prevent sticking, and a tight cover is used to hold in the steam. The vegetable is cooked over low heat until just tender.

ARTICHOKES

AVAILABILITY

Available all year, with peak supply in March, April and May.

HOW TO BUY

Select firm, heavy heads with compact leaves. Leaf scales should be of a good green color; browning may mean old age or injury, or frost damage (which may be harmless but it spoils appearance). Overmature artichokes have hard-tipped leaf scales which are open or spreading, and the center may be fuzzy and dark pink or purple in color.

Artichokes are generally found in three sizes . . . small, medium, and large—size has nothing to do with maturity or eating quality. Choose the size according to their use. Small for pickling, stews and casseroles; medium for salads; large for stuffing.

PREPARATION AND SERVING SUGGESTIONS

Fresh artichokes add a gourmet touch to any menu. The artichoke has a delicate nutty flavor which is prized in salads and hors d'oeuvers. It can be eaten in entirety or each leaf can be pulled off and dipped into a sauce. A Hollandaise sauce is appropriate with hot artichokes and a vinaigrette sauce when they are served cold.

Wash artichokes, trim stems, and remove the tough outside leaves from the base. Trim tips of leaves if desired. Spread leaves and remove the fuzzy thistle and tiny inner leaves with the tip of a teaspoon (this can be done before or after cooking).

To cook: stand artichokes upright in a deep saucepan just big enough to fit snugly, or tie them with a string so they will retain their shape. Add 1 teaspoon salt, 1 tablespoon of fresh lemon juice and boiling water to cover. Cook, covered, 45 to 60 minutes or until the base is soft. Lift out with two spoons and let drain upside down.

HOW TO EAT

This is one vegetable that can properly be eaten with the fingers. Simply pluck off each petal and dip into a savory sauce. When the prized heart is reached after all of the leaves have been removed, eat it with a fork.

When preparing stuffed artichokes, spread the leaves open, cut off some of the hard tips and remove some of the center leaves. Fill with a seafood or meat mixture and bake.

NUTRITIONAL VALUE

The composition of boiled, drained artichokes, 100 grams (3½ ounces) includes food energy of 8 to 44 Calories rising from time of harvest, plus a useful variety of other vitamins and minerals.

ARTICHOKES DELIGHT

4 artichokes, prepared as directed for stuffing
2 tablespoons butter or margarine
1 tablespoon lemon juice
½ pound mushrooms, sliced
1 tablespoon flour
¾ teaspoon salt
⅛ teaspoon pepper
1 tablespoon chopped parsley
½ cup milk
1 cup heavy cream
Grated Parmesan cheese

While artichokes are cooking, melt butter; add lemon juice and mushrooms. Cook until mushrooms are tender, stirring frequently; reserve a few slices for garnish. Stir in flour, salt, pepper and parsley. Gradually stir in milk and cream, blending until smooth. Cook stirring constantly, until sauce thickens. Pour sauce into hot cooked artichokes. Sprinkle with Parmesan cheese. Add mushroom slices and a little parsley, if desired. Makes 4 servings.

SAUCES FOR ARTICHOKES

LEMON-BUTTER SAUCE:

Melt ½ cup butter or margarine and add 2 tablespoons fresh lemon juice.
YIELD: ½ cup.

MOCK HOLLANDAISE SAUCE:

Blend ½ cup mayonnaise with 2 tablespoons fresh lemon juice. Heat over hot water, stirring constantly.
YIELD: ½ cup.

FRENCH FRIED ARTICHOKES

4 artichokes	**Dash Tabasco**
3 egg yolks, slightly beaten	**Flour**
½ cup milk	**Fine dry bread crumbs**
¾ teaspoon salt	**Solid all-vegetable**
½ teaspoon nutmeg	**shortening for deep**
Pepper to taste	**fat frying**

Wash and drain artichokes. Cut off top half of artichokes and trim stem. Snip off all outer leaves down to pale green leaves. Slice artichokes in half lengthwise; remove choke. Cut ¼ inch slices lengthwise. Blend together egg yolks, milk and seasonings. Coat artichoke slices with flour, dip into egg mixture, then coat with bread crumbs. Drop into skillet or deep fat fryer with shortening preheated to 375 degrees F. Fry until golden brown, about 1 minute. Remove with slotted spoon, or fry basket, drain and serve hot. Delicious as hors d'oeuvre or meat accompaniment. Makes about 24.

ARTICHOKES, ITALIAN STYLE

4 artichokes	⅛ teaspoon black pepper
¼ cup olive oil	1 teaspoon oregano leaves
¼ cup chopped onions	1 tablespoon chopped
1 clove garlic, minced	fresh parsley.
½ teaspoon salt	

Wash and prepare artichokes for cooking as given in preceding instructions. Cook 20 to 30 minutes or until partially cooked in boiling water to cover. Remove from water and drain, reserving the cooking water. Place remaining ingredients in saucepan and sauté until lightly browned. Place artichokes upright in a deep, round baking pan just large enough to fit snugly. Pour 1-inch of the reserved artichoke cooking water in the pan. Pour the sautéed onion sauce over the artichokes, allowing some to fall into the centers. Cover and simmer 45 minutes or until tender. Serve some of the liquid in a little cup with each artichoke. Makes 4 servings.

SHRIMP STUFFED ARTICHOKES

4 artichokes
1 teaspoon salt
1 tablespoon fresh lemon
   juice
   Boiling water to cover

Shrimp Stuffing
1-inch boiling water in
   baking pan
1 tablespoon fresh lemon
   juice

Wash artichokes, trim stems and pull off the tough outside leaves at the base of artichoke and discard. Cut off the top third and spread artichokes open by placing them upside down on a table and pressing ends firmly. Dig out the center leaves and fuzzy portion with a spoon. Stand artichokes upright in a deep saucepan just large enough to fit snugly or tie them with a string so they will regain their shape. Add 1 teaspoon salt, 1 tablespoon fresh lemon juice and boiling water to cover. Cook, cover 20 to 30 minutes or until partly tender. Remove from water with 2 spoons and drain up-side down. Fill centers with Shrimp Stuffing. Place in a 9x4x2-inch baking pan. Pour 1-inch boiling water and 1 tablespoon fresh lemon juice in the pan around the artichokes. Brush artichokes generously with olive or salad oil. Cover closely and bake in a preheated moderate oven 350°F. 20 minutes or until done. Top each serving with a whole cooked deveined shrimp. Serve with a wedge of fresh lemon. Makes serving for 4.

SHRIMP STUFFING:

1 cup (4½ ounces)
   cooked deveined
   shrimp
1½ cups soft bread crumbs
¼ cup finely chopped
   onion

½ teaspoon salt
2 teaspoons fresh lemon
   juice
1 egg, beaten

Break shrimp into small pieces and mix with remaining ingredients. Spoon into partially cooked artichokes. Bake as in above directions. Makes sufficient stuffing for 4 artichokes.

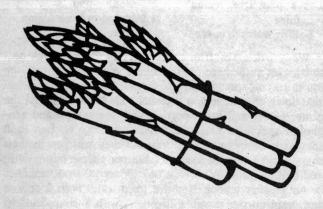

ASPARAGUS

AVAILABILITY

Almost the entire supply is domestic and is mostly available concentrated in the period *March through June, with peak in April.*

Asparagus is of two general types, that with spears that become dark green in sunlight and that which produce light green or whitish spears.

HOW TO BUY

Only the green portion of the asparagus usually marketed is tender, so the relative amount of green and white on the stalk is an important factor of quality. The asparagus should be fresh and firm with closed compact tips. Tender asparagus is brittle and easily punctured.

PREPARATION AND SERVING SUGGESTIONS

Asparagus is served in many forms as in salads, soups, hot dishes and in combination with various sauces. The whole spears may be served or only the green part, or as cuts or tips.

Fresh asparagus is a delight to the menu-maker; it goes with any meat, fish or fowl. It adds crisp-tender consistency and delectable flavor to egg, cheese or macaroni main dishes. Serve it hot with a luscious sauce. Or cook and chill asparagus spears and serve them with a well-seasoned french dressing garnished with bright red tomato quarters, rice, cooked egg yolk or strips of pimento.

One! Two! Three! Quick! That's the way to cook asparagus. Fifteen minutes cooking time when spears lie full length in boiling water makes them crisp-tender. This allows five minutes cooking time without lid, 10 additional minutes covered. When spears are cooked in an upright position in about 1½ inches of boiling salted water, allow an additional 3 to 5 minutes since the tips must steam while the lower parts cook in boiling water.

The simplest thing to do with a platter of steaming crisp-tender asparagus is to dress it with melted butter. Beyond that there are dozens and hundreds of delicious ways of preparing this springtime delicacy, such as fresh asparagus with butter and egg sauce on toast, fresh asparagus oriental style, fresh asparagus and chicken a la king on toast, fresh asparagus au gratin, or asparagus with chive mayonnaise, or with mustard butter, or with caper butter, or with black butter sauce, or with dilly butter.

To prepare for cooking: Cut or break off each stalk as far down as it snaps easily. Remove scales with a knife. Then wash thoroughly, using a brush.

To cook whole stalks in upright position: Tie 5 to 6 stalks of asparagus in a bundle with string. Stand upright in the bottom part of a double boiler. Sprinkle with 1 teaspoon salt. Pour in 1 to 1½ inches boiling water. Cover with the top part of the double boiler, inverted. Boil 15 to 20 minutes or until just crisp-tender. Lift out by catching tines of fork in string. Place on platter. Cut strings. The boiling water cooks the stalks while the rising steam cooks the tender heads. By this method the whole stalk is uniformly cooked.

To cook in skillet or large bottom saucepan: Place asparagus in 2 layers in a 9 or 10 inch skillet or saucepan. Sprinkle with 1 teaspoon salt. Pour on boiling water to a depth of 1 inch. Cover. Boil 12 to 15 minutes or until the lower part of the stalk is just crisp-tender. Lift out with a pancake turner or 2 forks. Serve with butter or margarine or one of the asparagus sauces.

NUTRITIONAL VALUE

A cup of cooked asparagus, 175 grams, provides three-fourths of the daily recommended allowance of vitamin C; a third of the vitamin A; and about a tenth of the iron for an adult. It is very low in sodium, with only 1 milligram per 100 grams of boiled spears. It is therefore an ideal vegetable for those on a low-sodium diet.

FRESH ASPARAGUS AND HAM CASSEROLE

2 pounds fresh asparagus, cooked	6 tablespoons butter or margarine
2 medium potatoes, cooked	3 tablespoons flour
4 hard-cooked eggs, sliced	1½ cups milk
2 cups diced cooked ham	¾ teaspoon salt
	¼ teaspoon pepper
	¼ teaspoon dry mustard
	½ cup soft bread crumbs

Place layer of cooked asparagus in bottom of 2-quart casserole. Slice cooked potatoes and place over asparagus. Cover with alternating layers of sliced hard-cooked eggs, diced ham and remaining cooked asparagus. Melt 4 tablespoons of the butter in a saucepan. Blend in flour. Stir in milk and cook until mixture thickens and comes to a boil, stirring constantly. Remove from heat. Add salt, pepper and dry mustard and pour over casserole. Melt remaining 2 tablespoons butter, mix with bread crumbs and sprinkle over the top. Bake in a 375°F. oven 20 to 25 minutes or until crumbs are brown. Makes 6 servings.

FRESH ASPARAGUS WITH ORANGE-LEMON SAUCE

1 bunch (2–2½ pounds) asparagus	4 teaspoons fresh lemon juice
¼ pound butter or margarine	½ teaspoon grated orange rind
¼ cup fresh orange juice	½ teaspoon grated lemon rind

Break off asparagus stalks as far down as they snap easily. Wash asparagus. Cook asparagus, covered, in small amount of boiling salted water until just tender. Drain, if necessary. Meanwhile, melt butter or margarine. Stir in remaining ingredients. Heat to serving temperature, stirring occasionally. Serve with cooked asparagus. Garnish with lemon slices, as desired. Makes about 6 servings.

BEANS, SNAP

AVAILABILITY

On the market all year rising from a low point in February to peak in the May-August period and tapering off again in late fall and winter.

Snap beans are of two types, the bush and the vining or pole bean. Within each type there are green-podded and yellow-podded varieties. Some beans are round-podded, some oval-podded and some flat-podded.

HOW TO BUY

Snap beans should be fresh appearing, clean, firm but tender, crisp, free from scars and reasonably well shaped. As the name implies, a good fresh bean snaps readily when broken. The seeds in bush beans should be small and immature. If seeds are half-grown or larger, the pods are likely to be tough. In pole beans, the seeds are large but this does not necessarily mean poor quality. Beans should have no strings. When breaking a bean pull the two halves apart gently to check for strings. A dull, lifeless or wilted appearance indicates beans have been held too long.

PREPARATION AND SERVING SUGGESTIONS

Some forms of snap beans can be used as food at various stages of maturity. The beans may be just appearing in the pod or they may be plump in the pod or they may be allowed to mature to the dry bean stage. In general, "snap beans" means to most people the bean harvested when immature at the stage when both seeds and pods are tender and edible. With today's stringless varieties, preparation is simple. Wash, snip off the stem end, or both ends if you like, and boil in a small amount of water until tender. Only the imagination of the cook limits the many ways of serving snap beans. The simplest method is to boil, flavor with salt and pepper and serve hot. If it pleases the palate, add butter.

For a more sophisticated dish, beans may be served like asparagus with a Hollandaise, cheese or mushroom sauce. Some folks like to add bacon or fatback to the cooking water to give a special flavor.

Beans may be served in vegetable salads, either hot or chilled. Often beans are marinated and served cold alone or with other salad vegetables. Snap beans are a good ingredient of stews and soups.

NUTRITIONAL VALUE

Fresh green and wax snap beans make a generally good contribution to the diet though they are not outstanding for any particular nutrient. Each 100 grams contain 32 calories.

MARINATED FRESH SNAP BEANS

1 pound fresh snap beans
1-inch boiling water
1 teaspoon salt

1 tablespoon chopped
   chives
½ cup French dressing
   Pimento strips

Wash snap beans, cut off tips and leave whole. Place in a saucepan with 1-inch boiling water and salt. Bring to boiling point and boil uncovered 5 minutes. Cover and cook until crisp-tender, 5 to 10 minutes. Cooking time depends upon the age and size of beans. Drain. Add chives and French dressing. Marinate at least one hour. Serve with Vegetable Sour Cream Mold. Garnish with pimento strips. Makes 6 servings.

SNAP BEANS WITH NUTMEG BUTTER

1½ pounds fresh snap
   beans
1 inch boiling water in
   saucepan
1 teaspoon salt

3 tablespoons butter or
   margarine
¼ teaspoon nutmeg
⅛ teaspoon pepper

Wash snap beans. Cut off tips and cut into 1-inch pieces. Place in saucepan with boiling water and salt. Bring to a boil and boil 5 minutes. Cover and continue cooking until just crisp-tender, about 10 minutes. Drain. Toss lightly with butter or margarine, nutmeg and black pepper. Makes 6 servings.

SNAP BEANS WITH SAUTÉED FRESH MUSHROOM CAPS

Wash and remove tips from fresh snap beans. Leave whole, cut into 1-inch pieces, or cut them French style. Place in a saucepan with ½ to 1 inch boiling water and ½ teaspoon salt. Bring to boiling point, uncovered, and cook 5 minutes without cover. Cover and cook 10 to 12 minutes or until crisp-tender. (Whole beans will take slightly longer to cook.) Drain if necessary, and turn into serving dish and top with *Sautéed Fresh Mushroom Caps*.

SAUTÉED FRESH MUSHROOM CAPS

1 pound fresh mushrooms	1 teaspoon fresh lemon
1 clove garlic	½ teaspoon salt
2 tablespoons butter or margarine	¹⁄₁₆ teaspoon pepper

Wash mushrooms, remove stems and save them to use in soups or sauces. Sauté mushroom caps and garlic in butter or margarine and lemon juice—about 5 minutes. Remove garlic and toss lightly with salt and black pepper. Makes 6 servings.

TUNA GREEN BEAN SALAD

½ pound fresh green beans	2 teaspoons fresh lemon juice
1 can (6½ ounces) tuna, drained	1 teaspoon minced fresh onion
⅓ cup thinly sliced celery	½ teaspoon salt
3 tablespoons salad oil	

Cut green beans into 1-inch pieces. Cook, covered, in small amount of boiling salted water until just tender. Drain, if necessary; cool. Combine beans with tuna and celery. Mix together remaining ingredients; toss lightly with green bean mixture. Chill about 1 hour. Mix lightly before serving. Makes about 4 servings.

BEETS

AVAILABILITY

Beets are on the market all year in moderate amounts, with the largest quantity available June through October. Globe-shaped or only slightly flattened beets are the most popular. They have alternate zones of purplish pink flesh in warm weather; but when reaching harvest stage in cool weather, they have darker flesh color with less differences between the zones.

HOW TO BUY

Good quality beets are smooth, firm and of good color. Beets that are soft, flabby, rough or shriveled should be rejected because they may be tough or woody.

Early beets are often marketed in bunches with tops attached. The condition of the tops does not indicate quality of the roots, but if tops are fresh and good they make for good eating. Late crop beets are usually sold topped. Beets of medium size of the late crop are less likely to be tough or woody than either large or very small ones.

PREPARATION AND SERVING SUGGESTIONS

In preparing beets, do not cut the stem or the root too closely or they will bleed in cooking. Cook them in the skins and the skins will slip off readily. Leave them in the cooking liquid until ready to use.

Beets may be served boiled, pickled and in salads. They can be steamed or cooked in a pressure cooker as well as in an ordinary kettle without loss of color as long as they are not pared or cut. Beet juice is a basic ingredient for the exotic Russian and Middle European borscht. Beet tops are prepared in the same manner as spinach. Sliced beets go well in salads, they are used molded in gelatin; as sweet and sour beets, they go well in soups; and can be baked or fried. A good dish is fresh beets with parmesan cheese; and another is fresh beets with sour cream; and there is a recipe for beets stuffed with a spicy egg mixture that is a gourmet delight.

NUTRITIONAL VALUE

In general, beets are low in calories and contribute a useful amount of vitamins and minerals. A cupful, 165 grams, provides only 50 Calories. Beet greens are high in vitamin A and iron. A cupful (180 grams) provides 80% more than the daily recommended allowance of vitamin A and a third of the iron.

FRESH BEETS WITH SCALLION BUTTER

8 medium-size fresh beets	1/3 cup chopped scallions
3 tablespoons melted butter or margarine	1/2 teaspoon salt
	1/8 teaspoon pepper

Remove greens from beets, leaving about 1-inch of the stem end intact. Cover and cook in a small amount of boiling salted water until just tender. Melt butter or margarine in a small skillet; add scallions and cook until tender. Slip skins off beets. Slice beets and toss with scallion butter. Season with salt and pepper. Makes 4 servings.

BROCCOLI

AVAILABILITY

Available all year, with period of greatest abundance in October through April and least in July and August.

HOW TO BUY

It should be fresh and green with compact bud clusters which have not opened to show the yellow flowers. The general color should be dark green, deep sage green or purplish-green depending on variety. Stalks and stem branches should be tender and firm. Yellowed and wilted leaves indicate staleness. If many of the bud clusters are open showing the flowers, the broccoli is overmature. Wilted, flabby or noticeably bruised broccoli should be avoided.

FRESH VEGETABLES
PREPARATION AND SERVING SUGGESTIONS

Broccoli is usually boiled but after that simple operation, it can be a surprisingly versatile vegetable. For example, here are some of its many uses: Broccoli on toast with a cheese sauce; fresh raw broccoli as an hors d'oeuvre with a cocktail dip or broken into small pieces and added to the tossed green salad; boiled broccoli with a creole sauce; left-over broccoli in tomato soup; broccoli with lemon sauce made of mayonnaise and fresh lemon juice; broccoli and ham casserole; broccoli au gratin; broccoli over slices of turkey or chicken; broccoli marinated in oil and vinegar and added to crisp greens; parboiled broccoli stalks sautéed in olive oil with sliced onions and minced fresh garlic; broccoli with egg sauce or hard-boiled egg slices; broccoli with vinaigrette sauce; broccoli with tomato sauce and grated parmesan cheese; broccoli with sour cream sauce; and cream of broccoli soup.

To prepare for cooking, wash broccoli and trim the main stem slightly. Do not remove the stem, since the whole stalk is edible. Make lengthwise gashes in the stems, almost to the flowerettes if they are more than a half inch in diameter.

Upright method: Tie in a bunch; stand upright in the bottom part of a double boiler, containing about 1 inch of boiling water and one-half teaspoon of salt. Bring to the boiling point and cook five minutes. Cover with the inverted top of the double boiler and cook 10 to 15 minutes or only until crisp-tender.

Saucepan method: Place broccoli loose in a saucepan with one inch of boiling water and one-half teaspoon of salt. Cook with cover off the first five minutes and then cook covered 10 to 15 minutes or only until crisp-tender. Or if desired, leave cover on during the entire cooking period, but lift the lid three or four times to permit the gases to escape, and thus protect the green color of the vegetable.

BROCCOLI

In general: Cook as briefly as possible in a small amount of water, both to preserve the crisp texture and to conserve nutrients. Good sauces for broccoli include Hollandaise, mayonnaise, polonaise and amandine.

NUTRITIONAL VALUE

In common with other leafy vegetables, broccoli is nutritionally rich. It is a good source of vitamin A and an excellent source of vitamin C. Broccoli is low in Calories, a cup (150 grams) has only 40 Calories.

BROCCOLI EGG DIVAN

1 bunch broccoli
4 hard-cooked eggs
½ teaspoon salt, divided
¼ teaspoon pepper
1 can (10½ ounces)
   condensed Cheddar
   cheese soup

⅓ cup milk
¼ cup fine dry bread
   crumbs
2 tablespoons melted
   butter or margarine

To prepare broccoli, cut off large leaves and the bottom of the stalk. Wash well. If stalk is more than ½ inch in diameter, make 2 lengthwise slits almost to flowerets. Cook broccoli, uncovered, in boiling salted water to cover until tender, about 15 minutes. Drain. Arrange broccoli, stems toward the center, in a 10-inch pie plate. Slice egg crosswise and layer over broccoli. Sprinkle with ¼ teaspoon salt and pepper. Mix undiluted soup with milk until smooth. Pour over broccoli and eggs in pie plate. Mix together bread crumbs, melted butter and remaining ¼ teaspoon salt. Sprinkle over cheese sauce. Bake in 375°F. oven 20 minutes, until cheese sauce is bubbly and bread crumbs lightly browned. Makes 4 servings.

FRESH BROCCOLI PARMESAN

1 bunch (1½ lb.) fresh
    broccoli
1 teaspoon salt
2 tablespoons olive oil
1 clove garlic, split

½ cup diced boiled ham
¼ cup grated Parmesan
    cheese
⅛ teaspoon pepper

Wash and trim broccoli; split all large stems to decrease cooking time. Place in medium-sized saucepan with 1 inch boiling water and salt. Cook, uncovered, for 5 minutes. Cover and simmer 5 minutes or until partially done. Drain, saving liquid to use later. Heat oil and garlic in 9-inch skillet. Add broccoli and sauté 3 to 5 minutes to finish cooking. If pan gets too dry add a little of the water drained from broccoli. Add ham and cook only until hot. Sprinkle with Parmesan cheese and black pepper. Serve at once. Makes 6 servings.

FRESH BROCCOLI WITH TOMATO SAUCE

¼ cup finely chopped
    onion
1 clove fresh garlic
2 tablespoons olive oil or
    butter or margarine
½ cup finely chopped
    fresh tomatoes
½ cup chicken stock
1 tablespoon chopped
    fresh parsley

1 teaspoon salt
¼ teaspoon pepper
1 tablespoon tomato
    paste
1½ pounds (1 bunch) fresh
    broccoli, cooked
Grated Parmesan
    cheese

Sauté onions and garlic in olive oil or butter or margarine until lightly browned. Add tomato, chicken stock, parsley, salt, black pepper and tomato paste. Stir and cook until hot. Serve over cooked broccoli. Sprinkle with grated Parmesan cheese. Makes 1 cup sauce.

BRUSSELS SPROUTS

AVAILABILITY

Supplies come on the market in September and rise to a peak in November. May to August is the slow time.

HOW TO BUY

Good sprouts are firm, compact, fresh, of bright appearance and good green color. Puffy or soft sprouts are usually poor in quality and flavor. Wilted or yellowing leaves indicate aging. Worm-eaten sprouts should be rejected, also sprouts with a smudgy, dirty appearance that indicates the presence of aphids.

PREPARATION AND SERVING SUGGESTIONS

Be sure that the stem ends of Brussels sprouts are not cut too closely during preparation or it will cause the outer leaves to fall off in cooking.

Brussels sprouts may be served boiled, baked, steamed, lyonnaise, French fried, au gratin, a la brigoule, buttered, creole, or amandine; also they may be served as casseroles, salads, or soufflés or with Hollandaise, peanut butter, mustard cheese, bechamel, paprika and sour cream, tomato, or parmesan sauces. They may be prepared with chestnuts, grapes, mushrooms, celery, sweetpotatoes, ham, squash, carrots, and tomatoes. To boil brussels sprouts trim them as may be needed and cook in one-inch depth of boiling water or stock. Let sprouts cook without a cover for about 5 minutes; then cover and cook about 10 minutes longer, or until just crisp tender. Be sure not to overcook.

NUTRITIONAL VALUE

Brussels sprouts are low in Calories (23 to a ½ cup portion) and yet provide a large amount of vitamin C and a good amount of other vitamins and minerals.

FRESH BRUSSELS SPROUTS IN ALMOND BROWN BUTTER SAUCE

1½ to 2 pounds (1 quart basket) fresh Brussels sprouts
1-inch boiling water in saucepan
½ teaspoon salt

3 tablespoons butter or margarine
¼ cup blanched almonds
Salt to taste
Black pepper to taste

Wash Brussels sprouts, remove wilted leaves and soak in salted water 20 minutes. Rinse and place in a saucepan with boiling water and ½ teaspoon salt. Bring to boiling point and boil 5 minutes without cover. Cover and boil 15 to 20 minutes or until Brussels sprouts are tender. Drain, if necessary. Place butter or margarine in a saucepan, melt, add almonds and cook until butter and almonds are brown. Add salt and black pepper to taste and pour over Brussels sprouts. Toss lightly. Serve at once. Makes approximately 6 servings.

BRUSSELS SPROUTS WITH PECAN BUTTER

1½ pounds (2 pints) Brussels sprouts
1-inch boiling chicken stock
2 tablespoons chopped onion
½ teaspoon salt

½ cup coarsely chopped pecans
½ stick butter or margarine
Pimiento strips
Fresh parsley

Wash and trim Brussels sprouts. Soak in salted water to cover 20 minutes, using 1 teaspoon salt to one quart water. Drain and rinse with cold water. Place them in a saucepan with 1-inch boiling chicken stock, onion and salt. Bring to boiling point and cook, uncovered, 5 minutes. Cover and cook 10 minutes or until just barely crisp-tender. Drain if necessary and keep hot. Sauté pecans in butter or margarine 2 to 3 minutes or until butter is golden. Pour over Brussels sprouts. Toss lightly. Garnish with pimiento strips and a sprig of fresh parsley. Makes 6 servings.

CABBAGE

AVAILABILITY

Cabbage is available all year round. There are a number of varieties of cabbage available which include:

DANISH

A term that is applied to solid-headed, late-maturing cabbage whose leaves are closely compacted and smooth, the heads being round or oval.

DOMESTIC

Heads are usually less compact than Danish type, and the leaves are generally crinkled or curly. There are both flat and round varieties.

POINTED

As the name indicates, this refers to conical or pointed heads with comparatively smooth leaf surfaces. It is marketed in the early spring as green cabbage; heads tend to be somewhat smaller than Danish or Domestic varieties.

RED

This variety is known by its reddish or purple color. It is used mainly for salads and pickling purposes.

SAVOY

This variety has very crinkled leaves; heads are loosely formed, usually flattened, and it has a yellowish-green color.

HOW TO BUY

Heads should be reasonably solid and hard, heavy or fairly heavy in relation to size and closely trimmed, with stems cut close to the head and only three or four outer or wrapper leaves remaining. Early cabbage need not be as solid or hard as that of late crop. Worm injury, yellowing of leaves, burst heads and decay are the most common defects of cabbage and are easily detected.

PREPARATION AND SERVING SUGGESTIONS

The smaller the pieces the faster cabbage will cook and the faster it cooks the better for flavor as well as nutrition. Cut it into portion size before cooking, but leave the core in because it will keep the leaves from falling apart. Lemon juice and/or vinegar added to the cooking water will help retain the color in red cabbage. Shredded cabbage makes an excellent hot vegetable in addition to being one of the top favorite raw salads (cole slaw). With hot shredded salad, try a mustard sauce. For better cole slaws, crisp the shredded cabbage in cold water; marinate in dressing for at least an hour and toss occasionally. Interesting additions include citrus segments or a combination of orange and onion. To avoid excessive loss of vitamin C, cutting with a knife is preferable to using a chopper—use within a short time after preparation. When cooking, to preserve nutrients use a minimum amount of water and do not overcook. Cabbage can also be baked in casseroles, with, for example, tomatoes. For boiling, it can be stuffed whole, cut into wedges or shredded. It is excellent for combination with meats, such as corned beef and sausages. Cabbage also mixes well with apples, pineapple and raisins for combination salads. Other interesting combinations include: cabbage and cucumber slaw; baked cabbage and egg casserole, and cabbage with sour cream.

NUTRITIONAL VALUE

Cabbage, especially green cabbage, is a rich source of vitamin C. Cabbage is so high in vitamin C that weight for weight it ranks with orange juice. Cabbage is also an ideal roughage and it is low in calories . . . 100 grams (3½ ounces) contains only 24 Calories.

RED CABBAGE, DUTCH STYLE

½ cup chopped onion
2 tablespoons butter or
   margarine
3 cups shredded raw
   cabbage
1 cup diced apples

3 whole cloves
1¼ teaspoons salt
⅛ teaspoon pepper
1 teaspoon wine vinegar
½ cup stock

Sauté onion in butter or margarine until they are limp and transparent. Add cabbage, apples, cloves, salt, black pepper, wine vinegar and stock. Cover and cook 10 minutes. Serve hot. Makes 4 servings.

CABBAGE SWISS STEAK DINNER

3 tablespoons flour
1 teaspoon salt
½ teaspoon paprika
¼ teaspoon dry mustard
¼ teaspoon pepper
3 pounds chuck or round
   steak, cut 1½ to 2
   inches thick

2 tablespoons oil
2 cups beef bouillon
2 large onions, sliced
1 medium-large cabbage,
   cut into 6 or 8 wedges

Combine flour, salt, paprika, mustard and pepper. Coat steak well on all sides with flour mixture. Heat oil in large skillet. Brown steak well on both sides. Pour off excess drippings, if necessary. Add bouillon and onions to meat. Cover and simmer slowly about 2 hours or until meat is tender. Add enough water if necessary to bring liquid level up to ½-inch. Arrange cabbage wedges around meat. Cover and simmer 10–15 minutes or until cabbage is just tender. Makes about 8 servings.

CREAM OF FRESH CABBAGE SOUP

10 cups coarsely cut
    cabbage (2½-3 pound
    head cabbage)
½ cup chopped celery
¼ cup chopped fresh onion
1 can (13¾ ounces)
    chicken broth

1 teaspoon salt
½ teaspoon caraway seeds
¼ teaspoon pepper
⅓ cup butter or margarine
⅓ cup flour
4 cups milk

Combine cabbage, celery, onion, chicken broth, salt, caraway seeds and pepper in large covered saucepan. Heat to boiling point over medium heat; simmer 10 minutes. Remove from heat. Do not drain. In another large saucepan melt butter or margarine; blend in flour. Gradually stir in milk. Cook over medium heat, stirring constantly, until mixture thickens and reaches boiling point. Add cabbage mixture and liquid. Heat to serving temperature, stirring occasionally. Season, as desired, with salt. Makes about 2 quarts.

RED AND GREEN COLE-SLAW

½ medium head green
    cabbage
¼ medium head red
    cabbage
⅓ cup finely chopped
    onions
⅓ cup finely chopped green
    pepper

1 teaspoon salt
¼ teaspoon pepper
2 teaspoons sugar
1 teaspoon fresh lemon
    juice
1 teaspoon cider vinegar
½ cup mayonnaise

Shred cabbage finely and combine with remaining ingredients. Mix well. Makes 6 to 8 servings.

BAKED CABBAGE AND TOMATO

1 lb. (4 cups) head
    cabbage
½ cup water
3 tablespoons vegetable
    oil
½ cup chopped onion
3 tablespoons flour
1 teaspoon salt
⅛ teaspoon pepper

¼ teaspoon ground
    marjoram
2½ cups tomatoes, cut up
⅓ cup stuffed green
    olives, sliced
1 cup cracker crumbs
1 cup (4 oz.) grated
    Cheddar cheese

Wash cabbage and cut into quarters. Discard core and shred coarsely. Cook in water for about 8 minutes, until tender then drain. Heat oil in saucepan. Add onion and sauté until transparent. Blend in flour, salt, pepper, marjoram and stir until thickened, adding tomatoes and green olives last. Place ⅓ of tomato mixture in individual casserole. Add 1 part cabbage, repeat. Cover with cracker crumbs and grated cheese. Bake in a preheated moderate oven (375°F.) for 25 minutes. Makes 6 servings.

CABBAGE CUCUMBER SLAW

2½ cups medium-fine
    shredded cabbage
1 cup coarsely shredded,
    unpeeled cucumber
½ cup finely diced celery
¼ cup finely chopped
    onion

1 teaspoon salt
¼ teaspoon pepper
2 tablespoons sour cream
    or mayonnaise
1 tablespoon French
    dressing

Combine all ingredients. Toss lightly and serve soon after making. Makes 6 servings.

CHINESE CABBAGE

AVAILABILITY

Chinese cabbage is available all year round. Peak period is Oct.-Dec.

The type usually found on most markets is pe-tsai which is headed, elongated, compact with green leaves slightly wrinkled and thin with a broad midrib.

HOW TO BUY

Select heads that are conical. They should be compact with crisp, clean, fresh green leaves. Reject any with yellowing or wilted leaves.

PREPARATION AND SERVING SUGGESTIONS

This is essentially a salad green which will bring interesting color, texture and flavor variety into any tossed salad. It does not have the strong flavor of true cabbage. While salads are the principal use, Chinese Cabbage can also be braised with bacon and onions to make a delicious cooked vegetable. When it is used in many Chinese dishes it is shredded or finely chopped.

NUTRITIONAL VALUE

Chinese cabbage nutritive values are similar to regular cabbage, however it is even lower in Calorie count, having only 14 Calories per 100 grams.

FRESH VEGETABLE AND CHICKEN, ORIENTAL STYLE

3 cups cooked white meat chicken
6 tablespoons butter or margarine
1 cup green pepper cubes
1 cup onion rings
3 cups sliced mushrooms
¼ head Chinese cabbage (celery–cabbage)

2 cups cooked snap beans, cut into 1″ pieces
¼ teaspoon salt
¼ teaspoon pepper
¾ teaspoon ground ginger
⅓ cup soya sauce
1 tablespoon cornstarch

Slice chicken in thin strips ¼ to ⅜ inches wide, and 2 to 3 inches long. Melt butter or margarine in a 10-inch skillet. Add green pepper and sauté until partially cooked, 4 to 5 minutes. Add onion rings and mushrooms, sauté until limp, 2 to 3 minutes. Cut Chinese cabbage into strips ½ inch wide. Cook just until wilted about 5 minutes, stirring often. Add snap beans that have been cooked only until crisp-tender, salt, black pepper and ginger. Blend soya sauce with cornstarch and pour overall. Heat thoroughly to slightly thicken sauce. Makes 6 servings.

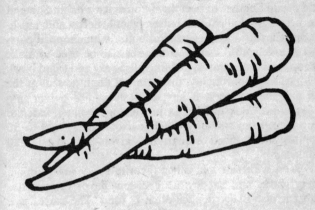

CARROTS

AVAILABILITY

Carrots are grown in all months and available all year round. There are types with long, tapered roots; others are shorter and cylindrical with a blunt tip. All usually now come to market topped, and this is advantageous, since the tops, when left on, remove water and nutrients from the roots.

HOW TO BUY

Select carrots that are firm, fresh smooth, well-shaped and well-colored. Reject wilted, flabby, soft or shriveled product. Check for decay which would appear as soft or watersoaked areas which may be partially covered with mold. Color is important; the deeper the orange color the more vitamin A the carrot contains.

PREPARATION AND SERVING SUGGESTIONS

Fresh carrots are truly an easy-to-prepare vegetable. One needn't bother to peel them unless it's a habit. Some of the best "go-alongs" are butter, gentle herbs and mushrooms. Carrots Vichy (glazed in butter with chopped parsley) is a delightful dish. Carrots can also be used to make a soup, and are mainstays of the relish tray and salad bowl.

First, wash thoroughly, then trim off the little scar at the top and the tap root, if any, then slice, dice or cut into shoestrings. Cook quickly in just enough boiling water to keep them from sticking. Whole carrots cook in 20 to 30 minutes; sliced, diced or quartered carrots cook in 10 to 20 minutes.

Season with salt and other favorite seasonings. Onion, celery leaves and parsley are excellent flavor companions with carrots. Black pepper often is used. The carrot is a versatile vegetable and is good when served alone, raw or cooked, or in combination with meats and other vegetables. Carrots may be boiled as a main fresh vegetable dish and served with butter or white sauce; diced and creamed with peas and new potatoes; roasted with meats; baked, fried, sautéed and pickled; they lend body and seasoning to soups. Carrots are good sliced raw in hors d'oeuvres; grated or sliced into thin strips in salads, and sliced into thin sticks and refrigerated for between-meal snacks for junior dynamos. They are also good when cut into long strips and simmered with frenched or plain green beans, tiny onions or cauliflower. Try glazing them with honey or brown sugar for serving with pork or poultry.

NUTRITIONAL VALUE

Carrots are one of the richest sources of vitamin A. They also provide many other important nutrients and are low in Calories—100 grams (less than a cup of grated carrots) contain just 42 Calories.

CARROTS NEWBERG

4 cups diced uncooked
   carrots
1-inch boiling water
1 teaspoon salt
½ teaspoon sugar
2 tablespoons butter or
   margarine
2 tablespoons flour
¾ cup chicken stock

¼ cup heavy cream
½ teaspoon chopped fresh
   parsley
¾ teaspoon finely chopped
   onion
2 teaspoons finely chopped
   green pepper
¼ teaspoon salt

Place carrots, 1-inch boiling water and 1 teaspoon salt and sugar in a saucepan. Cover and cook 12 minutes or until just crisp-tender. Melt butter or margarine in a saucepan. Blend in flour. Add chicken stock, cream, parsley, onion and green pepper and salt. Stir and cook 5 minutes or until of medium thickness. Add carrots. Serve hot. Makes 6 servings.

CARROTS WITH LEMON-CHEESE
SAUCE ON TOAST

18 small whole carrots
1 cup chicken or beef stock
½ teaspoon salt
2 tablespoons butter or
   margarine
1½ tablespoons flour
1 cup stock and milk

3 tablespoons grated sharp
   cheese
⅛ teaspoon white pepper
1 tablespoon fresh lemon
   juice
Toast
Fresh chopped chives or
   parsley

Scrub carrots. Place in saucepan with boiling stock and salt and cook, covered, until crisp-tender, 10 to 12 minutes. Drain and reserve liquid. Melt butter or margarine. Blend in flour. Add stock and milk and cook, stirring constantly, until sauce thickens. Add cheese and white pepper. Stir until cheese is melted. Stir in lemon juice. Serve on toast garnished with chopped chives or parsley. Makes 4 to 5 servings.

CREAM OF FRESH CARROT SOUP

1 lb. fresh carrots
2 tablespoons chopped onion
2 tablespoons butter or margarine
⅓ cup water
¾ teaspoon salt
½ teaspoon sugar
⅛ teaspoon pepper
2 tablespoons butter or margarine
1½ tablespoons flour
3 cups milk
1 tablespoon fresh lemon juice
Fresh parsley, finely chopped

Wash carrots, scrape and slice thinly. Prepare about 3 cups. In a small saucepan combine sliced carrots, onion, the 2 tablespoons butter or margarine, water, salt, sugar and pepper. Cover tightly and cook over very low heat 20 to 25 minutes or until carrots are tender. Mash carrot mixture with a fork. In the top of a double boiler melt the remaining 2 tablespoons butter or margarine. Blend in flour. Cook over low heat 5 minutes, stirring constantly. Add milk and continue cooking 5 minutes, stirring frequently. Add carrot mixture to milk mixture. Cook, covered, over hot water 30 minutes. Stir often. Stir in lemon juice. Serve hot garnished with chopped parsley. Makes 6 servings.

FRESH CARROT PIE

¾ cup sugar
½ teaspoon salt
½ teaspoon ground nutmeg
1 teaspoon ground cinnamon
1 teaspoon ground ginger
⅛ teaspoon ground cloves
½ teaspoon grated lemon rind
2 eggs, lightly beaten
2 cups cooked, sieved, carrots
1 cup undiluted evaporated milk
Unbaked 9-inch pie shell

Combine first 6 ingredients. Add remaining ingredients and mix well. Pour into pastry-lined pie plate. Bake in a preheated hot oven (400°F.) 40 to 45 minutes or until filling is firm. Makes 6 servings.

FRESH CARROT POTATO PATTIES

1½ cups cooked mashed
    fresh carrots
1 cup cooked mashed
    fresh potatoes
2 tablespoons butter or
    margarine
¼ cup grated Parmesan
    cheese

¼ cup snipped fresh
    parsley
2 tablespoons fine dry
    bread crumbs
1 egg yolk
Salt and pepper
Flour
Salad oil

Thoroughly mix together carrots, potatoes, butter or margarine, Parmesan cheese, parsley, bread crumbs and egg yolk. Season to taste with salt and pepper. Shape into 8 patties. Dust each patty lightly with flour. Sauté in a small amount of heated salad oil over medium heat until browned on both sides. Makes 4 servings.

SAVORY CARROT CASSEROLE

2 pounds carrot
1½ teaspoons salt
¼ cup fresh chopped
    onion

½ cup sliced celery
3 tablespoons butter or
    margarine
½ teaspoon nutmeg

In large saucepan, place carrots and 1 teaspoon salt in small amount of boiling water. Cover and cook until just tender; drain and mash well. Saute onion and celery in butter or margarine about 5 minutes or until just tender. Add to mashed carrots and season with remaining ½ teaspoon salt and nutmeg. Pile into lightly greased 1-quart casserole dish. Bake, covered in 375°F oven 15 minutes. Remove cover; bake 5 minutes longer. Makes 6-8 servings.

FRESH CARROT SOUFFLÉ

3 tablespoons butter or
margarine
3 tablespoons flour
¾ teaspoons salt
⅛ teaspoon pepper
¼ teaspoon powdered dry
mustard
¹⁄₁₆ teaspoon ground
cayenne pepper
1 cup milk

3 eggs, separated
3 cups cooked mashed
carrots
½ cup soft bread crumbs
⅓ cup chopped pimiento
½ cup thinly sliced green
pepper
1 tablespoon chopped
onion

Melt butter or margarine in a 2-quart saucepan. Add
flour and mix until smooth. Blend in seasonings. Stir in
milk and cook, stirring constantly, until the mixture has
thickened. Beat egg yolks and add. Stir in carrots, bread
crumbs, pimiento, green pepper and onions. Beat egg
whites until stiff and fold into the mixture. Turn into an
ungreased 1½ quart casserole. Place in a shallow pan of
hot water. Bake in a preheated moderate oven (350°F.)
1 hour. Serve at once. Makes 6 to 8 servings.

CAULIFLOWER

AVAILABILITY

Available in all months, but the supply rises sharply in September and peaks in October.

Cauliflower and broccoli are closely related, and *heading broccoli,* sometimes called cauliflower broccoli, is a late, long-season cauliflower. Early in the season, cauliflower is apt to run somewhat smaller than in mid and late season.

HOW TO BUY

Good quality is indicated by a white or creamy-white clean, firm, compact curd. If there are any jacket leaves, they should be fresh, green and brittle. Spotted, speckled or bruised curds should be avoided unless the bad parts can be trimmed with little waste. Size of the head has no relation to quality. Loose, open flower clusters indicate over-maturity.

PREPARATION AND SERVING SUGGESTIONS

After the leaves are removed, cauliflower is best cooked whole, in a steamer, or by boiling. Guard against overcooking. It is done when the stem end yields to the touch of a fork. The head is then separated into flowerettes or portion size. Styles include buttered, creamed, au gratin and Polonaise. Small bits of flowerettes are also used raw in salads, and the vegetable (any part of it) is useful in making a DuBarry soup.

A whole head of cauliflower needs not more than 25 minutes total cooking time. Set it in a 1-inch depth of boiling salted water. Let cook for 5 minutes, without lid, then cover and cook another 15 to 20 minutes, depending on the size of the head. Cauliflower is one of those white vegetables that can pick up an unattractive yellowish cast if cooked in "hard" or alkaline water. Add a teaspoonful of fresh lemon juice to the water and the cauliflower will stay nice and white. Cauliflower, like all other fresh vegetables, should not be over-cooked to a point of being very soft or mushy.

NUTRITIONAL VALUE

Cauliflower raw or cooked is a good source of vitamin C. One cup of raw cauliflower buds provides more than the recommended daily allowance of vitamin C for an adult. One cup of boiled and drained cauliflower provides 115% of the recommended daily allowance of vitamin C. Cauliflower is very low in calories while providing a good contribution of vitamins and minerals. There are only 22 Calories in a 3½ ounce portion.

FRESH CAULIFLOWER VEGETABLE SALAD

1 medium head (1½ pound) cauliflower
1 inch boiling water
1½ teaspoons salt
½ cup light cider vinegar
3 tablespoons olive or salad oil
1 tablespoon fresh lemon juice
1 clove garlic

1 tablespoon finely chopped green pepper
1 tablespoon sugar
¼ teaspoon salt
¾ teaspoon dill seed
1/16 teaspoon pepper
1½ cups cooked sliced fresh carrots
1½ cups cooked snap beans
1 cup onion rings
Salad greens

Remove outside leaves from cauliflower and wash. Place whole head in a saucepan with 1-inch boiling water and the 1½ teaspoons salt. Bring to boiling point without cover and boil 5 minutes. Cover and cook 10 minutes, turning head to cook uniformly. Cauliflower should be cooked *only* until crisp-tender. Drain off water. Combine vinegar, oil, lemon juice, garlic, green pepper, sugar, salt, dill seed and black pepper and pour over cauliflower. Add cooked vegetables and onion rings. Marinate overnight in refrigerator. To serve place cauliflower in center of serving platter and surround with carrots, beans, and onion rings. Garnish with salad greens. Makes 6 servings.

FRESH CAULIFLOWER AND TUNA FISH CASSEROLE

4 cups sliced fresh
  cauliflower
½ cup boiling water
1 teaspoon salt
2 tablespoons butter or
  margarine
2 tablespoons flour
1⅓ cups milk

⅛ teaspoon garlic powder
⅛ teaspoon thyme leaves
⅛ teaspoon pepper
7-ounce can tuna fish,
  drained
1 tablespoon butter or
  margarine, melted
½ cup soft bread crumbs

Place cauliflower, water and salt in a saucepan. Bring to boiling point, uncovered, and cook 5 minutes. Cover and cook 3 minutes or until partly done. Drain and set aside for later use. Melt butter or margarine in a saucepan. Blend in flour. Remove from heat and gradually stir in milk. Stir and cook over moderate heat until of medium thickness. Remove from heat and add seasonings and tuna fish. Arrange cauliflower and tuna fish mixture in alternate layers in a buttered 1-quart casserole. Combine melted butter or margarine and bread crumbs and sprinkle over the top. Bake in a preheated moderate oven (350°F.) 35 minutes or until golden brown. Makes 6 servings.

STUFFED CAULIFLOWER ITALIANNE

1 large head cauliflower
Boiling water
1 teaspoon salt
2 cups diced cooked ham
2 tablespoons finely
  chopped onion
⅛ teaspoon finely chopped
  garlic
2 tablespoons vegetable or
  salad oil
1 cup diced cooked beef
  or veal

1 cup chopped cooked
  cauliflowerets
¼ cup diced pimiento
1 tablespoon chopped
  parsley
½ teaspoon salt
¼ teaspoon pepper
½ cup dry white wine
¼ cup water
1 large egg yolk, lightly
  beaten

Remove tough outer leaves from cauliflower, cut off stems close to head and soak for 20 minutes in cold salted water. Drain and cook in boiling salted water only until crisp-tender, about 15 minutes. Drain; remove center flowerets to form a shell. Sauté ham, onion and garlic in oil until onion is limp and transparent. Stir in the next 6 ingredients; spoon mixture into cauliflower. Place in a buttered casserole. Combine wine and water; pour into casserole around cauliflower. Cover and bake in a preheated moderate oven (350°F.) 25 minutes. Remove cauliflower to a serving dish. Stir egg yolk into hot liquid; cook over low heat until slightly thickened, about 5 minutes. Spoon over cauliflower. Serve hot. Makes 4 servings.

CAULIFLOWER PARMESAN

1 large cauliflower
4 tablespoons butter or
    margarine, divided

½ cup bread cubes
1 tablespoon grated
    Parmesan cheese

Wash cauliflower; remove leaves and stalk. Place in boiling salted water in saucepan. Cook uncovered for 5 minutes, cover and cook 15 to 25 minutes, or until crisp-tender. While cauliflower is cooking melt 2 tablespoons of the butter; add bread cubes and brown, stirring occasionally. Remove from heat, stir in Parmesan cheese. Drain cauliflower; place in serving dish and spread with remaining 2 tablespoons butter. Top with bread cubes. Makes 4 to 6 servings.

SAVORY CAULIFLOWER

1 medium head
    cauliflower, about 2
    pounds
1-inch boiling beef or
    chicken stock in
    saucepan

½ teaspoon salt
⅛ teaspoon pepper
Chopped fresh parsley
    for garnish

Wash cauliflower and remove outside leaves (save for use in salads). Separate head into flowerets. Place in a saucepan with stock and salt. Cook, uncovered, 5 minutes. Cover and cook until cauliflower is tender, about 30 minutes. Season with black pepper and garnish with chopped parsley. Makes 3 to 4 servings.

FRESH CAULIFLOWER-TOMATO SCALLOP

1 large head cauliflower	¾ teaspoon salt
5 tablespoons butter or margarine	¼ teaspoon pepper
½ cup finely chopped fresh celery	¼ cup flour
	2 cups milk
¼ cup finely chopped fresh onion	1½ cups shredded sharp Cheddar cheese
¼ cup finely chopped fresh green pepper	3 large firm-ripe tomatoes, sliced
	½ cup soft bread crumbs

Break cauliflower into flowerets. Cook, covered, in 1-inch boiling salted water about 5 minutes or until crisp-.tender. Lift cover occasionally to allow steam to escape. Drain. In saucepan melt butter, add celery, onion and green pepper and sauté until onion is limp and transparent. Blend in salt, pepper and flour. Add milk and cook over low heat, stirring constantly, until thickened. Add cheese and stir until melted. Remove from heat. Arrange a layer of cauliflower in shallow baking dish or casserole. Top with a small amount of cheese sauce. Cover with sliced tomatoes and more sauce. Top with remaining cauliflower and sauce. Sprinkle with bread crumbs. Bake in a preheated hot oven (400°F.) 25 minutes or until brown. Makes 6 servings.

CELERY

AVAILABILITY

Celery is available all year round. Celery varieties may be classified by color as green and golden. The most popular type of green celery is called "Pascal". There are a number of Golden varieties which have a yellow-green to yellow foliage.

HOW TO BUY

Select celery that is fresh, clean, with stalks that are thick and solid, with good heart formation. Branches should be brittle enough to snap easily. Pithy, woody or stringy celery is undesirable. Seedstems appear as a solid, somewhat round stem replacing the heart formation. Celery with seedstems is undesirably mature.

FRESH VEGETABLES

PREPARATION AND SERVING SUGGESTIONS

Celery can be considered a "total vegetable" since all parts of it are suitable for one to another style of food service. The leaves are perfect for the stock pot (but use with discretion because they have the strongest flavor of any part of this vegetable). The outer ribe of the stalk are the ones best suits to use as a cooked vegetable. They are served creamed, au gratin, and braised (in chicken stock). The hearts are, of course, reserved for the relish tray.

NUTRITIONAL VALUE

Celery is extremely low in calories and may be eaten in unlimited quantities by persons seeking weight reduction. One pound contains only 77 calories. Celery is an excellent source of natural fiber.

CELERY STUFFING BALLS

1½ cups chopped celery	2 tablespoons water
¼ cup chopped fresh onion	1 teaspoon salt
	Few grains pepper
⅓ cup melted butter or margarine	3 cups day-old bread crumbs
1 egg	

Sauté celery and onion in butter or margarine in large skillet until tender. Beat egg slightly; mix in water, salt and pepper. Combine celery mixture, egg mixture and bread crumbs; toss lightly. Using a ¼ cup measure, shape into balls. Place in paper baking cups set in muffin pans. Bake in 375°F. oven 20 minutes or until lightly browned. Makes 4 servings.

CELERY SAUTÉ

3 tablespoons butter or
margarine
3 cups sliced celery

⅓ cup coarsely chopped
pecans
1 teaspoon salt
½ teaspoon dried dill weed

Melt butter in a skillet and add celery, pecans, salt and dill. Cook, stirring constantly, 4 or 5 minutes, until celery is crisp-tender. Makes 4 servings.

MOCK CRAB AND CELERY SALAD

1 pound perch fillets
2 cups boiling water
1 rib celery, chopped
1½ teaspoons salt
2 tablespoons fresh
lemon juice
2 cups diced celery

¼ cup chopped green
pepper
¼ teaspoon pepper
¼ cup mayonnaise
Head lettuce
Fresh parsley and
radishes

Tie fish in a cheese cloth bag or put in a sieve. Place in boiling water along with the 1 rib of celery and 1 teaspoon of the salt. Cook 6 to 7 minutes or until fish is flaky. Remove from water and sprinkle with lemon juice. Chill. Flake fish and toss lightly with diced celery, green pepper, black pepper, mayonnaise and remaining salt. Serve on head lettuce. Garnish with parsley and radishes. Makes 6 servings.

CELERY IN LEMON SAUCE

2 cups chicken broth
3 tablespoons fresh lemon
   juice
5 cups sliced celery
¼ cup chopped celery
   leaves
2 teaspoons flour

1 tablespoon cold water
2 egg yolks, slightly
   beaten
1 teaspoon salt
¼ teaspoon dried leaf
   tarragon

Combine chicken broth and lemon juice in a large skillet; add celery and leaves. Cover and simmer 20 minutes, or until tender. Remove celery with slotted spoon. Stir flour with water until smooth; stir into liquid in skillet. Cook, stirring occasionally, about 3 minutes. Stir a little sauce into the yolks and return to the skillet, along with celery. Add salt and tarragon and heat but do not allow to boil. Makes 6 servings.

FRESH CELERY POTATO SOUP

1 bunch celery (about 1½
   pounds)
4 cups water
2 teaspoons salt
3 medium-sized potatoes

2 cups milk
3 tablespoons butter or
   margarine
1 teaspoon salt
⅛ teaspoon pepper

Wash celery. Cut entire bunch crosswise into ¼-inch slices. Combine celery, water and 2 teaspoons salt in large saucepan or soup kettle. Cover and cook about 8 minutes or until celery is just tender. Drain; reserve cooking liquid and celery. Meanwhile, peel and quarter potatoes. Cook potatoes, covered, in celery liquid until tender. Remove from heat. Mash potatoes well in cooking liquid. Add celery, milk, butter or margarine, 1 teaspoon salt and pepper. Heat to serving temperature, stirring occasionally. Makes about 2 quarts.

CELERY HAM LOAF

1 cup soft bread crumbs	1 tablespoon
2/3 cup milk	Worcestershire sauce
2 tablespoons butter or margarine	1 teaspoon prepared horseradish
1/4 cup chopped fresh onion	1/2 teaspoon salt
1 cup finely chopped celery	1/2 teaspoon dried leaf thyme
1/2 pound *each* ground ham, pork, veal	2 tablespoons chopped celery leaves
2 tablespoons prepared mustard	1 egg

Soak bread crumbs in milk in large bowl. Melt butter in large skillet; add onion and celery, cook until tender. Add to bread crumbs. Add remaining ingredients and mix well. Pack in an 8 x 4 x 2¾-inch loaf pan. Bake in a 350°F. oven 1 hour. Let stand 5 to 10 minutes. Turn out onto platter and garnish with sautéed celery*. Makes 6 servings.

* *Sautéed Celery:* Melt 3 tablespoons butter or margarine in skillet. Add 2 cups sliced celery, sparkle with ½ teaspoon salt, and cook about 5 minutes, until crisp-tender.

HERBED SOUR CREAM DIP FOR CELERY HEARTS

1/2 cup sour cream	1/4 teaspoon ground basil leaves
1/4 cup mayonnaise	1/4 teaspoon salt
1/4 teaspoon garlic powder	Paprika for garnish
1/4 teaspoon onion powder	Celery hearts and
Dash white pepper	vegetable sticks
Dash ground cayenne pepper	

Combine first 8 ingredients. Serve, garnished with paprika, in a small bowl surrounded with celery hearts and raw vegetable strips. Makes about 2/3 cup.

ROQUEFORT CHEESE STUFFED CELERY

6 ribs celery
3-ounce package cream
    cheese
¼ cup crumbled Roquefort
    cheese

⅟₁₆ teaspoon cayenne
    pepper
Paprika
Chopped fresh parsley

Wash and cut celery ribs into 3-inch pieces. Combine cream cheese, Roquefort cheese and cayenne pepper. Mix well. Use to fill the grooves of celery pieces. Garnish with paprika and chopped parsley. Cut ribs in half. Makes 12 ribs, 3 inches long.

CREAM OF CELERY SOUP

½ stick (¼ cup) butter or
    margarine
2 cups thinly sliced celery
1 tablespoon finely
    chopped onion
4 tablespoons (¼ cup)
    flour

2 cups chicken stock or 2
    cups hot water and 2
    chicken bouillon
    cubes
2 cups milk
¼ cup finely chopped
    celery leaves
½ teaspoon salt
¼ teaspoon pepper
Pimiento

Melt butter or margarine in a saucepan. Add celery and onion and sauté 5 minutes or until celery is soft. Remove from heat. Blend in flour. Add stock and milk. Stir and cook until soup has thickened slightly. Stir in chopped celery leaves. Add salt and black pepper. Serve hot garnished with strips of pimiento. Makes 5 cups.

CELERY STUFFING

1 cup chopped onion	¼ teaspoon pepper
2 cups chopped celery	2 teaspoons poultry
¾ cup butter or margarine,	seasoning
melted	2 quarts toasted bread
2 teaspoons salt	cubes

Sauté onions and celery in ½ cup of butter or margarine until vegetables are limp. Combine with remaining ingredients. Mix well. Spoon lightly into the crop and body cavities of a 10 to 12 pound turkey. Close body openings with skewers. Make one-half of this recipe if you wish to stuff a 5 to 6 pound chicken or capon. Roast, using your favorite method. Makes sufficient stuffing for a 10 to 12 pound turkey.

BRAISED CELERY

2 tablespoons butter or	1 quart sliced celery
margarine	½ teaspoon salt
¼ cup chicken or beef	⅛ teaspoon pepper
stock	

Melt butter or margarine in a saucepan. Add chicken or beef stock, celery and salt. Cover and cook 20 to 25 minutes or until crisp-tender. Add black pepper. Serve at once. Makes 4 servings.

CORN

AVAILABILITY

Corn is available in all months; the high period is May through August and the low period is October through March.

HOW TO BUY

Sweet corn may be either yellow or white, but is mostly available as yellow. Ears should be well filled with bright, plump, milky kernels just firm enough to offer slight resistance to pressure. Look for fresh green husks. Husks that are dry, yellowed or straw-colored and husks with shrinking kernels are an indication of age or damage.

PREPARATION AND SERVING SUGGESTIONS

Today, corn is used with great frequency in many ways. It is boiled, steamed or roasted on the cob. It is also used in soups, chowders, souffles and fritters.

When boiling corn-on-the-cob, drop into enough boiling water to cover the ears. Add a teaspoon of sugar per quart of water. Cover and cook rapidly—about 5 or 6 minutes for tender young corn; about 10 minutes for more mature ears. A little milk in the water will help retain color and tenderness (use 1 tablespoon per quart of water). Serve piping hot with salt, pepper and butter, or a seasoned butter (with parsley, chive, chili, curry).

Foil-wrapped corn may be baked either over a charcoal grill or in a pre-heated hot oven set at about 425°F. Husk corn and remove silks. Sprinkle with salt, pepper and a generous dab of butter or margarine and then wrap in aluminum foil. Whether grilled or baked, allow 20 to 25 minutes cooking time.

NUTRITIONAL VALUE

Yellow varieties provide a fair amount of Vitamin A and C. Corn is very low in sodium.

HOW TO COOK FRESH CORN-ON-THE-COB

On the Range
1. Remove husks from ears of fresh corn and brush off silks.
2. Drop in a kettle of rapidly boiling water to cover.
3. Cover and cook only until milk is set, 5 to 7 minutes, depending upon maturity of the corn.
4. Remove from water and serve with salt and pepper to taste and butter or margarine.

In the Oven
1. Husk corn. Remove silks.
2. Place on squares of aluminum foil, one ear to a square.
3. Sprinkle with salt and pepper.
4. Top each with a pat of butter or margarine, ⅛-inch thick.
5. Wrap, making a double lengthwise fold over the top of the ear.
6. Turn up ends and fold against the top of the ear.
7. Bake in a preheated hot oven (425°F.) 20 minutes or until tender.
8. The baking time depends upon the size and the age of the ear.

On Outside Grill
1. Turn back the husks of tender, fresh corn to remove silks.
2. Place husks back over corn.
3. Line ears of corn on the grill over hot coals.
4. Cook only until husks are dry and browned, 15 to 20 minutes, turning to cook uniformly.
5. To eat, break off husks, spread with butter or margarine and sprinkle with celery, onion or garlic salt and pepper.

CHIVE BUTTER

½ cup (1 stick) butter or
   margarine, softened
4 teaspoons finely
   chopped chives

⅛ teaspoon pepper
¼ teaspoon salt

Combine all ingredients. Mix until thoroughly blended.
Spread over ears of hot corn-on-the-cob. Makes ½ cup.

FRESH CORN AND TOMATO SAUTÉ

3 cups fresh corn, cut off
   the cob
1 cup diced fresh
   tomatoes
¼ cup butter or margarine,
   melted

¼ teaspoon sugar
¼ teaspoon salt or salt to
   taste
1/16 teaspoon pepper

1. Combine all ingredients in an 8 or 9-inch skillet or in
   a 1-quart saucepan.
2. Sauté 5 to 8 minutes or until corn is tender, stirring
   frequently. Serve hot.
   Makes 4 to 5 servings.

BAKED FRESH CORN CASSEROLE

2 cups fresh corn, cut off
   the cob
1 tablespoon flour
1 tablespoon sugar
1 tablespoon butter or
   margarine

3 eggs, beaten
1½ teaspoons salt
⅛ teaspoon pepper
1 cup milk
½ cup heavy cream

Combine all ingredients. Turn into buttered 6-cup casserole. Place in pan of hot water. Bake in preheated slow
oven (325°F.) 1½ hours or until knife inserted in center
comes out clean. Makes 6 servings.

FRESH VEGETABLES

BROILED CORN AND BACON

4 ears fresh corn
 Boiling water to cover

½ teaspoon salt
8 strips bacon

1. Husk corn. Remove silks.
2. Drop into salted, boiling water.
3. Boil for 4 to 5 minutes or until almost tender.
4. Remove corn from water and wrap two strips of bacon around each ear.
5. Skewer ends of bacon with toothpicks.
6. Set broiler temperature to highest point and preheat.
7. Place ears 4-inches from source of heat.
8. Broil for 7 minutes or until bacon is crisp, turning once to cook bacon crisp on all sides.
9. Remove bacon and serve with corn.
 Makes 4 servings.

FRESH CORN AND TURKEY SALAD

1⅓ cups (approximately 4
     ears) cooked corn,
     cut off the cob
 1 cup chilled cooked
     turkey
 1 cup diced fresh green
     pepper
1½ teaspoons salt
 ½ teaspoon chili powder

⅛ teaspoon pepper
 2 tablespoons
     mayonnaise
 2 tablespoons fresh
     lemon juice
 Head lettuce
 Stuffed green olives
 Tomato wedges

Mix corn with turkey, green pepper and seasonings. Add mayonnaise and lemon juice and toss lightly. Serve on lettuce. Garnish with stuffed olives and tomato wedges. Makes 6 servings.

CUCUMBERS

AVAILABILITY

Cucumbers are available in all months, with the peak in June and July. Slicing cucumbers vary in length from 6 to 12 inches and are usually harvested at a more mature stage than those for pickles.

HOW TO BUY

Select cucumbers that are firm, fresh, bright green and well shaped. A small amount of whitish-green at the tip and on the ridged seams is not objectionable in some varieties. The flesh should be firm and the seeds immature and soft. Reject any cucumbers that are withered or shriveled.

FRESH VEGETABLES
PREPARATION AND SERVING SUGGESTIONS

Sliced cucumbers blend delightfully into a wide variety of raw salads, as with tomatoes, greens, peppers and radishes with any number of dressings and with or without meat, fish or cheese. They are excellent sliced, salted and peppered and allowed to marinate in vinegar and water, and can be combined in this marinade with other vegetables. Usually they are peeled before slicing, but some eat peel and all especially if the peel is not waxed. Most of the wax can be removed by placing the cucumber under a stream of very hot water, then wiping with a paper towel.

Slice lengthwise into sticks with the skin left on to add color to a relish tray; use sliced in sandwiches; cut in bits and serve with condiments and sour cream; combine pineapple, cabbage and cucumber in a molded salad; dice and add to any mixed salad; prepare a cucumber fresh fruit salad with such fruits as pears, grapes, oranges and lemons; cucumber slices go fine with lemonade; try a fresh cucumber lemon relish with chopped cucumber, some parsley, fresh lemon juice, and condiments; or a cucumber seafood cocktail sauce with chili sauce, chopped cucumber, lemon juice, horseradish and Tobasco.

Cucumber tartar sauce is chopped, cucumber, mayonnaise, lemon juice, chopped green olives, minced fresh onion, capers, salt and pepper. Cucumbers, thickly cut, are good as a hot vegetable sautéed 3 to 4 minutes in melted butter or margarine. Or spread cucumber slices with a cream cheese anchovy spread or curried egg spread or deviled ham spread for cucumber canapes. Wilt cucumbers by cooking for 3 or 4 minutes, slice and serve with dilly sour cream.

NUTRITIONAL VALUE

Cucumbers do not have any particular nutrients in an outstanding quantity; they are ideal for the calorie-conscious containing only 14 Calories per 100 grams.

CUCUMBER FLOUNDER ROLLS

4 cucumbers

2 tablespoons wine vinegar

1 teaspoon salt

⅛ teaspoon sugar

2 tablespoons butter or margarine

3 tablespoons chopped fresh onion

1½ cups soft bread crumbs

¼ cup chopped fresh parsley

1 teaspoon snipped fresh dill

1 tablespoon fresh lemon juice

1½ pounds flounder fillets (6 large fillets)

Pare cucumbers and cut in half lengthwise. With spoon, scoop out seeds. Cut into cubes. Mix together wine vinegar, salt and sugar in large bowl. Add cucumbers, mix well, and marinate at room temperature for 30 minutes. Drain and pat dry. Reserve 1½ cups cucumbers for sauce. Melt butter in large skillet. Add onion and cook until tender. Add bread crumbs, parsley, dill and lemon juice; simmer 10 minutes. Add remaining prepared cucumbers to stuffing mixture and cook slowly 5 minutes. Place ¼ cup stuffing on each fish fillet and roll up, securing ends with food picks. Place in shallow 1½-quart casserole and pour Shrimp-Cucumber Sauce* over all. Bake, uncovered, in 325°F. oven 20 to 30 minutes. Makes 6 servings.

*SHRIMP-CUCUMBER SAUCE

3 tablespoons butter or margarine

2 tablespoons chopped fresh onion

¼ cup flour

2 cups milk

3 tablespoons white wine

1½ cups reserved prepared cucumber

¼ teaspoon snipped fresh dill

¼ teaspoon salt

½ pound uncooked cleaned shrimp

Melt butter in large saucepan, add onion and cook until tender. Blend in flour. Stir in milk. Cook, stirring constantly, until mixture thickens and comes to a boil. Stir in wine, cucumber, dill, salt and shrimp. Simmer 5 minutes.

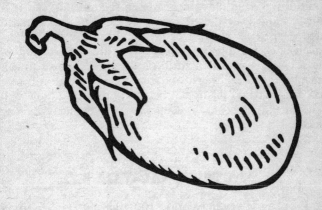

EGGPLANT

AVAILABILITY

Available all year with peak in August and September. In the United States, only large-fruited varieties of eggplant are grown commercially. Mostly they are dark purple, and vary from elongated egg shape to nearly globular. Shape has no relation to quality.

HOW TO BUY

Eggplants should be firm, heavy in relation to size, with a uniformly dark, rich purple color or color characteristic of the variety. They should be free from scars or cuts. A wilted, shriveled, soft or flabby eggplant will not only produce a low servable yield but also will usually be bitter or otherwise poor in flavor. Worm injury can be seen on the surface, and fruits so affected should be rejected.

PREPARATION AND SERVING SUGGESTIONS

Eggplant is becoming increasingly popular. For a long time it was seen only on European-style menus, but it is much more widely used today. Thick slices are breaded and deep fried, sautéed or grilled. Eggplant with a Parmigiana cheese topping is excellent as are eggplant chunks in a creole sauce. It used to be common practice to salt eggplant and keep weights on it in order to soften it before cooking. Today, this is not necessary since it is now well known that it cooks to tenderness very quickly by any method.

NUTRITIONAL VALUE

Eggplant is low in calories, 100 grams of edible portion of cooked eggplant contains only 19 Calories, along with moderate amounts of other important nutrients.

Storage Note:

Eggplant is a tropical-type plant and should be used as quickly as possible, or stored in the refrigerator (for a few days).

TUNA-STUFFED EGGPLANT

2 large eggplants (2 lb. each)
1 small onion, chopped
¼ cup butter or margarine
1 cup soft bread crumbs
2 cans (6–7 oz. each) tuna, drained

1 teaspoon salt
¼ teaspoon pepper
½ to 1 teaspoon ground thyme
1 cup bread cubes
2 tablespoons melted butter or margarine

Wash eggplants, wipe dry, and remove green tip. Then cut a lengthwise slice from each. Scoop out inside and reserve, leaving a wall ½ inch thick. Invert shells in a shallow baking pan; pour in 1-inch boiling water. Bake in 400 degrees F. oven 20 minutes (or until half done). Chop pulp and sauté with onion in ¼ cup butter. Add bread crumbs, tuna and seasonings. Spoon into eggplant shells and place in shallow baking dish. Mix bread cubes with melted butter. Sprinkle around edge of tops. Bake uncovered in 350 degrees F. oven 20 minutes. Makes 4 servings.

EGGPLANT AND TOMATO CASSEROLE

1 medium (1½ lbs.)
eggplant
½-inch boiling water
1½ teaspoons salt
2 tablespoons butter or
margarine
2 large eggs, beaten
¼ teaspoon pepper

1 teaspoon finely
chopped onion
½ teaspoon oregano
leaves
½ cup crumbled saltines
6 medium-size tomato
slices
½ cup grated American
cheese

Peel eggplant and cut into slices ¼-inch thick. Place in a saucepan with boiling water and salt. Cover, bring to boiling point and cook 10 minutes or until tender. Drain and mash. Blend in butter or margarine, egg, black pepper, onion, oregano and saltines. Turn into a buttered 1-quart casserole. Cover surface with tomato slices. Sprinkle with additional salt, black pepper and cheese. Bake in a pre-heated moderate oven (375°F.) 25 minutes or until lightly browned over the top. Makes 6 servings.

ESCAROLE-ENDIVE-CHICORY

AVAILABILITY

Available in ample supply every month of the year.

All these are the same species. From the buyer's stand-point, the curly type is generally marketed as either endive or chicory and the straight-leaved type as escarole. A light-colored, sometimes almost white form with compact tight leaves and shaped like a cigar is Belgian endive, sometimes called French endive or Witloof.

HOW TO BUY

Like all greens, they should be fresh, clean, crisp, and cold. They should not show dry or yellowing leaves, or seedstems. Flabby, wilted plants are suffering from old age or poor care. The bunches should not show discoloration of leaf margins or reddish discoloration of the hearts.

PREPARATION AND SERVING SUGGESTIONS

Endive makes a gourmet salad, its refreshing bitterness and interesting texture making delightful foils for savory salad dressings. French, garlic, vinaigrette and cheese dressings are particularly good with it. Braised endive is also a tasty vegetable.

Escarole is another green which adds pleasing texture and color contrast in a salad. Combine it with Iceberg, "chicory" and Romaine, for instance, and you have four distinctly different shades of green, shapes of leaves and flavors in the salad bowl. These and other greens are good mixed with hard-boiled eggs. Mix in some crisp bacon to tease the palate.

NUTRITIONAL VALUE

As in the case of greens generally, endive-escarole is high in vitamin A. One hundred grams, edible portion, has only 20 Calories.

GREENS

AVAILABILITY

The low period is July through September and then supply rises to top abundance December through April.

There are many types of greens which can be used more or less interchangeably. They include collards, turnip tops, mustard greens, kale, Swiss chard, dandelions, cabbage sprouts and beet tops.

HOW TO BUY

Best quality greens of any kind are fresh, young, tender and green. They should not show insect injury, coarse stems, seedstems, dry or yellowing leaves, excessive dirt or poor development. They should be crisp, never wilted or flabby. They need to be cold and moist at all times during the marketing process.

PREPARATION AND SERVING SUGGESTIONS

Such vegetables as collards, turnip greens, kale, mustard greens and Swiss chard are served hot more often than not. Ham or pork fat are the desired cooking fats, or they can be prepared tastily by cooking with bacon and onions.

NUTRITIONAL VALUE

Greens are an important source of essential vitamins & minerals and are high in vitamin A content, with low calorie content.

FRESH COLLARD GREENS WITH BACON

2 pounds fresh collard
   greens
½ cup boiling water
½ teaspoon salt

3 tablespoons bacon fat
3 strips crisp bacon,
   crumbled

Cut off coarse stems of collards, wash and cut into 2 to 3-inch lengths. Place in saucepan with about 1 inch of water with salt and bacon fat. Cover and cook only until tender, about 5 to 10 minutes. Remove from heat and toss lightly with crumbled crisp bacon. Serve hot.
Makes 6 servings.

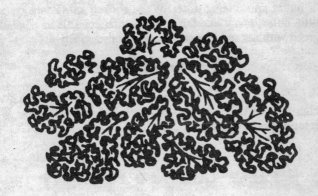

KALE

AVAILABILITY

Kale, a member of the cabbage family, is available all year long but is most abundant from December through April. There are several varieties including those with green leaves, bluish-green or yellowish-green leaves.

HOW TO BUY

Select plants whose leaves are crisp, green (or one of the characteristic varieties), and clean. Reject plants that have yellowed or brown leaves, bruises, coarse stalks and stems.

PREPARATION AND SERVING SUGGESTIONS

Kale's dark green leaves can add variety to meals. Young, tender kale should be cooked in a small amount of water. It is delicious served with a sprinkle of fresh lemon juice, butter or crumbled bacon. The flavorful leaves can also be cooked in a heavy frying pan with a small amount of butter and boiling water. While cooked kale is always a little bitter, many like this taste; raw tender kale as a salad green with oil and vinegar is sweet and distinctive.

NUTRITIONAL VALUE

Kale is rich in vitamins and minerals. It is noted for its high content of vitamin A and C; it is low in calories, 39 calories per 100 grams.

FRESH KALE AND POTATOES

1½ pounds fresh kale	¼ cup water
6 slices bacon	1½ teaspoons salt
2 cups diced raw potatoes	½ teaspoon sugar
	1/8 teaspoon pepper

Thoroughly wash kale; set aside. Saute bacon until crisp in pan large enough to cook kale; drain on absorbent paper. Pour off all but 2 tablespoons bacon drippings. Add kale, potatoes, water, salt, sugar and pepper. Cover and cook about 20 minutes or until vegetables are just tender. Top each servig with a slice of bacon. Makes about 6 servings.

LETTUCE

AVAILABILITY

Lettuce is an all-year vegetable with fairly even supplies available in such varieties as: ICEBERG, BUTTER-HEAD, ROMAINE, BIBB, AND LEAF.

ICEBERG

The Iceberg variety is the main type of lettuce, known for its solid head, it is sometimes also called "crisp head". The leaves overlap each other in a smooth, regular manner; veins are coarse and ribs prominent.

BUTTERHEAD

This variety is distinguished by its soft head, the inner leaves of which feel oily or buttery. The most common varieties of Butterhead are Big Boston, White Boston, and Bibb. The Big Boston is a medium-large plant.

241

BIBB

The Bibb variety is a small plant, with short leaves, clustered to form a compact head, leaves do not overlap. Bibb is usually a dark green color.

ROMAINE OR COS

This variety is distinguished by its elongated growth. The leaves are stiff and upright, giving the plant a somewhat cylindrical appearance. It has a loosely folded head.

LEAF LETTUCE

Has loose leaves which are clustered together but do not form a head. This variety is referred to as "garden" lettuce and is grown and sold locally.

HOW TO BUY

Iceberg lettuce should be fresh-looking, free from damage or blemishes. Heads should be "spring-firm" and give slightly to gently pressure. Avoid hard, heavy heads which are likely to be overmature and bitter. They have overdeveloped cores which yield less usable lettuce.

PREPARATION AND SERVING SUGGESTIONS

The word "lettuce" is virtually synonomous with "salad". All five types—crisphead, butterhead, Romaine, leaf and stem are basic ingredients of a wide variety of salads that can include other vegetables, fruits, seafood plus meats and dressings. Use Iceberg and Romaine lettuce whenever cripsness is desired. Use other varieties by themselves or in combination with other greens for additional texture and color variation. Romaine will not form crosscut slices "rafts" quarters or cubes (chunks) like Iceberg. The softer types of lettuce usually are combined with other greens or with somewhat dry ingredients such as seafood or cheese.But who shall say with firm authority what shall not be combined with something else. Let your imagination set the limits.

Use of lettuce in sandwiches is universal. But this champion of greens need not be limited to cold dishes. It may be braised or "wilted" and it makes a good soup when combined with a broth or bouillon and spices.

PREPARATION AND SERVING SUGGESTIONS

Here are some suggestions for serving Iceberg lettuce; toss shredded lettuce with fresh bean sprouts and sliced fresh mushrooms. Add chow mein noodle for crunch. Mix with a soy sauce dressing. Combine finely shredded lettuce, chopped avocado and tomato, dairy sour cream and oregano. Serve in prepared taco shells or over tortilla chips; lettuce wedges with a dressing made from mayonnaise, chili sauce and chopped cooked shrimp; main dish salad of shredded crisps lettuce tossed with fresh orange and grapefruit sections, grapes, diced pears and cubes of chicken; shredded lettuce floating on top of clear soup; steamed lettuce served as a vegetable with Hollandaise sauce; bite-size lettuce pieces tossed with fresh fruit and served cold with sliced turkey or ham: scalloped lettuce and tomatoes, alternating layers of shredded lettuce, tomatoes and onions in casserole.

NUTRITIONAL VALUE

Lettuce, especially the greener types, provides a useful amount of vitamin A, vitamin C, iron and other vitamins and minerals. Lettuce is very low in calories and can be eaten freely on a low-calorie diet. Lettuce also provides desirable roughage for good digestion.

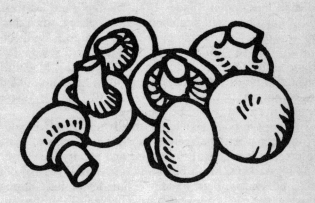

MUSHROOMS

AVAILABILITY

This vegetable, requiring no sunlight to grow, is produced in special, air conditioned houses and caves and is available all months.

HOW TO BUY

In the produce department you will find either white, tan, or cream colored mushrooms. The freshest mushrooms are closed around them stem by a thin veil. However, those having open veils, caused by loss of water as they mature, are just as nutritious but have a pungent flavor. In fact, many cooks prefer the flavor of open mushrooms which are delicious sauteed or in sauces. Closed capped mushrooms are excellent for marinating or eating raw.

PREPARATION AND SERVING SUGGESTIONS

Small mushrooms (under 1″), "buttons", are least expensive and best suited to chopping and slicing, when they are available. Next best in price for this purpose are mediums (1″ to 1⅛″), often labelled "fancy" or "extra fancy" (these terms do not refer to quality, but to size). Mediums might also be used for stuffing, but for a generous stuffed mushroom, the "large" size (1⅝″ to 3″) or the "extra large" (over 3″) would be preferred.

Fresh mushrooms should be stored "unwashed" in your refrigerator where they can be kept for two or three days. To prepare: wash just before using and pat dry, don't ever soak mushrooms. Mushrooms will turn dark if cut and not prepared quickly, but by adding a little lemon juice during cooking they can be prevented from darkening. Mushrooms do not have to be peeled, they can be cut into pieces or sautéed whole. Mushrooms add zest and flavor to gravies, sauces, soups and casserole dishes. They are a fine food in their own right when served as a vegetable or a main dish. Their delicate flavor blends well with other foods.

GOURMET STYLES OF PREPARATION

Whole and stuffed mushrooms with a savory filling become delicious hors d'oeuvres. A salad can combine lightly cooked mushrooms with a tangy french dressing, crisp celery and green pepper cubes. Pickled mushrooms are prized by many. Kebabs made by weaving strips of bacon between marinated mushrooms on a skewer . . . a fresh mushroom omelet or soufflé, all of these serving ideas are a gourmet's delight!

NUTRITIONAL VALUE

Although mushrooms will probably always be eaten for their innate flavor and taste appeal, they do possess definite food values and represent a fair source of vitamins and minerals; they are very low in calories, only 17 calories in each 100 grams (3½ ounces).

CREAMED FRESH MUSHROOMS AND CHICKEN IN POPOVERS

2 eggs
1 cup milk
1 cup sifted all-purpose
  flour

½ teaspoon salt
1 tablespoon butter or
  margarine, melted

Place eggs, milk, flour and salt in bowl. Beat with rotary beater. Add melted butter and continue to beat for one minute. Pour into buttered custard cups, filling each one half full. Place in preheated hot oven (450 degrees F.). Bake 30 minutes. Reduce heat to 350 degrees F. and bake 10 minutes longer. Cut off tops of popovers and fill with creamed chicken mixture. Place the tops back on. Makes 12 popovers.

CREAMED FRESH MUSHROOM CHICKEN FILLING

1 cup sliced fresh
  mushrooms
¼ cup butter or margarine,
  melted
¼ cup all-purpose flour
1 cup chicken broth

1 cup milk
1 teaspoon salt
¼ teaspoon pepper
2 cups diced cooked
  chicken

Lightly brown mushrooms in butter. Add flour: blend and add chicken broth, milk and seasonings. Cook until thick, stirring constantly. Add chicken. Serve in popovers. Makes 6 servings.

MUSHROOM SCRAMBLED EGGS
IN FRESH TOMATOES

6 fresh tomatoes	2 tablespoons light cream
6 thick slices Canadian bacon	1½ tablespoons butter or margarine
8 eggs	1½ teaspoons salt
1 cup sliced mushrooms	⅛ teaspoon pepper

Cut tomatoes in crosswise halves. Remove about half the pulp and save for use in tossed salads. Place tomatoes and bacon in baking dish and bake in preheated moderate oven (375 degrees F.) 20 minutes. Beat eggs; add mushrooms, cream, salt and pepper. Heat butter in skillet. Add egg mixture and cook over low heat until thickened, stirring constantly. When tomatoes are baked, place tomatoes on Canadian bacon slices. Fill with the hot egg mixture. Serve for brunch. Makes 6 servings.

FRIED ZUCCHINI WITH MUSHROOMS

Wash 1½ pounds zucchini and cut into slices ¼ inch thick. Saute ½ cup sliced fresh mushrooms, ⅔ cup chopped green pepper and 1 tablespoon chopped onion in ¼ cup hot olive oil or in butter or margarine for 3 to 4 minutes. Add zucchini, ¼ cup chicken stock or bouillon, ¾ teaspoon salt, dash ground black pepper and ½ teaspoon crumbled whole oregano leaves. Cook, covered, until zucchini is tender, about 10 minutes.
YIELD: 4 to 5 servings.

ONIONS, DRY

AVAILABILITY

Dry onions are available in large amounts throughout the year. There is no way to classify the pungency of onions by variety, color, shape or size. The same variety, grown in different areas on different soils, often has quite a different taste. Most of them can be called mild-sweet but some are strong.

BERMUDAS

They are thick and flat to top-shaped, mild and often yellow. Usually they are early onions.

GLOBES

These are mostly late-crop onions, generally spherical with many variations, with yellow, white or red skins and mild flavor. The term "Spanish" is applied to some globes but lacks definite meaning.

CREOLES

This is a general term for very strong onions of which there are several varieties, with skins that may be red, brown or white.

HOW TO BUY

Select bright, clean, hard, well-shaped onions with dry skins and without seedstems. Check for a thick, tough, woody or open condition of the neck or a visible portion of the stem which indicates seedstem development. Color, shape or size do not necessarily indicate strength of flavor. shape is only important depending upon the use which may result in excessive waste in preparation of off-shape bulbs. Check for moisture at the neck of any onion—it is an indication of decay, which may not be visible but may make the onion unfit for use. Sprouted onions or those showing new neck or root growth are undesirable because these growths are at the expense of the bulb.

PREPARATION AND SERVING SUGGESTIONS

Here are some suggestions for usage, depending upon the type of onion involved.

Large—all purpose, but excellent for stuffing and a good buy for slices with hamburgers; also good for french fried onion rings.

Medium—good for chopping, boiling, stuffing.

Small—a good choice for boiling and use in stews and casseroles.

Picklers or Pearls—good for pickles and relishes.

Red onions—good for salads and garnishes.

Onions are used as a main vegetable dish or as a flavorful ingredient of main meat dishes. They are good boiled, broiled, baked, creamed, steamed, fried, french fried, roasted, pickled, in soups and stews, for onion rings, sliced raw and diced raw in salads. A glance through any good cookbook reveals few recipes, other than desserts, which do not include at least a suspicion of onion.

PREPARATION AND SERVING SUGGESTIONS

There are enough variations to keep the onion a popular repeater on the menu circuit. It develops different and interesting nuances without ever losing the distinctive individuality of its flavor. It contributes zip and nip even to such mild dishes as the soufflé. And think of the lovely aroma of onion and steak over the charcoal broiler on a summer evening.

Here are some menu suggestions: cream of onion and celery soup; baked whole onions; creamy onion casserole; onions and peas aromatique; chili creamed onions and peppers; breast of veal with onion stuffing: beef liver creole; baked fresh onion and tomato casserole; onion and mushroom casserole; curry topped onion pot pie; little onion pies with fresh mushroom sauce; shish kebab with onion; baked stuffed onions; stuffed onions with spinach and bacon crumbs; French fried onion rings; sage flavored onion stuffing for poultry; onion and potato au gratin; french onion soup; scalloped meat with eggplant and onion; open-faced onion and cheese sandwich; baked onion and beef casserole. The list is endless.

The redolence of onion recalls memories of pleasant feasting and arouses appetite for delights to come. "Without it there would be no gastronomic art", declares one 19th century epicure. "Banish it from the kitchen and all pleasure of eating flies with it. Its presence lends color and enchantment to the most modest dish.

NUTRITIONAL VALUE

Onions are low in calories and contain moderate amounts of important vitamins and minerals.

ONIONS, GREEN

AVAILABILITY

Green onions are available all year, but are most abundant April through August.

A green onion is an onion which has been harvested very young. There are several types of onions classified under the green onion catagory, they include:

SCALLIONS which are any shoots from the white onion varieties that are pulled before the bulb has formed. LEEKS, which are similar to scallions but have flat leaves. SHALLOTS, which are similar to green onions, but whose bulbs grow in clusters like garlic cloves. CHIVES also are classified in the onion catagory; they have thin, grasslike blades and are sold in clumps.

253

HOW TO BUY

Good quality green onions, leeks or shallots should have green, fresh tops, medium-sized necks well blanched for 2 or 3 inches from the root, and they should be young, crisp and tender. Yellowing, wilted or discolored tops indicate flabby, tough fibrous necks or other undesirable qualities. Except for appearance, bruised tops are unimportant, unless they are to be cut up and used.

PREPARATION AND SERVING SUGGESTIONS

While green onions are principally served on the relish tray, small quantities also make a good addition to tossed salads. The green tops, which are usually cut off, may be used as a garniture in soups, sauces and hash. If green onions are blanched, for about 5 seconds in boiling water, they will become soft and pliable for use in cold buffets.

Green onions are a savory morsel eaten raw with meat, cheese or fish. Many like to munch on the tops as well as the small bulb. Sometimes the greens are chopped and mixed with cottage cheese.

SCALLIONS are ideal for use as appetizers and for salads.

LEEKS which are sold in bunches can be cooked and served like asparagus.

SHALLOTS are much like green onions and can be used similarly.

CHIVES which are thin, grasslike blades can be used for flavoring or garnishing many dishes.

NUTRITIONAL VALUE

Green onions are low in calories and contain moderate amounts of important vitamins and minerals.

FRENCH ONION SOUFFLÉ

2 cups peeled, quartered onions	½ teaspoon salt
½ cup water	½ teaspoon paprika
3 tablespoons butter or margarine	⅛ teaspoon pepper
	1 cup light cream
3 tablespoons flour	3 eggs, separated

Make a collar for a 5-cup soufflé dish with waxed paper. It should extend 2-inches above rim of dish. Wrap around soufflé dish. Overlap ends and tie on with string. Cook onions, covered, in water until just tender (about 10 minutes). Purée onion liquid and onions with food mill; reserve. Melt butter or margarine in medium saucepan; stir in flour, salt, paprika, and pepper. Mix in cream. Cook over medium heat, stirring constantly until mixture thickens and reaches boiling point. Beat egg yolks slight; stir in a little hot mixture; return to saucepan and cook 1 minute stirring constantly. Remove from heat; stir in puréed onions. Cool. Beat egg whites stiff; fold in onion mixture. Pile into ungreased soufflé dish (7-inches in diameter). Bake in preheated moderate oven (350°F.) about 40 minutes or until knife inserted in center comes out clean. Remove collar and serve immediately. Makes 4 servings.

*FRITTER BATTER

1 cup sifted all-purpose flour	¼ teaspoon pepper
	1 egg, slightly beaten
1 teaspoon double-acting baking powder	¾ cup milk
½ teaspoon salt	1 tablespoon shortening, melted

Sift the first 4 ingredients together into a mixing bowl. Combine beaten egg and milk and stir into the flour mixture along with the melted shortening. Mix only until ingredients are blended. Makes sufficient batter for 6 servings French Fried Onions.

FRENCH FRIED ONION RINGS

Peel mild-flavored onions and cut into crosswise slices
¼ inch thick. Dip a few rings at a time into Fritter Batter*
and drop into hot, deep fat preheated to 375°F. Fry until
golden brown. Lift out and drain on absorbent paper. Serve
at once.

ONION BAKED EGGS AND CHEESE

Butter or margarine
¾ cup grated American
   cheese
2 teaspoons fresh minced
  onion

6 eggs
½ teaspoon salt
⅛ teaspoon pepper
Paprika

Butter a baking dish. Mix cheese with minced onion and
sprinkle a layer over bottom of buttered baking dish. Break
in eggs and sprinkle with salt, black pepper, and remaining
cheese. Bake in preheated hot oven (400 degrees F.) 20
minutes or until eggs are firm. (Do not bake too long since
eggs continue cooking after removal from oven.) Garnish
with paprika. Serve for brunch. Makes 6 servings.

FRENCH ONION SOUP

1½ cups sliced yellow
  onions
3 tablespoons butter or
  margarine
1½ quarts beef bouillon
¼ teaspoon salt or salt to
  taste

¼ teaspoon pepper
¼ cup grated sharp
  Cheddar cheese
6 slices French bread
Grated Parmesan
  cheese

Sauté onions in butter or margarine. Add bouillon, salt
and black pepper. Simmer 30 minutes. Pour into a casserole or soup tureen. Sprinkle grated Cheddar cheese over
slices of toasted French bread. Place under broiler for
cheese to melt. Float over top of soup. If desired, sprinkle
with grated Parmesan cheese. Makes 6 servings.

HERBED CREAM ONIONS

1½ pounds small white
    onions
1-inch boiling water in
    saucepan
1 teaspoon salt
3 tablespoons butter or
    margarine
3 tablespoons flour
1½ cups milk

½ teaspoon salt or salt to
    taste
⅛ teaspoon pepper
⅛ teaspoon crumbled
    whole rosemary or
    thyme leaves
Fresh parsley for
    garnish

Peel onions and place in a saucepan with 1-inch boiling water and the 1 teaspoon salt. Bring to boiling point and boil 3 minutes. Cover and cook until tender, 12 to 15 minutes. Remove from heat and drain. In the meantime, melt butter or margarine in a saucepan. Blend in flour. Remove from heat. Gradually stir in milk. Add salt, black pepper and crumbled rosemary or thyme leaves. Return to heat. Cook until medium thickness, stirring constantly. Pour over drained, cooked onions. Garnish with chopped fresh parsley. Makes 6 servings.

GOURMET BAKED ONIONS

6 large onions
½ cup water
2 tablespoons butter or
    margarine

1 beef bouillon cube
½ cup dry white wine
2 tablespoons chopped
    fresh parsley

Cut slice from both ends of onions; peel thinly. Place onions in shallow baking dish. Combine water, butter or margarine and bouillon cube; heat until butter and bouillon cube dissolve. Stir in wine and parsley; remove from heat. Pour over onions. Cover casserole tightly. Bake in 350°F, oven 1-½ hours or until onions are tender. Before serving, garnish with parsley as desired. Makes 6 servings.

PARSLEY

AVAILABILITY

Available all year.

Varieties are unimportant in buying, but there are two general types, the curly-leaved and the plain-leaved. In quality they are alike but the curly-leaved is more attractive and is the kind that is grown most.

HOW TO BUY

Parsley should be bright, fresh, green, crisp, and free from yellowed leaves or dirt. Wilting and yellowing denote age or damage.

PREPARATION AND SERVING SUGGESTIONS

This most frequently used of all garnishes needs to be bright green and fresh looking to be completely effective. For best results, place it in a large jar and add just enough water to cover the bottom. Close tightly and refrigerate. Chopped parsley should be folded into a towel and wrung out thoroughly, so that it dries out quickly and can be kept very well in the refrigerator for two or three days if it is kept in the towel used for drying it. An interesting parsley garnish can also be made by dipping sprigs in deep fat for 2 or 3 seconds.

The foliage parsleys are used for garnishing and for flavoring soups, stews, gravy, and poultry stuffings. Parsley is usually an ingredient of *fines herbes,* a combination of several herbs finely chopped and thoroughly mingled, used in omelets and sauces. Parsley may be chopped and mixed in salads, added to butter to make parsley butter, and may be made into a jelly. Gourmet Magazine suggests fried parsley. It says that "fried parsley is crisp, tasty and tasteful." A recipe for drying parsley is also given by Gourmet. "Strip the clusters of parsley leaves from the stalks and plunge them into boiling water for 30 seconds. Drain, spread the leaves on a wire screen, and dry them in a slow oven (300 degrees F.) until they are crisp. Leave the oven partially open. Store dried parsley—in clusters or powdered —in a tightly closed container." Parsley is very versatile. Its ability to stimulate the appetite recommends its use with hors d'oeuvres and canapes. It seems to go well with everything but sweetmeats. It is cooked and served as other root vegetables. It is also popular in stews.

NUTRITIONAL VALUE

Parsley is very high in vitamin C, it has about four times as much as an equal weight of fresh oranges—however, since little is consumed it is not an important source of this vitamin.

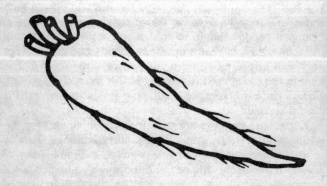

PARSNIPS

AVAILABILITY

Available in all months, with largest supplies October through March and least in July and August.

HOW TO BUY

Parsnip flavor is not fully developed until prolonged exposure to temperatures around 40 degrees F. or lower. Parsnips should have been stored and have reached the right flavor. They should be smooth, firm, clean, well-shaped, of small to medium size. Soft, flabby or shriveled roots are usually pithy or fibrous. Softness may also be an indication of decay. Misshapen roots are objectionable because of waste in preparation. Large, coarse parsnips are apt to have tough, woody cores. Discoloration may be an indication of freezing.

FRESH VEGETABLES
PREPARATION AND SERVING SUGGESTIONS

Stews, soups and mashed probably offer the best potentials for serving parsnips. However, they are delicious when creamed or sautéed or deep fat fried in thin slices in batter.

Use methods for storing and cooking carrots for parsnips.

NUTRITIONAL VALUE

Parsnips are nutritious but do not have an outstanding quantity of any particular nutrient.

OVEN POST ROAST
WITH FRESH PARSNIPS

2½ pounds boneless pot
    roast (round, rump,
    or chuck)
1 tablespoon shortening
½ teaspoon salt
¼ teaspoon black pepper
½ cup boiling water
2 pounds fresh parsnips
½ teaspoon salt
Parsley for garnish

Brown meat on all sides in shortening in heavy skillet. Mix ½ teaspoon salt with black pepper and sprinkle lightly over entire surface of meat. Place on rack in a roaster or casserole. Pour boiling water into pan. In the meantime, peel parsnips and place around the meat and sprinkle with the remaining ½ teaspoon salt. Cover. Cook in a preheated slow oven (325°F.) until tender 2 to 2½ hours. Remove meat and parsnips to a warm platter. Garnish with fresh parsley. Makes approximately 6 servings.

FOR GRAVY: Mix 3 tablespoons flour with 1 cup water or beef broth (if water is used add 1 beef bouillon cube for flavor). Cook until medium thickness. Add salt and black pepper to taste, if desired. Color with ¼ teaspoon kitchen bouquet.
YIELD: 1 cup gravy.

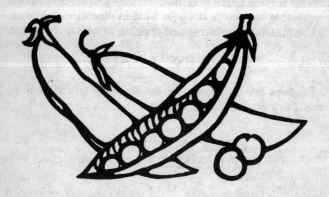

PEAS, GREEN

AVAILABILITY

Available all year, but largest supplies April through July and few September through December.

HOW TO BUY

It is essential that peas, having been picked at the right stage, be quickly cooled and kept cold throughout the marketing process. They lose sugar quickly if kept warm. Peas should be young, tender and sweet with pods fresh appearing, uniformly light green, slightly velvety to the touch and fairly well filled with well developed peas. A large proportion of pods that are flat and quite empty should cause rejection. On the other hand, pods noticeably light in color and of swollen appearance may be over-mature and contain tough peas.

FRESH VEGETABLES
PREPARATION AND SERVING SUGGESTIONS

A menu that can boast fresh peas is sure to stand out for the excellence of its service. Most people seem to agree that properly cooked fresh peas all by themselves represent a sufficient treat. However, a dressing of butter or a little addition of mint flavor will give them even more appeal. Sliced mushrooms make another good teammate.

NUTRITIONAL VALUE

Peas are an excellent source of many essential vitamins and minerals, notably iron.

SNOW PEAS
(Sugar Peas, China Peas)

These translucent green pods contribute color, crunchy texture, and delicious taste to Oriental and traditional dishes alike. Choose fresh, crisp pods and use as soon as possible. If they must be stored, seal unwashed pods in a plastic bag and keep in the refrigerator. To prepare them, wash and snip off both tips, removing the string, if any, from the pod. Stir-fry or boil quickly, only about 2 to 3 minutes, to retain their peak of crispness.

A summer romance between a standard pea and the completely edible Snow Pea has produced a stir the vegetable world hasn't seen for half a century. It's a one-in-a-million mutant called Sugar Snap peas that combine the best features of both parents, are best eaten raw, and taste like an incredible green bean, with plump, juicy, kernels and a sweet, crunchy, pod. Nature has provided a handy zipper: Nip the end away from the stem and pull up the tough little string that guards the pea's side.

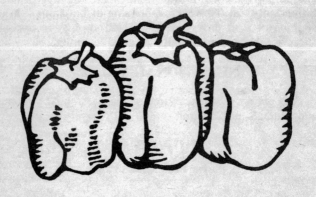

PEPPERS, SWEET

AVAILABILITY

On market all year in good volume.

Pepper types can be divided into mild or sweet-fleshed fruits, and the hot or pungent-fleshed fruits. The kind most used taper slightly and are often called "bell" peppers.

HOW TO BUY

Peppers should be fresh, firm, bright in appearance, thick fleshed, and either bright green or with more or less red. Immature peppers are usually soft, pliable, thin-fleshed and pale green. Stale peppers may be shriveled, soft and dull in appearance. Constricted, crooked or deformed peppers of otherwise good quality are objectionable only if the use to which they are to be put would result in undue waste.

FRESH VEGETABLES

PREPARATION AND SERVING SUGGESTIONS

Sweet peppers are one of the vegetables that are called on to flavor other foods as frequently as they are expected to be a food themselves. As a vegetable, they are most often stuffed and this has become a very popular dish. There are, however, many interesting stuffings for peppers that are not often seen. Among these would be chicken, tuna or turkey a la kind or hash. Chili con carne would be another. When served raw, pepper rings are most apt to be the style of preparation. If the raw pepper is first stuffed with cream cheese and then cut into thin rings, the stuffed rings make especially flavorsome and eye-catching salad additions. See recipes pages 39–40, omit avocados.

Sweet peppers are good either raw or cooked but do not over-cook them. Brief parboiling is desirable if peppers are to be stuffed, but 3 to 5 minutes in boiling salted water is long enough if they are to have additional cooking . . . Stuffed peppers are easily prepared. Remove the "lid" of the pepper pod by cutting away a thin slice at the stem end. Remove seeds and membrane (placenta). Parboil in boiling salted water to cover. Invert, drain and fill with some well-seasoned mixture of cooked meat and vegetables . . . Sweet peppers are delicious, too, cut in strips and sautéed briefly in garlic-flavored olive oil. Especially good with beef or fish . . . In the hors d'oeuvres department, one quick-to-fix idea is stuffed pepper quarters. The stuffing can be cottage cheese which has been tossed with minced chives, carrot shreds and crisp celery bits. For a final touch of color, sprinkle minced chives and paprika lightly over the top.

In the salad realm, the ways of stuffing green peppers seem to be never-ending. As a starter, try filling the cavity with a mixture of lightly cooked and marinated vegetables —carrot cubes, snap beans and tiny cauliflowerettes make a colorful trio. A gourmet alternative is a mixture of corn, potato cubes, and shreds of raw cabbage topped with a dollop of sour cream. To give company dinners an extra flourish, fill peppers with a piquant Roquefort cheese and ham stuffing.

NUTRITIONAL VALUE

Green sweet peppers are very high in vitamin C content. One medium raw pepper provides more than the recommended daily allowance of vitamin C for an adult. Sweet peppers are low in calories (only 15 calories to a medium pepper, about 62 grams) and supply some vitamin A and a variety of other vitamins and minerals, plus bulk for good digestion.

GREEN PEPPER BURGERS

1 pound ground beef chuck	1 tablespoon minced fresh onion
¼ cup finely chopped green pepper	1 teaspoon salt
	1 teaspoon chili powder (optional)

Lightly blend together all ingredients. Shape into 4 patties. Broil in preheated broiler about 3 inches from heat source 10 minutes, turning once, for medium doneness. Serve on buns with a cheese slice, tomato slice, green pepper ring and stuffed olives, as desired. Makes 4 servings.

FRESH VEGETABLES
PEPPER & HAM ELEGANT

½ cup chopped green
  pepper
⅓ cup chopped fresh
  parsley
3 tablespoons grated
  Parmesan cheese
1 tablespoon minced fresh
  onion

1 teaspoon salt
⅛ teaspoon pepper
2 tablespoons butter or
  margarine
1 dozen medium-sized
  eggs
12 slices boiled ham (about
  ⅟₁₆-inch thick

Combine green pepper, parsley, Parmesan cheese, onion, salt and pepper; reserve. Melt butter or margarine in 10-inch skillet over very low heat. Break whole eggs into skillet one at a time until all are used. Sprinkle vegetable mixture over eggs. When whites of eggs just begin to set, stir whites lightly with fork. When partially set, break egg yolks individually and mix into whites until each yolk is well mixed into whites. Stir briskly with fork until eggs are blended but moist and fluffy. Remove from heat. Place a spoonful of egg mixture on each ham slice. (Distribute egg mixture evenly over ham.) Roll ham around egg mixture. Place ham rolls, seam side down, in shallow baking pan. Bake in 400°F. oven 10 minutes. Makes 6 servings.

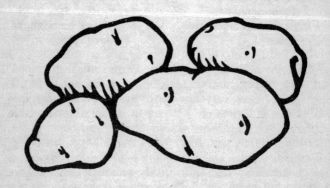

POTATOES

AVAILABILITY

Potatoes are in good supply all year long. The types of potatoes generally found on the market include: long russet, long white, round russet, round white and round red tubers. It really takes an expert to distinguish between some of the varieties; these varieties include: Russet Burbank, Kennebec, Katahdin, Norchip, Norland, Red Pontiac, White Rose, and others. Most potatoes are identified by the areas in which they are grown, for example: "Idaho" or "Maine" potatoes. Practically all supermarket potatoes are "U.S. No. 1" grade, which is reasonable assurance of freedom from major defects. You will find, however, that size and quality varies a great deal in this grade.

FRESH VEGETABLES
HOW TO BUY

Potatoes of any kind or size should be firm, relatively smooth, clean and reasonably well-shaped. Avoid product that is wilted, sprouted or any with a green tinge. Green colored potatoes indicate poor quality. Size does not affect quality and is a matter of choice for particular use.

Cooking quality varies by variety and production areas. Some types from some areas are known to be good bakers and french fryers; this is because they have a high content of dry matter. For boiling and salads, potatoes of slightly higher moisture content is desirable. Early or "new" potatoes are good for boiling, frying and salads; and this is true of most late round varieties.

PREPARATION AND SERVING SUGGESTIONS

Potatoes are one of the most popular vegetables in the world. They offer high mineral and vitamin content and are easily digestible. There are almost endless methods of preparing and serving potatoes: baked, roasted, boiled, mashed, fried from raw strips or pieces from boiled or baked pieces, french fried, creamed, hash browned . . . and how about potato salads, potatoes in stews, soups, casseroles . . . in pancakes and pastries; au gratin, curried, in soufflés, in chowders, in croquettes, in dumplings, scalloped and lyonnaise.

Potatoes also are excellent "go-alongs" with meat, fish, fowl, and a wide variety of other vegetables.

General preparation—scrub potatoes well, but leave the skins on; if potatoes are peeled, the paring should be very thin. Use a sharp knife to remove the eyes.

PREPARATION AND SERVING SUGGESTIONS

Cooking: potatoes should be cooked in a covered pan with a small amount of salted boiling water, preferably with the skins on. Medium-sized potatoes take approximately 30 minutes to cook—don't overcook or potatoes will be mushy. Drain off the water and shake pan over low heat briefly to dry potatoes.

Baking potatoes: Prick skins before baking. Bake in preheated 450°F oven for about 1 hour depending on size of potato.

NUTRITIONAL VALUE

Fresh potatoes contain a wide variety of valuable nutrients. For example, one good sized baked potato—about 200 grams or 7 ounces—supplies two thirds the vitamin C recommended daily for adults. It also makes a contribution of B vitamins—especially thiamine—plus iron, calcium, fiber and protein.

POTATO BEEF PIE

3 cups seasoned fresh mashed potatoes	2 tablespoons salad oil
1 medium-sized onion, chopped	1 pound ground beef chuck
½ cup thinly sliced celery	1 teaspoon salt
½ cup chopped green pepper	⅛ teaspoon pepper

Spread mashed potatoes into an even layer over bottom and sides of buttered 9-inch pie plate. Sauté onion, celery and green pepper in a salad oil until tender. Stir beef into vegetable mixture. Sauté until meat loses red color, stirring frequently. Mix in salt and pepper. Turn into potato shell. Bake in moderate over (375°F.) 15–20 minutes or until piping hot. Makes about 4 servings.

FRESH VEGETABLES

SHRIMP STUFFED POTATOES

6 medium potatoes
1½ tablespoons butter or
   margarine
1¾ teaspoons salt
¼ teaspoon pepper

½ cup milk
6-ounce can shrimp
1 teaspoon fresh lemon
   juice

Bake potatoes in a very hot oven (450°F.)* 40 to 50 minutes or until tender when tested with a fork. Cut a ¾-inch slice off the top. Scoop out potato. Add butter or margarine and mash. Beat in salt, ground black pepper, and milk. Save 6 shrimp for garnish. Break remaining shrimp into pieces, add to potatoes along with lemon juice and mix well. Garnish each with a whole shrimp. Makes 6 servings.

* If oven is set at a temperature lower than 450°F., for another dish, bake potatoes at the same time, until tender.

HOT CURRIED POTATO SALAD

6 medium potatoes
⅓ cup butter or margarine
2 tablespoons chopped
   onion
3 tablespoons flour
1 teaspoon curry powder
½ teaspoon salt

1¼ cups chicken broth
2 tablespoons vinegar
1 red apple, cored and
   cut in wedges
½ cup sliced celery
½ cup halved, seeded
   grapes

Place unpared potatoes in a large saucepan. Add water to cover. Bring to a boil and simmer until potatoes are tender, 30 minutes or longer. Drain and cool slightly. When potatoes are cool enough to handle, peel and cut into ¼-inch slices. In large skillet heat butter; add onion and cook until transparent. Blend in flour, curry powder and salt; cook, stirring constantly, for 1 or 2 minutes. Slowly stir in chicken broth and vinegar; cook, stirring constantly, until thickened. Add potatoes, apple, celery and grapes. Heat 5 minutes. Serve immediately. Makes 4 to 6 servings.

FRESH POTATO ONION PUFF

2 pounds potatoes, pared
    and cubed (about 4
    medium-sized)
½ teaspoon salt
½ cup chopped fresh
    onions

¼ cup melted butter or
    margarine
¾ cup milk
½ teaspoon salt
Dash pepper
2 eggs, separated

Cook potatoes with ½ teaspoon salt in covered sauce-pan in small amount of boiling water until just tender. Drain well. Sauté onions in butter or margarine until tender. Mash potatoes. Beat onions, milk, ½ teaspoon salt and pepper into potatoes. Add egg yolks; beat well. Beat egg whites until stiff; fold into potato mixture. Pile into buttered 6-cup casserole. Bake in 375°F. oven 30 minutes or until lightly browned. Serve immediately. Makes 4–6 servings.

POTATO SHRIMP CHOWDER

2½ cups cubed potatoes
1 cup water
½ teaspoon salt
1 can (10-ounces) frozen
    condensed cream of
    shrimp soup

½ cup light cream
2 tablespoons snipped
    parsley
Dash pepper

Cook potatoes with water and salt in covered saucepan until just tender; do not drain. Add shrimp soup. Cook over medium heat, stirring constantly, until mixture reaches boiling point. Add cream, parsley and pepper; heat but do not boil. Serve with lemon wedges, if desired. Makes about 1 quart.

POTATO TOPPED BEEF STEW

2½ pounds cubed beef
    chuck
2 tablespoons salad oil
⅔ cup sliced celery
½ cup chopped fresh
    onions
3 cups boiling water

2 beef bouillon cubes
1½ teaspoons salt
⅛ teaspoon pepper
4 carrots, cut into 1-inch
    lengths
⅓ cup flour
⅓ cup cold water

Brown beef well on all sides in salad oil in large heavy pan. Move meat to one side. Add celery and onions and cook until tender. Add boiling water, bouillon cubes, salt and pepper. Cover and simmer about 1-¼ hours or until meat is almost tender. Add carrots; cover and simmer 15 minutes longer. Mix flour and cold water to form a smooth paste; stir in a little hot mixture. Return to stew. Cook, stirring, until thickened. Top with mounds of Fluffy Mashed Potatoes.*

*FLUFFY MASHED POTATOES

2½ pounds potatoes (about
    6 medium)
2 teaspoons salt

¼ cup butter or
    margarine
½ cup milk
Few grains pepper

Pare and quarter potatoes. Cover and cook in small amount boiling water with 1 teaspoon salt until tender (about 15 to 20 minutes). Drain, if necessary. Mash potatoes well. Add remaining ingredients; beat until fluffy. Pile by spoonfuls over stew. Serve from cooking utensil. Makes about 6 servings.

PUMPKINS

AVAILABILITY

Pumpkins have their peak season in October for Halloween, approximately 80% of the supply is available at this time. Technically, pumpkins are a member of the squash family; sizes vary from large to extremely large.

HOW TO BUY

Pumpkins should be well matured, not broken or cracked, free from soft rot and excessive scarring. They should have a rich, orange color.

PREPARATION AND SERVING SUGGESTIONS

Aside from the artistry of making a scary jack-o-lantern, pumpkins provide the makings of spicy pumpkin pie; pumpkin bread or muffins; various puddings and custards; and a small pumpkin may be used for stuffing with meats and vegetables or meats and seafood for an interesting change.

FRESH VEGETABLES

Here are basic cooking directions for pumpkin: halve or quarter the pumpkin; remove seeds and stringy portions; cut into small pieces; cut off rind. Cook, covered, in small amount of lightly salted boiling water 25–30 minutes. Since pumpkin is a watery vegetable, a large amount of cooking water is undesirable. When cooked, drain; mash well; place mashed pumpkin in strainer; let drain about 30 minutes to remove excess liquid. One 5-pound pumpkin yields about 4½ cups of mashed cooked pumpkin.

NUTRITIONAL VALUE

Pumpkins are a source of vitamin A and other vitamins and minerals; they are low in calories—100 grams contains 33 Calories.

OLD FASHIONED FRESH PUMPKIN PIE

1 cup sugar
1 tablespoon flour
½ teaspoon salt
1 teaspoon ground ginger
1 teaspoon ground cinnamon
⅛ teaspoon ground nutmeg
⅛ teaspoon ground cloves
3 eggs
1½ cups cooked mashed pumpkin
1 cup milk or light cream
Pastry for one-crust 9-inch pie

Mix sugar with flour, salt, ginger, cinnamon, nutmeg and cloves. Beat in eggs. Stir in pumpkin and milk or cream. Mix well. Pour mixture into a 9-inch pie pan lined with unbaked pastry. Bake in a preheated hot oven (400°F.) 50 minutes or until a knife inserted in the center comes out clean. Makes 6 servings.

RADISHES

AVAILABILITY

Available all year in good volume with peak period March through June.

They are not usually bought by variety but rather by type, such as globular red, globular red and white, globular white, long red, long white or long black.

HOW TO BUY

They should be fresh, well-formed, smooth, firm, tender, crisp, mild in flavor and not showing any large number of black spots and pits. Pithy, spongy, or wilted radishes are undesirable. Generally medium or large radishes are preferable, but size in itself is not a quality factor.

PREPARATION AND SERVING SUGGESTIONS

Naturally, the best appearing medium to large-sized radishes are reserved for use as radish roses. Others are perfectly suitable for slicing. While it is not difficult to fashion roses with a paring knife, a cutter does the job faster and more uniformly. After cutting, they should be held in ice water.

NUTRITIONAL VALUE

Radishes have a fair contribution of minerals to offer, but they are not eaten in sufficient quantities to be an important nutrient source. They are low in calories, 17 Calories per 100 grams.

CRUNCHY RADISH SALAD

4 bunches (1 quart) radishes
1/3 cup thin onion rings
1 cup finely diced fresh tomato
1 1/4 teaspoons salt
1/8 teaspoon finely chopped fresh garlic
1/8 teaspoon ground black pepper
1 teaspoon finely chopped fresh mint
2 tablespoons fresh lemon juice
2 tablespoons salad or olive oil
Fresh parsley

Wash radishes and slice. Add onion and tomatoes. Combine seasonings, lemon juice and oil. Mix well and pour over the salad. Toss lightly. Garnish with fresh parsley. YIELD: 6 servings.

SPINACH

AVAILABILITY

Available all year in good volume.

Almost all spinach marketed fresh is of the savoy or crumpled-leaf type. Hybrids are now produced in large amounts. It is not generally bought by variety.

HOW TO BUY

If in the form of plants, the plants should be well developed and relatively stocky. Straggly overgrown plants or plants with seedstems are undesirable. Leaves should be clean, fresh, tender and of good green color. Yellow, discolored, wilted, bruised or crushed leaves should be avoided. Small, yellowish-green undeveloped heart leaves are natural and should not be considered objectionable.

PREPARATION AND SERVING SUGGESTIONS

Properly cooked (steamed) fresh spinach, possibly seasoned with a bit of onion, is a tasty dish. The trick is in a very quick cooking to slightly crisp tenderness in only the water which clings to the leaves after washing! The onion, which has been sautéed, is simply tossed with the cooked spinach. Other interesting methods of preparing include the addition of cream sauce with mushrooms and a nutmeg flavored cream sauce.

Serving suggestions include: plain spinach with melted butter and seasoned to taste; with hard-boiled chopped eggs; escalloped; molded or creamed; in a spinach ring; a fondue; soufflé or served with cheese; Dutch style with bacon, vinegar and sugar; cream of spinach soup; with mushroom sauce; spinach roulade; spinach with eggs Florentine; spinach and herbs omelet; and raw spinach salad with eggs and anchovies.

NUTRITIONAL VALUE

Spinach has high nutritional value, as a relatively rich source of vitamins A, C and folic acid (a B vitamin). It is also relatively high in iron and takes top rank for content of vitamin K (a blood coagulation factor). A 100 gram serving of boiled spinach contains 23 Calories.

FRESH SPINACH WITH LEMON-NUTMEG BUTTER

1 pound fresh spinach
¼ cup butter or margarine
¼ teaspoon nutmeg

1 teaspoon finely grated lemon rind
1 tablespoon fresh lemon juice

Cook spinach, covered, with water clinging to the leaves after washing, until just tender. Drain, if necessary. Meanwhile, combine remaining ingredients. Cook over low heat, stirring occasionally, until butter or margarine is melted. Serve over spinach. Makes about 4 servings.

SPINACH SALAD

3 tablespoons wine
    vinegar
6 tablespoons salad oil
½ teaspoon salt
⅛ teaspoon pepper
¼ teaspoon dry mustard
2 tablespoons chopped
    parsley

1 clove garlic, cut in half
½ pound (5 to 6 cups)
    fresh spinach leaves
½ cauliflower, cut into
    flowerets
1 avocado, peeled and
    sliced
½ red onion, sliced and
    separated into rings

Mix together wine vinegar, oil, salt, pepper, dry mustard, parsley and garlic; let stand for 30 minutes. Remove garlic. While dressing is standing, wash the spinach and remove stems. Dry well and combine with cauliflowerets, avocado and red onion in salad bowl. Add dressing and toss lightly to mix well. Makes 6 servings.

FRESH SPINACH POTATO SOUP

1 pound beef chuck, cut
    into ½-inch cubes
⅓ cup chopped celery
1 medium-sized onion,
    chopped
2 cups water
1 beef bouillon cube

1 tablespoon salt
2 cups diced potatoes
1 pound fresh spinach,
    coarsely chopped
3½ cups milk
½ cup light cream

Combine chuck, celery, onion, water, bouillon cube, and salt in large saucepan. Cover and cook about 1 hour, or until meat is tender. Add potatoes; cook 5 minutes. Add spinach; cook 3 to 5 minutes or until vegetables are just tender. Add milk and cream. Heat to serving temperature, stirring occasionally. Makes about 2½ quarts.

SQUASH

AVAILABILITY

Available all year 'round, with largest quantity June—Nov. Squash comes in many different shapes, sizes and colors. It is usually classified as "winter" or "summer" squash, but this does not refer to the season but rather to the stage of maturity when harvested. Summer squash is immature, soft-skinned, and small; winter squash is mature, hard-shelled and ranges from small to large. Here is the best way to break down the main varieties:

HOW TO BUY

Soft-shelled squashes, which are eaten skin and all, including seeds, should be tender, crisp, fresh and fairly heavy in relation to size. They should be free from cuts or bruises. Tenderness is the main thing. Squash which has developed into the hard rind stage, also has hard or semi-hard seeds, and is not usable as a whole.

The hard-shelled squashes, on the other hand, should not have any softness of rind which would indicate immaturity, thin flesh and probably watery texture and lack of flavor in this variety.

SOFT-SHELLED SQUASH (SUMMER)

COCOZELLE—Cyclindrically shaped with alternating dark green and yellow ribs. Choose squash about 6" to 8" long.

CHAYOTE—Round or pear-shaped. The green rind can be smooth, ribbed or covered with smooth white to dark green spines. Choose firm, hard squash.

SCALLOP—Also known as cymling and pattypan. Small, flat and pie-shaped with a scalloped edge. They can be white, yellow, light green or striped. Select small squash, 3" or 4" in diameter.

YELLOW CROOKNECK—Bright yellow and lightly pebbled skins, about 4" to 6" long with a curved neck.

YELLOW STRAIGHTNECK—Similar to crooknecks with either a smooth or lightly pebbled skin.

ZUCCHINI—Slender, dark green, cyclindrically shaped. Thin, smooth skins are frequently striped with pale yellow or white. Choose squash 4" to 9" long.
There's a squash for every season and every taste—so many varieties in different colors, shapes and sizes.

HARD-SHELLED SQUASH (WINTER)

ACORN—Wide ribbed, slightly oval and pointed at one end. Dark green shell changes to orange in storage.

BANANA—Large, long and cyclindrical, pointed at both ends. Moderately thick, pale gray to creamy white shell which can be smooth or somewhat wrinkled.

BUTTERCUP—Dark green with grayish spots and stripes. It is drum-like in appearance, about 4" to 5" long, and is crowned with a grayish turban-like top. Sweet orange fresh.

PREPARATION AND SERVING SUGGESTIONS

BUTTERNUT—Cyclindrically shaped with a thick neck. Smooth creamy brown or dark yellow shell, deep orange flesh.

HUBBARD—Large, about 10" to 16" long, spherically shaped, tapering at both ends. The shell is ridged and warted and varies in color from dark blue, gray or orange red. Sweet orange flesh.

TURBAN—Used for ornamental purposes. Drum-shaped with a striped red-orange, warted shell. Like buttercup, they are turban-shaped.

For those who have never attempted cooking hard-shelled squash like Hubbard, Butternut or Acorn, get ready for a dining adventure! There's no need to be afraid of them; they're so easy to prepare.

What is inside these mysterious, gourd-like vegetables? Delicious golden meat! You have to know that there are fibers and seeds which need to simply be scooped out, and then you're ready to cook these fine, nutritious vegetables.

Take the delightfully shaped acorn squash. You can make a wonderful sausage and cabbage stuffing and bake it for a most interesting main dish. Apples also contribute to the flavor of this stuffing.

Butternut squash has a fine, old-fashioned flavor that you'll enjoy. A good idea is to cut it in cubes after paring, sprinkle with spices and brown sugar, drizzle melted butter over it and add a tang of fresh lemon juice. Bake this delicious mixture for a wonderful vegetable that holds the essence of the season.

Hubbard squash is delicious many ways, but especially good mashed and seasoned lavishly with maple syrup and butter. It's sprinkled with chopped toasted pecans just before serving—a fine dish for company or to surprise the family with your knowledge of the variety of fresh, delicious vegetables at your market.

The big, hard-shell squashes, which are normally peeled before cooking, are best served mashed. For additional appeal, some butter, brown sugar or maple syrup, and cinnamon may be added before mashing. Small hard-shells, particularly acorn, are often served in the shell. Some butter and either brown sugar or maple syrup placed in the hollow of the seed cavity is a tasty idea.

Zucchini and the yellow straightnecks or crooknecks are simply cut into small pieces and cooked. Zucchini is especially good with a Creole sauce. It also makes an interestingly different raw relish offering.

PREPARATION AND SERVING SUGGESTIONS

Cooking methods: Squash may be prepared in any of the usual ways for boiling and baking vegetables, and may also be fried. Winter or hard-type squashes are cut in halves or pieces, seeds are removed, and the squash is then baked, steamed or boiled. Where water is used in cooking, the quantity of water should be kept small to avoid taking flavor and nutrients out of the vegetable. In the case of the small delicate summer squashes, especially, the flavor may be lost by cooking in a large volume of water. Squashes of the small, hard-type such as Acorn and Butternut frequently are cut in half and baked and served in the shell. When large squashes are cooked, pieces may be served in the shell or the pulp may be removed and mashed. Squash pulp is also used for pie, and may be served in casseroles, soufflés, pancakes and custards.

NUTRITIONAL VALUE

Squash, especially the mature type, contributes a good range of nutrients but is not outstanding for any one, except vitamin A, in the mature types. Squash is low in calories and sodium, which is advantageous to those on a restricted sodium diet.

MAPLE NUT HUBBARD SQUASH

**3 pounds HUBBARD
  squash**
½ cup butter or margarine

¾ cup maple syrup
Salt and pepper to taste
**½ cup chopped toasted
  pecans**

Cut squash into pieces, pare, remove seeds and fibers. Cook covered in boiling water for 20 to 30 minutes, or until tender. Drain and mash well. Beat in butter, maple syrup, salt and pepper. Sprinkle with pecans. Makes 6 servings.

BAKED BUTTERNUT SQUASH

**1 large BUTTERNUT
  squash, pared and cut
  into 1-inch cubes
  (remove seeds and
  fibers)**
¼ teaspoon cinnamon

¼ teaspoon nutmeg
½ cup packed brown sugar
**½ cup butter or margarine,
  melted**
**2 teaspoons fresh lemon
  juice**

Place squash cubes in 2-quart casserole or baking dish. Sprinkle with spices and brown sugar. Drizzle with melted butter and lemon juice. Bake uncovered in 375°F. oven for 45 minutes, or until tender. Makes 4 servings.

ACORN CABBAGE BAKE

2 large ACORN squashes
½ pound sausage meat
2 tablespoons butter or
  margarine
1 medium onion, chopped
1 small apple, pared and
  chopped
2 cups shredded green
  cabbage

2 tablespoons slivered
  almonds
¾ teaspoon salt
¼ teaspoon pepper
¼ teaspoon dried leaf
  thyme
½ teaspoon dried leaf sage,
  crumbled

Cut ACORN squash in half lengthwise and scoop out seeds and fibers. Place in baking pan, cut side down, and add ½-inch water. Bake in 400°F. oven for 20 minutes.

Meanwhile, cook sausage meat in skillet until browned. Drain off excess fat, and add butter to pan. Add onion, apple, cabbage and almonds; cook until vegetables are tender. Add seasonings and mix well.

Turn squash halves cut-side up and fill centers with cabbage mixture. Return to baking pan and bake in 400°F. oven 30 minutes longer. Makes 4 servings.

ZUCCHINI CASSEROLE

¼ cup butter or margarine
½ cup onion rings
2 cups sliced zucchini
2 cups sliced summer
  squash

1 tablespoon salt
¼ teaspoon pepper
3 cups diced fresh
  tomatoes

Melt butter or margarine in a skillet. Add onion rings and cook about 5 minutes or until transparent. Add squashes and seasonings and cook 10 to 15 minutes. Add and stir in tomatoes and cook another 10 to 15 minutes until squash is tender. Makes 6 to 8 servings.

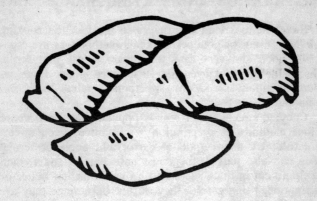

SWEETPOTATOES (YAMS)

AVAILABILITY

Available all year, with heavy supplies in October through December, lighest in June and July.

Sweetpotatoes may be divided into *soft-fleshed* and *firm-fleshed,* also into red-fleshed and yellow-fleshed. The Porto Rico type is the most extensively grown soft-fleshed kind and the one dominant in the South. There are many variants of this type. The flesh is orange-yellow to salmon color. There are newer soft-fleshed varieties with deeply copper-colored skin. Sweetpotatoes often are called "yam" but they are not related to the true yam.

HOW TO BUY

Sweetpotatoes should be clean, smooth, well-shaped, firm and bright in appearance. Type, whether yellow-fleshed or orange-fleshed, copper-skinned or light-skinned is a matter of choice. Seriously misshapen tubers and those showing growth cracks or wireworm injury are undesirable. A damp appearance may indicate decay in the package.

PREPARATION AND SERVING SUGGESTIONS

Sweetpotatoes lend themselves to most of the cooking methods used for potatoes. Baked sweetpotatoes are especially good and very easy to prepare. Wash and scrub, then bake in a hot oven for 40 minutes to one hour depending upon size. Many sweetpotato eaters like them skin and all.

Candied sweets are extremely popular, but don't ignore other methods of preparation . . . sautée sliced sweetpotatoes; try a sweetpotato, carrot and apple casserole. You can also parboil them just until barely tender, then peel and cut in thick slices and brown in melted butter or margarine, being careful they do not burn since they are so high in sugar.

You can also whip the sweetpotato into succulent softness, add some brown sugar and a nip of fresh lemon tartness, then bake. Combine leftover chicken and sweetpotatoes in a casserole, lusciously creamed and buttered, with crisp bacon slices adding a salty allure. And what could be finer than baked or fried ham with sweetpotatoes.

Remember, sweetpotatoes should be cooked in their jackets to give their best nutriment and flavor. Never store sweetpotatoes in your refrigerator, as cold is harmful to them.

NUTRITIONAL VALUE

Sweetpotatoes are one of the most all-round nutritious foods available anywhere. The deep-yellow (or orange) soft-fleshed varieties are exceptionally high in vitamin A. A 100-gram serving of baked sweetpotato contains 141 Calories.

SWEETPOTATO PUFF

2 pounds sweetpotatoes,
  cooked and mashed (3
  cups)
3 tablespoons butter or
  margarine

¾ cup milk
  Few grains pepper
2 eggs, separated
¼ teaspoon salt

Whip together sweetpotatoes, butter or margarine, milk
and pepper. Beat in egg yolks. Whip egg whites with salt
until stiff; fold into sweetpotato mixture. Pile into buttered 1½ quart casserole. Bake in 375°F. oven 30 minutes, or until puffed and top surface is lightly browned.
Makes 4–6 servings.

STUFFED BAKED SWEETPOTATOES

4 sweetpotatoes
3 tablespoons butter or
  margarine
2 tablespoons milk

1 teaspoon salt
⅛ teaspoon pepper
⅓ cup toasted slivered
  almonds

Wash and scrub the sweetpotatoes. Bake in a 375°F.
oven for 45 minutes to 1 hour, until tender when tested
with a fork. Cut lengthwise slice from side of sweetpotatoes. Scoop out sweetpotatoes, being careful to keep skins
intact, and mash in bowl with butter, milk, sale and pepper. Stir in almonds and spoon into sweetpotato shells.
Return to 375°F. oven and heat for 12 to 15 minutes.
Makes 4 servings.

SWEETPOTATO CHICKEN CASSEROLE

4 medium-sized
    sweetpotatoes
¼ cup flour
1 teaspoon salt
Few grains pepper
1 chicken (about 2½
    pounds) quartered
2 tablespoons butter or
    margarine

1 medium-sized onion,
    sliced
1 green pepper, cut into
    strips
1 cup fresh orange juice
2 tablespoons dry sherry
    (optional)
1 chicken bouillon cube
½ teaspoon ginger

Cook sweetpotatoes in covered saucepan in small amount boiling water 5 minutes. Drain. Pare when cool enough to handle. Cut sweetpotatoes in half lengthwise; set aside. Combine flour, salt and pepper. Coat chicken with flour mixture. Melt butter or margarine in oven-proof casserole. Brown chicken on all sides. Remove chicken from casserole. Add onion and green pepper to drippings in casserole. Sauté 5 minutes. Stir in orange juice, sherry, bouillon cube and ginger. Blend well. Arrange chicken and sweetpotatoes in casserole. Cover and bake in 350°F. oven about 1 hour. Makes 4 servings.

MASHED SWEETPOTATO PATTIES

2 tablespoons finely
    chopped fresh onion
2 tablespoons butter or
    margarine
2 cups mashed fresh
    sweetpotatoes

2 tablespoons finely
    chopped parsley
¾ teaspoon salt
Dash pepper
Flour
Butter or margarine

Cook onion in the 2 tablespoons butter or margarine until tender. Combine onion-butter mixture with sweetpotatoes, parsley, salt and pepper. Shape into 6 patties and chill until firm.* Coat with flour. Sauté in butter or margarine until browned on both sides. Makes 6 potato patties.

* To serve for breakfast: prepare the night before. Cook just before serving.

SWEETPOTATO-SAUSAGE STUFFING

2 cups mashed sweet potatoes	2½ teaspoons salt
6 cups toasted bread cubes	½ teaspoon pepper
1 cup chopped celery	2 teaspoons poultry seasoning
⅔ cup chopped onion	¼ cup butter or margarine, melted
8 sausage links	

Combine sweetpotatoes, toasted bread cubes, celery and onion. Cut sausage links into 1-inch pieces, brown, and add to the mixture. Add seasonings and melted butter or margarine. Mix well and spoon lightly into the crop and body cavities of a 10 to 12 pound turkey. Close openings with skewers. Make half of this recipe if you wish to stuff a 5 to 6 pound chicken or capon. Makes sufficient stuffing for a 10 to 12 pound turkey.

SWEETPOTATO STUFFING FOR TURKEY

2 cups mashed sweet potatoes	2½ teaspoons salt
6 cups toasted bread cubes	½ teaspoon pepper
1 cup chopped celery	2 teaspoons poultry seasoning
⅔ cup chopped onion	¼ cup butter or margarine, melted
8 sausage links	

Combine sweetpotatoes, toasted bread cubes, celery and onion. Cut sausage links into ½-inch pieces, brown and add to the mixture. Add seasonings and melted butter or margarine. Mix well and spoon lightly into the crop and body cavities of a 10 to 12 pound turkey. Close openings with skewers. Make half of this recipe if you wish to stuff a 5 to 6 pound chicken or capon. Makes sufficient stuffing for a 10 to 12 pound turkey.

TOMATOES

AVAILABILITY

Available all year in large volume, with most from May through August and least November through February.

Varieties within types are of more interest to growers than distributors, and varietal names are not used in the marketplace. Types can be indicated as field-grown vine pink (often spoken of as "vine ripe"); field-grown mature green; plum type; cherry type; greenhouse; and hydroponic. The term "beefsteak" does not indicate a distinct variety but is applied often to large slicing tomatoes.

HOW TO BUY

A tomato picked truly "mature green," not just green, will attain just as much flavor and succulence as a so-called "vine ripe." However, many tomatoes are not picked quite mature, and in that case, though they redden fully, they will not attain good taste and texture. Tomatoes picked with any degree of pinkness or redness will ripen fully if shipped at the right temperature. They must not be chilled. No attempt should be made to interrupt ripening with cold, since tomatoes thereafter do not ripen properly. After they are ripe, they can be refrigerated. Good quality tomatoes are well formed and plump, of uniform red color, free from bruise marks and not over-ripe or soft. But as indicated above, they can be all of this and still fall short in flavor, so flavor is a definite quality factor. Use the taste test.

PREPARATION AND SERVING SUGGESTIONS

Small sizes are good for sauces and casseroles. Mediums are usually preferred for slicing, since fewer need be handled and yet the slices are still manageably sized for sandwiches and salads. Largest sizes are good for stuffing* or when slices are served separately (not in salad). Cherry tomatoes served whole are increasingly popular in salads. Hard or firm-ripe tomatoes are preferred for cooked applications. They are served cooked in many delicious forms, such as stewed, fried and baked. Large green tomatoes are often used for frying while small green ones are excellent for pickling.

* See pages 39–40 for stuffing recipes, omit avocado.

NUTRITIONAL VALUE

Tomatoes raw or cooked are a valuable source of vitamin C, vitamin A, and other vitamins and minerals. Raw, 100 grams (3½-ounces) of tomato contains only 22 Calories.

FRESH TOMATO ASPIC

2 pounds fresh tomatoes,
  peeled and quartered*
¼ cup sugar
2 envelopes unflavored
  gelatin
1 cup beef bouillon

¼ teaspoon salt
½ teaspoon Worcestershire
  sauce
⅛ teaspoon Tabasco
2 tablespoons fresh lemon
  juice

Combine tomatoes and sugar. Cover and simmer 15 minutes, stirring occasionally. Put tomato mixture through sieve or food mill. Reserve. Soften gelatin in ½ cup bouillon. Dissolve gelatin over low heat. Remove from heat. Stir in remaining bouillon, tomato purée, salt, Worcestershire sauce, Tabasco and lemon juice. Pour into lightly oiled 4-cup mold. Chill until firm (about 4 hours). Garnish with softened cream cheese, as desired. Makes 4 servings.

* To peel tomatoes, dip into boiling water with a fork. Cool slightly. Slip off skins. Remove stem ends.

FRESH TOMATO VEGETABLE STEW

1 cup chopped fresh
  onions
¼ cup melted butter or
  margarine
2 pounds fresh tomatoes
1½ teaspoon salt
¼ teaspoon sugar
⅛ teaspoon pepper

2 cups cubed pared
  potatoes
1½ cups fresh corn kernels
  or cut fresh green
  beans
1 cup sliced pared fresh
  carrots

In large saucepan, cook onions in butter until tender. Dip tomatoes into boiling water; peel off skins. Cut tomatoes into wedges. Add tomatoes, salt, sugar and pepper to onions. Cover and simmer 20 minutes. Add potatoes, corn and carrots. Cover and cook about 20 minutes, until vegetables are tender. Makes 6 servings.

LOW-CALORIE STUFFED TOMATO

6 medium-large firm ripe
tomatoes
12-oz. package (1½ cups)
cottage cheese
¼ cup finely chopped
celery
1 tablespoon minced fresh
onion
½ teaspoon salt

1 tablespoon sour cream
or skim milk
¹⁄₁₆ teaspoon white pepper
¼ teaspoon minced fresh
garlic
30 slices cucumber
Salad greens
6 slices hard-cooked eggs

Wash tomatoes, cut into 5 petals, starting at the bud end and cutting not quite through the stem end. Spread the petals slightly. Set aside to use later. Combine cottage cheese, celery, onion, salt, sour cream or milk, pepper and garlic. Spoon into centers of tomatoes. Insert a slice of cucumber in between each tomato petal. Top with a hard-cooked egg slices. Serve on lettuce. Makes 6 servings.

COLE-SLAW STUFFED TOMATOES

6 medium-large firm ripe
tomatoes
Salt
2 cups finely chopped
shredded raw cabbage
¼ cup chopped green
pepper
1 tablespoon minced
onion

⅓ cup diced celery
2 tablespoons mayonnaise
1 tablespoon fresh lemon
juice
½ teaspoon salt or salt to
taste
⅛ teaspoon pepper
Salad greens

Wash tomatoes, cut a slice from the stem ends and carefully scoop out some of the pulp and seeds, leaving the cups intact. (Save pulp to mix with soup, sauces or with other vegetables.) Drain well. Sprinkle inside with salt. Combine cabbage, green pepper, onion, celery, mayonnaise, lemon juice, salt and black pepper. Mix and spoon into tomato cups. Garnish with pieces cut from stem end of tomatoes. Serve on salad greens. Makes 6 servings.

HAM AND CHEESE STUFFED TOMATO

6 large tomatoes
1 cup American cheese,
   cut in small cubes

½ cup diced ham or
   bologna
6 toasted bread rounds

Cut ½ inch thick slice from stem end of each tomato. With spoon, scoop out a hollow about 1 inch deep in each tomato. Fill tomatoes with cheese and meat. Place each tomato on toasted bread rounds. Serve with salad dressing. Makes 6 servings.

STUFFED TOMATO SALADS

Prepare 4 medium-large tomatoes, as desired, by slicing tomatoes and reassembling into original shape, or cut into wedges without cutting through bottom, or hollow out tomato to form tomato "cup." Fill with one of the following:

POTATO FILLING

Combine 2 cups cubed cooked potatoes, 1 cup chopped celery, 1 teaspoon grated fresh onion, 1 teaspoon salt and enough mayonnaise to moisten. Season to taste with salt and pepper. Chill until serving time.

CABBAGE FILLING

Combine 3 cups shredded cabbage, 1 tablespoon fresh lemon juice, 2 teaspoons sugar, ¼ cup chopped green pepper, ½ teaspoon salt and enough mayonnaise to moisten. Chill until serving time. Garnish salads with hard-cooked eggs, as desired.

MOLDED FRESH TOMATO RING

4 cups uncooked fresh
tomato juice
3 tablespoons fresh lemon
juice
½ teaspoon minced onion

3 teaspoons salt
⅛ teaspoon pepper
2 envelopes unflavored
gelatin
½ cup water

To make fresh tomato juice, mash fresh tomatoes and put through a sieve. Measure 4 cups, add lemon juice, onion, salt and pepper. Soften gelatin in water in a custard cup. Place in hot water (not boiling) to dissolve and add to tomato juice. Rinse a 5-cup ring mold in cold water. Fill with tomato juice mixture. Chill until ready to serve. Turn out on a serving plate. Fill center with mayonnaise. Makes 6 to 8 servings.

FRESH TOMATO SAUCE

2 pounds fresh tomatoes
⅓ cup chopped celery
½ teaspoon salt
½ teaspoon sugar
⅛ teaspoon pepper
1 bay leaf

1 beef bouillon cube
2 tablespoons chopped
fresh onion
6 tablespoons melted
butter or margarine
⅓ cup flour

Remove stem ends of tomatoes; chop coarsely. Combine tomatoes, celery, salt, sugar, pepper, bay leaf and bouillon cube in large saucepan. Cover and simmer 20 minutes. Strain mixture or put through food mill; reserve. Saute onion in butter or margarine in same saucepan 5 minutes. Blend in flour. Cook over low heat, stirring constantly, until lightly browned. Stir in tomato purée. Cook over medium heat, stirring constantly, until mixture reaches boiling point. Serve with London broil, or other sliced beef, as desired. Makes about 2¼ cups sauce.

TURNIPS-RUTABAGAS

AVAILABILITY

On market in all months. The volume is greatest October through March and least June through August.

There are white-fleshed and yellow-fleshed kinds of both turnips and rutabagas, but generally, as designated in the market, "turnips" have white flesh and "rutabagas" have yellow flesh and are usually larger. Turnips are white, turning purplish at the top. Rutabagas have a smooth yellowish skin.

HOW TO BUY

Turnips should be heavy in relation to size, smooth and firm, with few leaf scars around the crown and with very few fibrous roots at the base. When tops are present, they should be fresh, green, young, crisp. Shriveled or soft turnips are likely to be tough when cooked. Large, coarse, overgrown turnips, especially if light in weight for their size, are apt to be tough, woody, pithy, hollow or strong in flavor.

FRESH VEGETABLES

PREPARATION AND SERVING SUGGESTIONS

White turnips are especially good in soups and stews. Raw, thinly sliced white turnips are also good in salads and are frequently used in buffet decorations. Yellow turnips and rutabagas are most often mashed. The addition of a little mashed potato, plus butter and seasonings, enhance the turnip for many people.

Rutabagas, being large, are usually cut up before cooking. They may be boiled or roasted with meat and eaten in pieces; or boiled and mashed; or cut into julienne strips and boiled with other vegetables such as carrots, turnips and celery; and made into various savory combinations and even into puddings. Other serving ideas include rutabaga and potato salad; rutabaga parmesan; french fried rutabagas and raw rutabagas and apple salad.

NUTRITIONAL VALUE

Turnips are a good source of vitamin C and contain other vitamins and minerals. Raw turnips, 100 grams (3½-ounces) contain 30 Calories. Rutabagas have much more vitamin A than turnips and more of other vitamins, but less iron.

SAVORY MASHED RUTABAGAS

1½ pounds (4 cups) peeled, diced rutabagas
3 medium-size potatoes peeled and diced
½ cup beef stock

1 teaspoon salt
1 teaspoon sugar
¼ teaspoon white pepper
2 tablespoons butter or margarine

Place rutabagas, potatoes, stock and salt in a saucepan. Bring to boiling point and boil 5 minutes, uncovered. Cover and boil 30 minutes or until rutabagas and turnips are tender. Drain, if necessary, and mash until smooth. Add sugar, white pepper and butter or margarine. Beat until fluffy and well mixed. Makes 6 servings.

TURNIP CASSEROLE

2 cups mashed cooked
    yellow or white turnip
3 tablespoons butter or
    margarine
1 tablespoon sugar
1 teaspoon salt

$\frac{1}{16}$ teaspoon pepper
1 cup soft bread crumbs
2 eggs, beaten
1 tablespoon butter or
    margarine, melted

Combine turnip, the 3 tablespoons butter or margarine, sugar, salt, black pepper, ¾ cup of the bread crumbs and eggs. Mix well. Turn into a buttered 1-quart casserole. Mix remaining bread crumbs with the 1 tablespoon melted butter or margarine and sprinkle over the top. Bake in a preheated moderate oven (350°F.) 30 minutes or until brown. Makes 6 servings.

RUTABAGAS IN CREAM

4 cups diced rutabagas
1 inch boiling water
1 teaspoon salt
¼ cup thin cream

½ teaspoon sugar
⅛ teaspoon pepper
Salt to taste
Butter or margarine

Cook rutabagas in 1-inch boiling water and the 1 teaspoon salt in an uncovered saucepan 5 minutes. Cover and cook until almost tender, about 30 minutes. Drain if necessary. Add cream, sugar, black pepper and salt to taste. Simmer, do not boil, 5 minutes. Add butter or margarine. Shake the saucepan over low heat until butter is melted and perfectly blended. Serve at once. Makes 6 servings.

GLAZED RUTABAGAS

4 cups cubed rutabagas	⅛ teaspoon pepper
1 inch boiling water	½ teaspoon salt
1 teaspoon salt	1 teaspoon sugar
¼ cup butter or margarine	⅓ cup stock

Peel rutabagas and cut into 1-inch cubes. Place in a saucepan with 1-inch boiling water and the 1 teaspoon salt. Bring to boiling point and cook until almost tender. Place rutabagas in a buttered 9-inch pie plate. Melt butter or margarine and pour over rutabagas. Combine black pepper, salt and sugar and sprinkle over the top. Pour in stock. Cook in a preheated moderate oven (350°F.) 45 minutes until browned and nicely glazed; basting 2 to 3 times with the liquid in pan. Serve hot. Makes 6 servings.

BAKED RUTABAGAS

2 pounds rutabagas	½ teaspoon salt
1 inch boiling water	1 teaspoon sugar
1 teaspoon salt	3 tablespoons butter or
2 tablespoons chopped	margarine
parsley	2 tablespoons milk
⅛ teaspoon black pepper	

Wash and peel rutabagas. Cut them into slices ½-inch thick. Place in a saucepan with 1-inch boiling water and the 1 teaspoon salt. Cover. Bring to boiling point and parboil about 10 minutes. Drain well and arrange slices in layers in a buttered baking dish, sprinkling each layer with chopped parsley, and a mixture of black pepper, the remaining ½ teaspoon salt and sugar. Dot with butter or margarine and sprinkle with milk. Cover and bake in a preheated moderate oven 350°F. for 50 to 55 minutes or until rutabagas are tender.

WATERCRESS

AVAILABILITY

On the market all year in small amounts.

HOW TO BUY

Watercress should be fresh, young, crisp, tender, rich medium-green in color and free from dirt or yellowed leaves. Wilting or discoloration indicates overage or lack of freshness.

FRESH VEGETABLES
PREPARATION AND SERVING SUGGESTIONS

The most critical factor in watercress is maintaining its fresh appearance. A tired sprig of watercress can detract from, rather than enhance, the food it garnishes. One of the simplest and most effective methods of protecting it is by refrigerating it in a large, tightly-covered jar to which a very small amount of water has been added.

The tangy leaves and tender stems of watercress lend an interesting flavor to soups and may be braised or cooked with other vegetables or added to sauces.

NUTRITIONAL VALUE

Watercress is high in vitamins and minerals and low in calories; however not a large enough quantity is eaten to consider this as an important source of nutrients.

DID YOU KNOW . . . THESE VERY INTERESTING FACTS ABOUT FRESH FRUITS AND VEGETABLES?

- Almost half of the vitamin A in the food supply (50%) is from fruits and vegetables.
- Unless fruits and vegetables are consumed regularly, it is next to impossible to obtain enough vitamin C from food.
- Almost all fruits and vegetables are very low in fat in their natural state.
- Almost half (43%) of the folic acid, an anti-anaemia B-vitamin, comes from fruits and vegetables.
- Virtually all fresh fruits and vegetables have an *alkaline* reaction in the body, whether or not they have an "acid" taste.
- The most economical sources of vitamin C in the food supply are in order: (1) citrus fruit and tomatoes; (2) potatoes; (3) green and yellow vegetables and (4) other fruits and vegetables.
- The most economical source of vitamin B1 in the food supply is potatoes.
- For the over-weight, consuming carbohydrates in the form of bulky fruits and vegetables with low carbohydrate content is one means of lowering the total calorie intake and yet eating a considerable amount.
- Crisp apples cleanse the teeth and are recommended by the American Dental Association for both children and adults.
- Bananas fit well into reducing diets, because they are high in bulk, low in calorie content, cause satiety and give flavor satisfaction.

FRESH VEGETABLES
DID YOU KNOW ...

• Bananas have virtually no fat. The smooth, apparently oily texture of the pulp may cause belief that bananas contain considerable oil, but they don't. The fat content of bananas, weight for weight is on a par with that of lettuce.

• Broccoli is a good source of vitamin A and an excellent source of vitamin C. One cup of cooked broccoli (150 grams) provides 75% of the recommended daily allowance of vitamin A for an adult, and twice the vitamin C.

• One cup of cooked Brussels sprouts (130 grams) provides 190% of the recommended daily allowance of vitamin C for an adult.

• Cabbage is so high in vitamin C that weight for weight it ranks with orange juice.

• The golden color of cantaloupe flesh is due to carotene, which the body converts to vitamin A.

• Speaking of vitamin A . . . a single carrot (5½ x 1 inch) will give you more than the daily recommended allowance.

• One cup of boiled and drained cauliflower provides 110% of the daily recommended allowance of vitamin C.

• Celery is ideal for nibbling by the overweight since it is very low in calories, yet provides a useful amount of vitamins and minerals.

• One cup of raw grapefruit sections (194 grams) provides 120% of the daily recommended allowance of vitamin C.

• Adding lettuce to a sandwich not only makes it more palatable but improves digestion.

• A cup or orange juice provides 1½ to 2 times the recommended daily allowance of vitamin C.

• Parsley is very high in vitamin C. Only 1.2 ounces provides the recommended daily allowance for an adult.

DID YOU KNOW...

• One medium-sized cooked pepper provides the entire daily recommended allowance of vitamin C for an adult.

• Potatoes contain virtually no fat. They are low in sodium and fit for low sodium diets. Potatoes are highly digestible—the carbohydrate is 92–99% usable; the iron is 93% usable; and the potato vitamin B1 is more usable than even a like dose of the purified vitamin.

• One cup (288 grams) of cooked pumpkin provides one and a half times the recommended daily allowance of vitamin A.

• Spinach is especially high in iron and is used in diets to increase iron intake.

• Ten large strawberries provide 100% of the recommended daily allowance of vitamin C.

• Sweetpotatoes are one of the most all-round nutritious foods of the world.

• Watermelon is surprisingly nutritious. A 4 x 8 inch wedge, which is just a "sample" for a real watermelon eater, provides half of the recommended dietary allowance of vitamin C and half the allowance of vitamin A, as well as a good contribution of other vitamins and minerals.

FRESH FRUIT CALORIE AND CARBOHYDRATE CHART

Food	Amount	Calories	Carbohydrates (no. Grams)
APPLE, raw	1 small (2 inch dia.)	58	15
APRICOTS, raw	3 medium	51	13
AVOCADOS	half, peeled	167	6
BANANA	1 small (6 inches)	85	22
BERRIES (Blackberries, Boysenberries, Dewberries) raw	5/8 cup	58	13
BLUEBERRIES, raw	5/8 cup	62	15
CRANBERRIES, raw	1/2 cup	23	5
RASPBERRIES, black, raw	2/3 cup	73	16
Red, raw	3/4 cup	57	14
STRAWBERRIES, raw, whole	10 large	37	8
CANTALOUPE	1/4 melon (5 inches dia.)	30	8
CHERRIES, sweet, raw	15 large, 25 small	70	17
FIGS, raw,	3 small, 2 large	80	20
Dried	2 small	82	21
GRAPEFRUIT, fresh	1/2 medium (4 inches dia.)	40	10
GRAPES	24 medium	67	17
HONEYDEW MELON	1 wedge (2 inches wide, 6½ inches dia.)	49	12
LEMONS, peeled	1 medium	27	8

FRESH FRUIT CALORIE AND CARBOHYDRATE CHART

Food	Amount	Calories	Carbohydrates (no. Grams)
LIMES	1 medium	28	10
NECTARINES, raw	2 medium	64	17
ORANGES, peeled	1 small (2½ inches dia.)	49	12
PEACHES, raw	1 medium	38	10
PEARS, raw	½ pear (3 inches x 2½ inches)	61	15
PINEAPPLE, raw	¾ cup, diced	52	14
PLUMS, raw	2 medium	50	13
RHUBARB, raw	¾ to 1 cup	16	4
cooked, sweetened	⅜ cup	141	36
TANGERINES	1 large, 2 small	46	12
WATERMELON	1 slice (6 inches dia. x 1½ inches)	156	38

FRESH VEGETABLE CALORIE AND CARBOHYDRATE CHART

Food	Amount	Calories	Carbohydrates (no. Grams)
ARTICHOKES, Globe, cooked	Base and soft ends of leaves	44	10
ASPARAGUS, raw	5–6 spears	26	4
cooked	⅔ cup cut pieces	20	4
BEANS, Lima, cooked	⅝ cup	111	20
SNAP BEANS, cooked or fresh	¾ cup	24	5
BEAN SPROUTS, Soya, cooked, drained	¾ cup	38	4
BEET GREENS, cooked	½ cup	18	3
BEETS, cooked, diced	½ cup	27	6
BROCCOLI, cooked	⅔ cup	26	5
BRUSSEL SPROUTS, cooked	⅔ cup	36	6
CABBAGE, raw, shredded	½ cup	12	3
cooked	½ cup	20	5
CABBAGE, Chinese, raw, shredded	2¼ cups	14	3
cooked	½ cup	8	1
CARROTS, raw	1 large, 2 small	42	10
cooked, drained	⅔ cup	32	7
CAULIFLOWER, raw	½ cup	14	3
cooked, drained	½ cup	13	3

FRESH VEGETABLE CALORIE AND CARBOHYDRATE CHART

Food	Amount	Calories	Carbohydrates (no. Grams)
CELERY, raw,	½ cup diced	9	2
cooked, drained	½ cup	11	2
CHARD, cooked	⅔ cup	18	3
COLLARDS, cooked	½ cup	29	5
CORN, fresh cooked	1 small ear	100	21
CUCUMBERS, raw	1–1¼ inch	5	1
DANDELION GREENS, raw	½ cup	45	9
cooked	½ cup	33	6
EGGPLANT, cooked, drained	½ cup	19	4
ENDIVE, raw	20 long leaves, 40 short	20	4
ESCAROLE	7 small inner leaves	4	1
KALE, cooked with stems	½ cup	19	3
LETTUCE, Iceberg	3½ ounces	14	3
MUSHROOMS, raw	10 small or 4 large	28	4
MUSTARD GREENS, cooked	½ cup	23	4
OKRA, cooked	8–9 pods	29	6
ONIONS, raw	1 medium	38	9
cooked	½ cup	29	7
PARSLEY, raw	3½ ounces	44	9

FRESH VEGETABLE CALORIE AND CARBOHYDRATE CHART

Food	Amount	Calories	Carbohydrates (no. Grams)
PARSNIPS, cooked	½ cup	66	15
PEAS, green, cooked or fresh	⅔ cup	71	12
PEPPERS, GREEN, raw	1 large empty shell	22	5
cooked	3½ ounces	18	4
POTATOES, baked	1 medium	93	21
boiled, peeled	1 medium	65	15
French fried	10 slices (½ inch x ½ inch x 2 inch)	137	18
mashed (milk and butter)	½ cup	94	12
RADISHES	2 small	3	1
RUTABAGAS, cooked	½ cup diced	35	8
SPINACH, raw	3½ ounces	26	4
cooked	½ cup	21	3
SQUASH, soft skin, cooked	½ cup	14	3
hard skin boiled and mashed	⅝ cup	38	9
SWEET POTATOES, baked	1 small	141	33
TOMATOES, raw	1 small	22	5
cooked	½ cup	26	6
TURNIP GREENS, cooked	⅔ cup	20	4
TURNIPS, raw, diced	¾ cup	30	7
boiled, drained	⅔ cup, diced	23	5

INDEX

ALL ABOUT FRUITS

INDEX

INDEX

ALL ABOUT VEGETABLES

INDEX

INDEX

INDEX

MY FAVORITE RECIPES

MY FAVORITE RECIPES

MY FAVORITE RECIPES